THE METACOGNITIVE preschooler

How to Teach Academic, Social, and Emotional Intelligence to Your Youngest Students

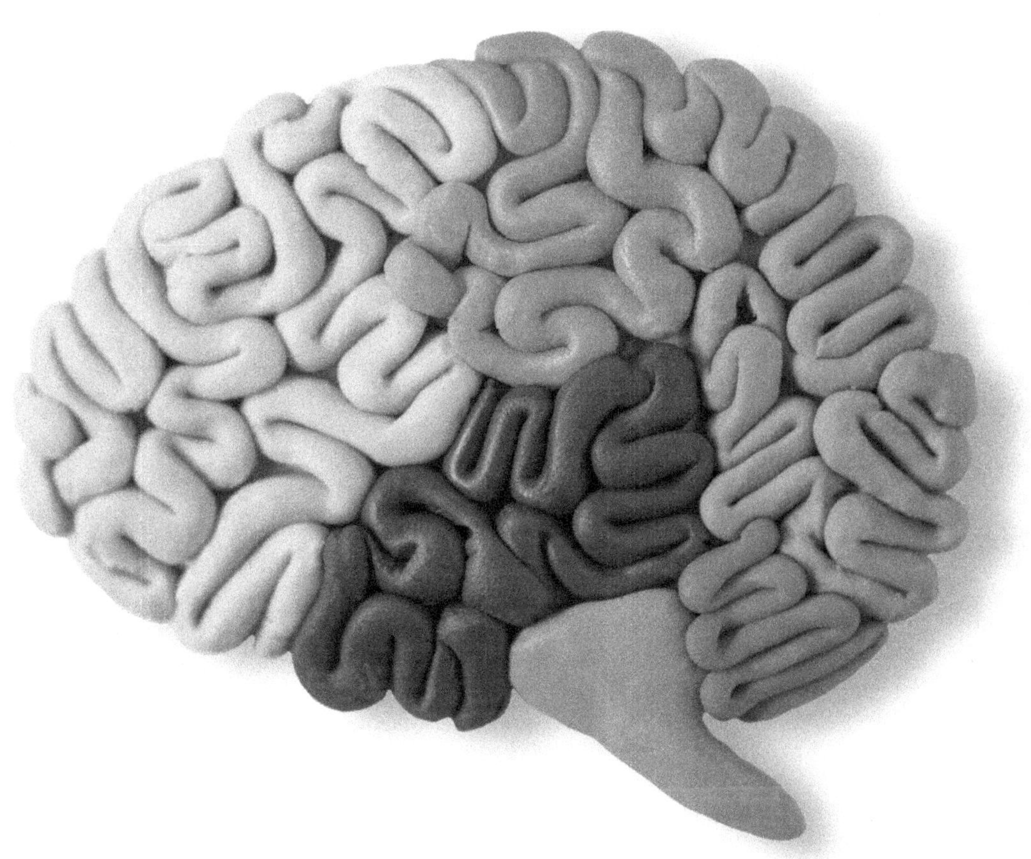

Richard K. COHEN Michele A. HEROLD
Emily R. PELUSO Katie UPSHAW Kelsee G. YOUNG

Foreword by Martín Blank

Solution Tree | Press

555 North Morton Street
Bloomington, IN 47404
800.733.6786 (toll free) / 812.336.7700
FAX: 812.336.7790

email: info@SolutionTree.com
SolutionTree.com

Visit **go.SolutionTree.com/instruction** to download the free reproducibles in this book.

Printed in the United States of America

Library of Congress Control Number: 2024012249

ISBN: 978-1-958590-41-6

Solution Tree
Jeffrey C. Jones, CEO
Edmund M. Ackerman, President

Solution Tree Press
President and Publisher: Douglas M. Rife
Associate Publishers: Todd Brakke and Kendra Slayton
Editorial Director: Laurel Hecker
Art Director: Rian Anderson
Copy Chief: Jessi Finn
Production Editor: Alissa Voss
Copy Editor: Charlotte Jones
Proofreader: Evie Madsen
Text and Cover Designer: Kelsey Hoover
Acquisitions Editors: Carol Collins and Hilary Goff
Assistant Acquisitions Editor: Elijah Oates
Content Development Specialist: Amy Rubenstein
Associate Editor: Sarah Ludwig
Editorial Assistant: Anne Marie Watkins

Acknowledgments

This is now my second book that stems from the incredible work of Dr. Maurice J. Elias and his colleagues. Thank you, Dr. Elias, for always serving as an incredible role model of academics, social and emotional intelligence, and character. I also wish to acknowledge the inclusive and all-around heartwarming staff, parents, students, and community of Metuchen School District.

I would especially like to thank the entire Moss School Staff and, of course, my coauthors, Emily, Katie, Kelsee, and Michele. I have been blessed to work with so many amazing teachers. These four educators have elevated themselves through passion, perseverance, curiosity, collaboration, and love for their students from the most amazing teachers to now the most amazing teachers of teachers. You are changing the field or preschool education in so many wonderful ways.

We would all like to express our gratitude to Solution Tree Press, and specifically, Douglas Rife, Alissa Voss, and Todd Brakke. (You are the man, Todd; we can't thank you enough for everything.)

I would like to thank my formative friends for life, Don Cipriani, Daniel Johnson, James Savage, and the late James Foley. I would never have written a book without your inspiration, support, or off-the-hook antics.

I would like to thank my parents for giving me everything I ever needed in life to pursue my dreams and achieve them. To my sister Lonni, you mean more to me than you may ever know; thank you for always being there for me and guiding me throughout my life.

Finally, I would like to thank my family who I adore. To my wife Camila, I could not love you more; and to my children, Sarah, Benny, and Sofia, I could not be more proud of you. I will always love, and hate, your jokes about the "Ricky process."

—Rick

First, I would like to thank Alissa Voss, Todd Brakke, and the entire team at Solution Tree for their time and support throughout our writing process.

I would also like to thank my amazing coauthors Rick Cohen, Katie Upshaw, Kelsee Young, and Emily Peluso for being there for me both personally and professionally. Thank you for your guidance, kindness, and perseverance throughout this process!

Thank you to my wonderful parents, Joanne and Perry Reed, my in-laws, Michele and Robert Herold, and sister-in-law, Caitlin Herold, for always believing in me!

An extra special thank you goes to my loving husband, Robert Herold Jr., for always being in my corner and lifting me up when I need it most! To my dear son, Robert Herold III, I hope you always know your dreams have no limits and neither does our love for you!

Thanks to you, reader, for taking the time to learn this strategy we are all so proud of!

—Michele

Thank you to our publishing team at Solution Tree, especially Alissa Voss and Todd Brakke, for excellent guidance and being patient with me as I learned how to be a coauthor and all that goes into writing a book.

Big thanks to my coauthors and colleagues, Rick Cohen, Michele Herold, Katie Upshaw, and Kelsee Young, for inspiring me to continue to grow personally and professionally.

Thank you to Karen Calantoni, Lori-Anne DiSerio, and Caroline Mandel for always supporting and raising me up.

Thank you to my in-laws, Diana and Vince Peluso, and my parents, Meg and Tom Walsh, for loving me and encouraging me to be all that I can be. Thank you to my husband, Vince Peluso, my true partner in life, with whom I can do anything. Last but certainly not least, thank you to my children, Vincent and Juliet, my greatest blessings. I want you to see yourself in me and know you can accomplish leaps and bounds more. All that we do is because of and for you.

Thanks to you, the reader, whether you're an educator, related service provider, administrator, or parent for wanting to learn how to do your best for your students and our children.

—Emily

I would like to start by giving the biggest thank you to the Solution Tree team for all of their guidance and support through our process of writing this book!

I extend my deepest appreciation to my coauthors Rick Cohen, Emily Peluso, Kelsee Young, and Michele Herold, whose dedication, knowledge, and collaboration were invaluable throughout this journey.

I am immensely grateful to my husband Bryan, whose steadfast support and encouragement gave me the strength to push through the highs and lows of the writing process.

I want to say a special thank you to the exceptional teachers whose passion, dedication, and perseverance inspired me in my teaching journey. Your tireless efforts in shaping the lives of students with diverse needs is unwavering.

Lastly, I would like to thank my family for their understanding, patience, and encouragement as I poured my heart into this project. My mom and grandmother brought teaching into my life and without their inspiration I would not be where I am today.

This book stands as a testament to the collective effort and commitment of every author involved, every teacher who has inspired us, and all the teacher this book goes on to support.

—Katie

Thank you to the publishing team at Solution Tree, especially Alissa Voss and Todd Brakke, for all your efforts and contributions.

I acknowledge my coauthors, Rick Cohen, Michele Herold, Emily Peluso, and Katie Upshaw, for sharing their expertise and knowledge of our youngest learners.

I admire the dedication of the administrators and teachers who bring structured SELf-questioning to life daily within the Metuchen School District.

Working with my preschool students and their families, past and present, has also been a blessing and an inspiration.

I express gratitude to my late grandparents, Joan and Richard Gentile, who taught me at an early age the belief that I could achieve anything through determination.

With love and appreciation, I recognize my mother, Kim Gentile-Young, and my father, Larry Young. Their unwavering devotion has compelled me to believe in myself.

—Kelsee

Solution Tree Press would like to thank the following reviewers:

Gina Cherkowski
Education Researcher
Headwater Learning
Calgary, Alberta, Canada

Barbara Cirigliano
Education Consultant
Woodstock, Illinois

John D. Ewald
Education Consultant
Frederick, Maryland

Lauren Smith
Assistant Director of Elementary Learning
Noblesville Schools
Noblesville, Indiana

Visit **go.SolutionTree.com/instruction** to download the free reproducibles in this book.

Table of Contents

Reproducibles are in italics

About the Authors

Richard K. Cohen is chief academic officer for secondary education of Edison Township Public Schools in New Jersey. He is the former assistant superintendent and principal of Moss School of Metuchen School District (preK and kindergarten) in New Jersey. He serves as faculty for Rutgers University in New Brunswick, New Jersey. He served as the principal of Red Bank Primary School (preK to third grade) in New Jersey for six years. Prior to Red Bank, Rick was the founding director of a new bilingual school, Colegio Americano (preK to twelfth grade), in San Salvador, El Salvador. Rick began his teaching career as a Teach for America corps member in 1996 in Phoenix, Arizona. Rick's first formal teaching assignment was in juvenile detention centers in Washtenaw County, Michigan, as a University of Michigan Project Community service-learning student facilitator.

Rick has served as a leader of social-emotional learning (SEL) at the district, county, state, and national levels. His work infusing academic state standards and SEL skills together along with evidence-based character education has won multiple National School of Character and National Promising Practice Awards from Character.org. In 2015, Rick served on the New Jersey State Standards Revision Committee, helping add self-reflection and metacognition into academic state standards. Rick is the coauthor of *The Metacognitive Student: How to Teach Academic, Social, and Emotional Intelligence in Every Content Area*. His work has also been published in *Educational Leadership*, *Edutopia*, *District Administration*, Character.org's *11 Principles Framework for Schools*, and *NJEA Review*'s Great Ideas column.

Rick received a bachelor's degree in political science from the University of Michigan and a master's degree in educational administration from Rutgers University.

To learn more about Rick's work, visit TheMetacognitivePreschooler on Facebook, @MetacognitivePK on X, and the_metacognitive_preschooler on Instagram.

Michele Antonia Herold has been an integrated preschool teacher in the Metuchen School District since 2018. She is an active member of the school leadership team. Throughout her teaching career, Michele has provided training on SEL and metacognition at the district, national, and international levels through professional organizations. Overall, Michele's educational philosophy is to create an uplifting, compassionate, and nurturing classroom that encourages her students' confidence, kindness, and love for learning!

Michele is a member of Character.org and represented her school in accepting the National School of Character Award and National Promising Practice Award. She received the Moss Teacher of the Year Award for the 2020–2021 school year.

Michele is a graduate of Monmouth University and received her bachelor's degree in early childhood education and English. Most importantly, Michele is a proud wife and mother!

Emily Rose Peluso is a school-based speech-language pathologist (SLP) at Moss Elementary School of Metuchen School District. She formerly worked as a school-based SLP for the Plainfield School District and First Children's School. In addition to the school setting, she has experience working in the home setting through New Jersey Early Intervention Services for Children's Specialized Hospital and the private practice setting at Reach for the Stars. Emily has been practicing since 2016 and has evaluated and treated children of various ages who present with a range of speech and language abilities and needs. As a school-based SLP at Moss Elementary School, Emily provides speech and language services to preschool and kindergarten students to facilitate their speech clarity and receptive, expressive, and pragmatic language skills.

Emily is a member of the American Speech-Language-Hearing Association (ASHA) and maintains the ASHA Certificate of Clinical Competence. Always the learner, Emily received an award for continuing education from ASHA in 2019 and 2020. She was also named 2019–2020 Educational Services Professional of the Year at Moss Elementary School. Emily has implemented meaningful child-directed services and worked collaboratively with colleagues and families to help students understand the power of communication.

With a focus on speech-language pathology, Emily received a bachelor's degree in science from Towson University in Towson, Maryland, and a master's degree in arts from Kean University in Union, New Jersey. Emily considers being a mother and wife her greatest achievements.

Katie Upshaw is a preschool special education teacher in the Metuchen School District in New Jersey. Katie serves as a teacher leader and teacher union representative, school leadership team chair, and member of many district committees. Katie comes from a generational teaching family and has been involved in the classroom since her grandmother and mother were teachers. Her first formal role in special education was as a children's program coordinator until she received her job in the Metuchen School District. Her informal and formal experience as an educator has only fueled her focus on helping all students succeed!

Katie is a member of Character.org and served as a school representative in accepting the New Jersey School of Character Award and National Promising Practice Award from Character.org in 2023. Katie continues to be a member of the Rutgers Labor Management Collaborative. Katie has provided training on SEL and metacognition at the district, national, and international levels through professional organizations and universities.

Katie received a bachelor's degree in early childhood education and English from Monmouth University and is pursuing her master's degree in educational leadership from William Patterson University.

You can follow Katie's work on Instagram at @mrs.upshaw_prek.

Kelsee Gentile Young has been a special education preschool teacher at Moss School in Metuchen, New Jersey, since 2020. Her educational philosophy is to create a warm and nurturing environment for her students to play, grow, and thrive, upholding compassion over compliance. Kelsee has presented about structured SELf-questioning at Rider University and is a Class Dojo mentor for her school. She is a member of the Metuchen School District's Special Education Parent Advisory Council, the special education district leadership team, and the school leadership team. Kelsee received the Moss School Teacher of the Year Award for the 2023–2024 school year.

Kelsee is pursuing her master's degree in special education autism and developmental disabilities through William Patterson University in Wayne, New Jersey. She recevied her bachelor's degree in early childhood special education from Kean University in Union, New Jersey, and her associate degree in liberal arts from Middlesex College. Kelsee received registered behavior technician training from the Autism Partnership Foundation and enjoys studying behavior intervention.

You can follow Kelsee's work on X at @kelsee_young.

To book Richard K. Cohen, Michele A. Herold, Emily R. Peluso, Katie Upshaw, or Kelsee G. Young for professional development, contact pd@SolutionTree.com.

Foreword

by Martín Blank

A few years ago, I was in Tulsa, Oklahoma, giving a talk. Later that day, I met a young man working in the hotel lobby who had recently been released from prison for domestic violence. As we sat talking on that humid evening, he shared with me, "Nobody ever taught me what to do with my fear, with my anger." Most of us didn't learn this in school nor at home. There are real repercussions to neglecting this core area of education. Mental health struggles, incarceration, family separations, alcohol and drug use, impulsivity, all of these go up when we don't study the universe within us.

One day, our students will create, sustain, and rethink the systems we all will depend on and benefit from. Helping them learn to identify, understand, regulate, and manage their thoughts and feelings is arguably the single most important intervention we can put in place for a better, kinder, and more connected world. Society moves in one direction or another because someone at some point made a decision, and how this person feels impacts the quality of those decisions.

Schools have traditionally focused on helping us learn about the external world. Social-emotional learning—as implemented in great detail in this book in the form of SELf-questioning—is a gentle invitation for early childhood students to explore their internal worlds. These inner worlds are rich with messages, only audible and discernable once we develop our listening muscles. SELf-questioning *is* the development of these listening muscles. It empowers even the youngest students to consider simple but powerful questions and then be open to the answers. What more valuable skill can we teach students than the ability to tune into their own bodies, feelings, and thoughts and understand their triggers and reactions so that they can make more informed decisions about how to flourish in their lives?

The idea that emotions matter is the premise of social-emotional learning. Marc Brackett's (2019) *Permission to Feel* invites us to be what he calls "emotion scientists." We can become curious about these messengers from beyond—beyond our conscious, everyday awareness. Our emotions help us make sense of our relationship with the world. They are the way our bodies communicate with us, driving us to move toward something. The word *emotion* even has the word *motion* built into it.

Yet, we often resist fully acknowledging or noticing our emotions. They can be scary. They can mean things. They can tell us something. What if they tell us something about ourselves that we don't want to hear? Very often, we resist them. And the things we resist tend to persist, especially pain. And what emotions give us pain? Typically sadness, guilt, shame, and so on. So we resist those, and they show up, and then we can't get away from them. They represent parts of ourselves that have a deep need for love—not from anyone else, but from ourselves.

All of this starts in earnest after you've graduated preschool. But when you're *in* preschool, it's a whole different story. Preschool-aged students don't resist emotions. They allow them to come, often in ways that challenge teachers. The lesson our young students need to learn is how to effectively regulate emotions *without* resisting them, to express themselves without shame, judgment, or fear of retaliation. So then, why do so many preschoolers become elementary students, secondary students, and even adults who resist their emotions?

Adults are often uncomfortable when children show emotions. When a child displays deep sadness, frustration, anger, or rage, especially to an adult who has experienced deep trauma, it might be too much to bear for the adult. Thus, the child learns to repress and resist emotions to avoid making others uncomfortable. But was it the emotion that caused the discomfort for the adult or the underdeveloped skill in its expression?

SELf-questioning, as you will learn from this book, is an effective methodology for helping children and adults work together toward becoming more emotionally intelligent. And the learning doesn't stop with the student: every time a teacher or student asks a metacognitive question, a stepping back occurs. Emotions have a way of getting messy, often *very* quickly, and structured SELf-questioning is an invitation for adults and students to empower themselves, take ownership of their emotions, and thrive.

Because we are only as good as our best questions, structured SELf-questioning gives adults and students the tools to get curious about their emotional realities. Every student deserves a caring adult, and when you get curious about a student's feelings, you send them a message of love and acceptance. You are telling them that they matter enough to you for you to get curious about how they're feeling. They are worthy of your time, attention, and interest. And they deserve your interest. Saying "emotions matter" really means saying "you matter." Structured SELf-questioning is a language to communicate this core message to every student: I care about you because you matter.

I'm grateful to Richard K. Cohen, Michele A. Herold, Emily R. Peluso, Katie Upshaw, and Kelsee G. Young for bringing this framework into the hands of so many preschool educators. As you'll read in the coming pages, they've tinkered, redesigned, and tested theories that could have stayed on paper but instead have been brought to life through their effort. I can think of no better ambassadors for this work. It's a simple yet profound approach to supporting students' social and emotional development, but it's really doing much more than that: it's creating a legacy of socially and emotionally prepared future leaders.

Despite the played-out adage, children are *not* our future. They are our present. And when we remember that, we more effectively invest in their well-being. This book describes that investment. I hope you heed its call!

Martín Blank, MAPP, RYT, is the founder and CEO of School Wellbeing Solutions (https://schoolwellbeingsolutions.com), applying his expertise in positive psychology, resilience, and social-emotional learning to help K–12 schools and districts create environments that support the well-being of leaders, teachers, staff, and students. For more than two decades, he has worked with hundreds of schools and learning organizations to create the conditions that lead to flourishing leaders, staff, educators, and students.

Introduction

As early as age 4, children can learn that behavior has causes, that people have feelings, and that there is more than one way to solve a problem.

—Myrna B. Shure

At the start of the 2020 school year, three-year-old Ben experienced success for much of the day at Moss Elementary. A preschool student, Ben loved painting, drawing, and making up his own stories. At the block center, he would create cityscapes and tell stories about the characters living there. But sometimes, when Ben got frustrated—if a peer took something from him, or if he couldn't figure out a problem—he exploded. Most often, Ben screamed. His cries carried through classroom walls and down the hall. Ben's screaming frightened his classmates, shattered everyone's focus, and disrupted learning time for his teacher and peers.

It was concerning for the staff at Moss School, a half-day preK and kindergarten school in Metuchen, New Jersey, to see Ben so upset and all the other students frightened. Katie Upshaw, Ben's preschool teacher and coauthor of this book, did all she could to intervene. So did the speech therapist, coauthor Emily Peluso, as did the child study team members, including certified behaviorists, the learning disabilities teacher consultant, and the school psychologist. All would come to help, all to no avail—at first.

Once Ben started screaming, like with any preschool student having an emotional meltdown, Moss staff tried as many precise interventions from Ben's "self-calming toolbox" as they could. In instances when those precise interventions did not lead to any de-escalation, all the adults around resorted to a less precise, any-intervention-known-to-humankind approach. The hope was to keep Ben from getting physical (throwing chairs, tossing all the materials in bins across the room, kicking, punching, or spitting). After trying every trick they knew and feeling like they could not do anything else to help Ben calm down, staff guided Ben into the hallway to ensure the other students in the classroom were not in harm's way.

Once in the hallway, a still-screaming Ben threw himself to the ground, pinned his own shoulders to the floor, and arched his back. The principal of Moss School, coauthor Rick Cohen, hearing the screams from his office, walked over to make sure the situation was safe.

Emotional outbursts like these had become noticeably more frequent and more intense by October 2020. As he made the long walk down the hallway, Rick (who could often identify who the upset student was by the sound and tone of the screams) asked himself, "What can I do?" to help bring calm—to himself, to the student, to the staff members, and to the situation.

When Rick arrived at the end of the hallway, staff were standing in a circle around Ben to make sure he didn't hurt himself. Ben laid himself out across the hallway floor and flailed his arms and legs as if he were making snow angels on the carpet, staring up intently at the lights and screeching at the top of his lungs with his mouth wide open. The only thing Rick was confident of at that point was that any intervention he tried would only make matters worse. Rick, Katie, Emily, and the circle of certified specialists and paraprofessionals looked up at each other and shrugged their shoulders. The only precise intervention left was for all of them to wait until Ben tired himself out while ensuring he avoided hurting himself or others. In the meantime, the rest of the students and staff in Mrs. Upshaw's preschool classroom would wait out the disruption to the best of their abilities. This happened again and again and again.

The story of Ben's frequent, intense, and emotionally-charged behaviors is all too familiar, especially since COVID-19 emerged. More and more preschool students walk into preschool classrooms with increasing difficulty recognizing their feelings, communicating their feelings, asking for the help they need, or calming themselves down. This introduction refers to studies that started to emerge in 2023 about the impact of COVID-19 on preschoolers' social and emotional well-being. As expected, the findings of these studies confirm what many preschool teachers and administrators already know all too well.

The problem of missing or underdeveloped social and emotional learning (SEL) competencies among preschool-aged children is widespread. We wrote *The Metacognitive Preschooler* to offer a lifeline to preschool educators across the globe. The need for a singular, practical solution to overcome the SEL gaps of so many of our youngest students has never been greater. In this introduction, we show what this singular, practical solution looks like. We also give an overview of how this book will be a vital support for you in filling the SEL gap with all your early childhood students. We have a lot of ground to cover, and we guarantee it will be worth it!

The Need for One Practical Strategy

As the experience with Ben demonstrates, and studies are now showing, COVID-19 is having a big impact on preschoolers. In practice, many of the tools from everyone's tool kit are no longer working consistently. Since COVID-19, things are different. Preschoolers are among those students hit hardest.

In a *PLoS ONE* article about the impact of COVID-19 lockdown on preschool children and their parents, researchers Irina Jarvers and colleagues (2023) conclude:

> Preschool children's mental health is strongly and negatively influenced by the ongoing COVID-19 pandemic and its lockdown measures. . . . It is estimated

> that up to 15 % of children and adolescents worldwide suffer from mental health problems, which constitute the number one cause of disability. In consequence of the ongoing COVID-19 pandemic, even larger percentages have been reported. . . . For preschool children, the increase in parental stress and parental depressive and anxious symptomatology explained a large portion of the increases in children's own internalizing and externalizing problems during the COVID-19 pandemic.

As a result of COVID-19 (both during its height and since), preschool teachers are witnessing firsthand the increase in preschoolers' internalizing and externalizing problems. These disruptive behaviors are markedly more frequent, more extreme, and demand more adult intervention for longer periods of time.

According to an article written in the *International Journal of Clinical and Health Psychology* (Ding et al., 2022):

> The severe impact of the COVID-19 pandemic on family life significantly increased the risk for exacerbated emotional and behavioral health among preschool children. . . . It is considered vital to identify risk factors for vulnerable families and then to implement precise interventions when necessary for emotional and behavioral health of children in these families.

While this guidance from researchers is sound, it is easier said than done, and it is not always effective. Identifying the risk factors of students and their families takes time (and sometimes, families are hard to reach or less eager to share such sensitive information), as does training on the precise interventions, the mastered delivery of which also takes time. As we saw in the case of Katie Upshaw's classroom, even when she and other well-trained staff and specialists had identified risk factors and implemented precise interventions, the situation remained unsafe and completely disruptive.

What can be done for our youngest students? What can be done for preschoolers who lack the SEL competencies needed for success at school and in life? What can be done for preschoolers who may have identified, or not yet identified, executive function deficiencies? What is the best way for preschool staff members and parents to manage all of this?

It is clear that an effective and practical strategy is desperately needed.

The Importance of Social and Emotional Learning (SEL) Competencies

Fortunately, as the epigraph for this introduction states, we know that all preschool students are capable of learning the social and emotional skills they need to better manage the social and emotional challenges they are experiencing (Shure, 2001). This book dives deep into how the one practical, easy-to-learn-and-implement, metacognitive strategy we call *structured SELf-questioning* teaches all preschoolers SEL competencies and develops preschoolers' academic skills at the same time. But first, it's important to establish a common definition of exactly what the SEL competencies are that students so desperately need for greater success in any K–12 system of education, as well as greater success in college, careers, and life.

The learning objectives that empower all students to develop into emotionally self-regulated and independent social problem solvers and decision makers are categorized as SEL competencies by organizations such as the Collaborative for Academic, Social, and Emotional Learning (CASEL; n.d.). CASEL (n.d.) has developed a framework built around five core social and emotional competencies that can be taught and applied at various developmental stages from childhood to adulthood and across diverse cultural contexts. Many school districts, states, and countries have used the *CASEL 5* to establish preschool to high school learning standards and competencies that articulate what students should know and be able to do for academic success, school and civic engagement, health and wellness, and fulfilling careers.

The CASEL 5 core SEL competencies are as follows (CASEL, n.d.).

1. **Self-awareness:** The ability to understand one's own emotions, thoughts, and values and how they influence behavior across contexts.
2. **Self-management:** The ability to manage one's emotions, thoughts, and behaviors effectively in different situations and to achieve goals and aspirations.
3. **Social awareness:** The ability to understand the perspectives of and empathize with others, including those from diverse backgrounds, cultures, and contexts.
4. **Responsible decision making:** The ability to make caring and constructive choices about personal behavior and social interactions across diverse situations.
5. **Relationship skills:** The ability to establish and maintain healthy and supportive relationships and to effectively navigate settings with diverse individuals and groups.

Does teaching three-, four-, and five-year-olds *self-awareness*, *self-management*, *social awareness*, *responsible decision making*, and *relationship skills* before entering kindergarten sound too far-reaching, or even unreasonable? Metacognition is the key to success. *The Metacognitive Preschooler* will show you how easy it is to teach our youngest students far-reaching learning objectives, including awareness of self and others, management of their own emotions and behavior, and complex problem-solving skills, with just one metacognitive strategy of structured SELf-questioning.

Before we begin our deep dive into the what and how of this one metacognitive strategy, it's important to note that this book focuses on four of the five SEL competencies previously listed (self-awareness, self-management, social awareness, and responsible decision making). It does not focus on teaching relationship skills. With preschoolers, we find that growth with relationship skills is an inevitable byproduct of teaching the other four competencies. Perhaps most importantly, the benefits of teaching preschoolers SEL competencies are astounding. According to Myrna Shure (2001), psychology professor at Drexel University and coauthor of the book from which this introduction's epigraph comes, the outcomes for students who learn SEL competencies like those we listed are numerous:

> Research has shown that when children learn to use problem-solving thinking, their social adjustment improves, with significant reductions in nagging and demanding, emotional upset, and social withdrawal. Children become more able to wait, share, and take turns, as well as to get along with others . . . In brief, children who have learned [personal and interpersonal cognitive problem-solving skills] concepts are more successful in getting what they want when they can have it and are better able to cope with frustration when they cannot. Finally, [teaching preschoolers personal and interpersonal cognitive problem-solving skills] not only helps lessen problem behaviors, but 1- and 2-year follow-up studies suggest that it can actually prevent their occurrence. (pp. 1–3)

Many researchers' subsequent findings since Shure's 2001 work agree. According to a meta-analysis by education scholars Joseph A. Durlak and colleagues (2011), teaching SEL competencies for student populations:

- Reduces aggression and emotional distress among students
- Increases helping behaviors at school
- Improves positive attitudes toward self and others
- Increases students' academic performance by 11 percentile points

Another meta-analysis, "Promoting Positive Youth Development Through School-Based Social and Emotional Learning Interventions" (Taylor, Oberle, Durlak, & Weissberg, 2017), confirms the benefits of increased SEL skill competencies and reports that these benefits, such as reduced conduct problems and emotional distress as well as increased academic performance, lasted years after programming. Findings within this research also report that increased SEL competencies were the best predictor of long-term benefits and that these benefits were experienced equally, regardless of students' socioeconomic status, race, or zip code (Taylor et al., 2017).

So, the researchers are in agreement, and the research is clear. SEL competencies can be learned as early as ages three and four, and the benefits are life-changing.

Challenges Teaching SEL in Preschools

A great deal has been learned about teaching SEL to all students. One lesson is very clear. For students of any age to actually learn SEL competencies and reap the benefits of evidence-based SEL, these skills need to be embedded into academic core content areas (Durlak et al., 2011) and daily routines at school. About SEL competencies, CASEL CEO Karen Niemi (2020) writes:

> When SEL is woven into the daily life of school—from academic instruction to discipline practices—it is more likely to produce the many benefits that research has documented, including the promotion of students' skills and attitudes, improved school climate and long-term academic achievement.

Even though preschool teachers fully understand the benefits of and need for SEL, trying to embed evidence-based SEL into academic preschool instruction and daily routines has been difficult. As a result, an increasing number of students are leaving preschool systems of education without the core SEL competencies needed for success in K–12.

This deficiency occurs for a variety of reasons. Among them, we see three major challenges that all preschool educators face when it comes to developing SEL competencies for all preschool students.

1. Students come into preschool from very diverse educational backgrounds (from limited or no school experience to extensive daycare programming experiences and everywhere in between) and with an even wider range of academic, social, and emotional needs. While there exists a multitude of resources and specialized programs (and a multitude of isolated, precise strategies that teachers can utilize to individualize preschool programming and interventions), preschool teachers need one easy-to-learn, multitiered strategy that can help all students academically, socially, and emotionally.
2. Three- and four-year-old students seem to be entering preschool classrooms with fewer SEL competencies than ever before. More and more three- and four-year-old students are struggling day to day to cope (emotionally, socially, and academically). Preschool teachers have observed there is a lot more SEL ground to cover.
3. Parents lack a practical strategy they can use at home. Without a practical strategy that all preschool parents can learn and apply with ease at home, the comprehensive partnerships between preschools and parents that support preschoolers academically, socially, and emotionally are extremely hard to establish within the short timeline of preschool education.

This book explains how all three challenges can be easily and effectively addressed when preschool educators sprinkle eye-dropper doses of the one simple, practical, metacognitive strategy, *structured SELf-questioning*. This book shows how easy it is to use this one strategy with all preschool students to embed SEL competencies into already existing academic curricula, preschool programming, and the daily routines of preschool life.

Structured SELf-questioning is not a new curriculum or program. It is one metacognitive strategy that can easily be embedded into any and all existing preschool state standards, preschool curricular and instructional programs—like *The Creative Curriculum for Preschool* (https://teachingstrategies.com/product/the-creative-curriculum-for-preschool) and Tools of the Mind (www.toolsofthemind.org), to name a few—and into any home.

After over a decade of collaboration and partnership with Maurice Elias, psychology professor at Rutgers University and coauthor of *Social Decision Making/Social Problem Solving [SDM/SPS]* (Butler, Romasz-McDonald, & Elias, 2011), we find that structured SELf-questioning is a strategy that is effective toward far-reaching ends for students across preK–12. This book's previously published companion, *The Metacognitive Student: How to Teach Academic, Social and Emotional Learning in Every Content Area* (Cohen et al., 2021), was written for K–12 teachers and parents. *The Metacognitive Student* has won two Gold Medals for Best Indie Book in Education (Foreword Reviews 2021 and IPPY Awards 2022), and this follow-up explains why and how it is as effective and easy for preschool teachers to apply across all classrooms as it is for educators who teach in K–12.

Why Teach Metacognition to Teach SEL?

The coauthors of this book have found that metacognition is the key to success when aiming to teach preschoolers the five CASEL (n.d.) SEL competencies of (1) self-awareness, (2) self-management, (3) social awareness, (4) responsible decision making, and (5) relationship skills. (Again, the fifth competency will result as an intentional byproduct of students using this book's strategy to gain proficiency with the first four.) Our favorite definition of *metacognition*, and the one we will use throughout this book, is "awareness and management of one's own thoughts" (Kuhn & Dean, 2004, p. 270), to which we would also add *feelings*. Since the first four of CASEL's five total SEL competencies involve awareness (self-awareness and social awareness) and management (self-management and responsible decision making), metacognition is a perfect match. When preschoolers are metacognitive, they are not only aware of their thinking and feelings, they are also able to take a step back, consider their situations, and manage their thinking and feelings. In other words, when preschoolers are metacognitive, they are able to calmly manage their thinking through complex emotions as well as multistep problem solving across academic content areas and social contexts.

There are seemingly endless reasons backed by researchers to teach metacognition. Teaching metacognition:

- Can be successful with students as young as age three (Wilson & Conyers, 2016)
- "Actually changes the structure of the brain, making it more flexible and open to even greater learning" (Price-Mitchell, 2015)
- Is ranked fourteenth among 150 educational influences by authors and educators Douglas Fisher, Nancy Frey, and John Hattie (2016)

Unfortunately, metacognition is not often taught explicitly in schools and especially less so in preschools. Indeed, you may not be convinced that very young students can learn such complex thinking. Is it really possible to overcome all these challenges and teach all three- and four-year-olds the ability to self-manage their thinking and their own emotions? Or to teach them responsible decision making and complex problem solving across academic content areas as well as social and emotional contexts? We fully understand any doubts you may have about this.

Fortunately, this book provides very clear evidence (chapter 1) and details the neuroscience (chapter 2) underpinning the teaching of one metacognitive strategy; it also provides simple and practical guides (chapters 3–7) on how to do so, with countless examples of success and resources you can immediately use in your classrooms and provide to your students' parents or caregivers.

What a Metacognitive Preschooler Looks Like

Before we dive into the rest of the book, we want to paint one more picture for you to illustrate what a metacognitive three- or four-year-old looks and sounds like. What in the world does a metacognitive preschooler actually do?

Let's take a look again at our friend Ben, mentioned in the vignette at the beginning of this introduction. After just a few months, Ben learned how to go from a student with underdeveloped executive function skills, who could be heard screaming uncontrollably throughout our hallways, to a student capable of using the metacognitive strategy of structured SELf-questioning across academic, social, and emotional challenges in his classroom with independence. The following real-life example depicts his growth and provides a mental movie of what a metacognitive preschooler looks like.

While still in his first year of preschool, Ben is at the blocks center working independently, building a structure with large snap blocks. While building, Ben takes the first step of the academic and social SELf-question set (Select a Focus), with prompting by his teacher Katie, who says, "Let's ask ourselves the SELf-question, What is my goal?" Ben says he wants to construct a second tower alongside the first tower he had just built.

From his training in structured SELf-questioning, Ben already knows the next step is to gather information. He asks himself internally, *What do I need?* He needs a block to be the start or foundation for the second tower he imagined. He finds one piece that is well-suited and connects it to the foundation of the first tower. Next, he steps back and scans the available pieces. He selects one to use as the first-floor wall. He stops, takes a step back literally to have a think about his thinking. After a few seconds, he moves into the third step in the structure (Brainstorm) and asks himself internally, *What can I do?* but he struggles to find where to place the wall so that it stands upright on its own power. He takes a step back and comes up with another brainstorm, and another and another, but every attempt he makes to place the wall leads to failure.

Ben begins to show mild frustration. Katie starts to get a little nervous and says in her head, *C'mon Ben, I can see you're frustrated. . . . Use your SELf-questioning.* Ben pauses and takes another step back from the tower. Katie watches, inferring that he is taking a step back to take the first step in the social and emotional question set now, having a think about his feelings (Identify Feelings) and asking himself, *How am I feeling?* Ben looks at the bin of snap blocks, chooses another piece, and tries again. It doesn't work. Ben tries to use a lot of force. He becomes visibly frustrated as he tries to jam the piece in the way he wants.

When Ben first arrived at Moss School in the fall of 2020, these moments were typically when he lost it. But it is now the spring of 2021, and Ben has been doing a lot of practicing. Ben takes a step back from the tower and says to himself, "I can do it!" Katie infers that Ben has asked himself what he can do to self-calm or accomplish his goal. Katie infers that he chose this positive affirmation, which she taught him to say when he gets frustrated during challenging academic tasks. Ben tries to place the wall again and fails again.

By this point, his frustration has grown, but the teacher sitting by his side continues to watch, waiting to see if he would use the structured SELf-questioning further to guide his self-talk through emotional coping skills. His frustration is visible, but instead of letting that frustration take control, Ben stops again and takes another step back. At this point, the solution is clear to him. After having tried multiple ways to build the tower without success, after trying positive affirmations without success, Ben decides that the best way forward is to ask a trusted adult for help. He turns to his teacher and says, "I need help."

Katie responds, "I can help you." No disruption occurred, no staff had to be called up to help or keep others safe. Rick continued working undisturbed in his office, and Ben stayed on task, as did his classmates. Ben persevered and kept practicing his strategy without scaffolding from his teacher, a result that was fast becoming routine for him.

Countless stories of these successes occur at Moss School on a daily basis. As a result of implementing structured SELf-questioning schoolwide at Moss School, preschool teachers, educational specialists, paraprofessionals, administrators, and parents in Metuchen School District have been able to figuratively step inside their students' (or children's) heads and develop habits of mind that enable even the youngest of students to take a step back, be aware of, and manage their thinking and feelings. By implementing the one metacognitive strategy of structured SELf-questioning, these educators have taught their preschool students how to guide their self-talk. And, as this book will demonstrate with countless examples and anecdotes from preschool classrooms across the full spectrum of preschool programming, the benefits are palpable.

About This Book

As we've established throughout this introduction, this book shows how any preschool teacher, paraprofessional, education specialist, daycare provider, school leader or administrator, parent, or other individual who works with our youngest learners can overcome academic, social, emotional, and behavioral challenges by simply sprinkling on eye-dropper dosages to their already existing daily routines and curricula of this one simple metacognitive strategy—structured SELf-questioning. This book shows how this strategy works with all students from all backgrounds and all types of abilities and needs to facilitate their learning of four SEL competencies that we know will help them pass the tests of school and life: (1) self-awareness, (2) social awareness, (3) self-management and (4) responsible decision making (CASEL, n.d.).

Know that you can embed these competencies directly into your existing daily routines and academic curricula without the need for additional instructional time, without having to learn a new program or implement a new curriculum, and without the need for costly resources or subscriptions. In fact, structured SELf-questioning can be taught with just the resources we show in chapter 1.

Readers of *The Metacognitive Preschooler* will finally be empowered to actualize the limitless benefits that evidence-based SEL interventions present with all three- and four-year-olds, regardless of background, home situation, strengths, talents, and developmental needs.

This book provides a practical how-to guide for teachers that makes it easy for educators to embed structured SELf-questioning into already existing curricula, management systems, and best practices, including the following.

- Morning meeting or circle time
- Inquiry-based units of study, inquiry-based learning, or problem-based learning
- Situations needing social conflict resolution, social decision making, or social problem solving
- Forms of literature for shared reading and read alouds
- Classroom management systems

This book is not intended nor recommended to be used to supplant existing curricula, daily routines, or classroom management systems. Rather, it explains how to embed structured SELf-questioning into teachers' existing preschool routines, curricula, instructional programs, and pedagogy across the entire spectrum of preschool programming and services.

The first and second chapters explain the research-based, evidence-based, and brain-based components that the metacognitive strategy of structured SELf-questioning has been built on and why it is thus so easily embedded by preschool teachers and internalized by preschool students. Chapters 3–7 explain the *why* and the *how* of this metacognitive strategy in all aspects of a preschooler's day, showing how to develop each student's academic, social, and emotional intelligence. These chapters include scenarios or small moments that serve as clear examples of what effective instruction using the strategy looks and sounds like. The last of these chapters, chapter 7, dips its toes into transfer theory and demonstrates how preschoolers easily achieve transfer with this strategy independently across academic content areas and social and emotional contexts.

Note that because this book talks about how to teach students to independently transfer SELf-questioning across content and contexts, we find that the best and most effective pedagogy to teach metacognition is for the teacher to conduct think alouds and facilitate gradual release of responsibility. To that end, chapters 3–7 include ample models of what teachers think and say out loud for students to see and hear what thinking about thinking and feelings looks and sounds like, and they explain how to use think alouds via a gradual release of responsibility.

To close, we would like to share two inspiring findings. The National Scientific Council on the Developing Child (2020), published by Harvard University's Center on the Developing Child, summarizes the following in an article titled "Connecting the Brain to the Rest of the Body: Early Childhood Development and Lifelong Health Are Deeply Intertwined:"

> The rapidly advancing frontiers of 21st century biological sciences now provide compelling evidence that the foundations of lifelong health are also built early. . . . This understanding can stimulate a new conversation about early childhood investment in a post-pandemic world. . . . By intervening early, we can

> prevent the physiological disruptions that lead to problems in early learning, social-emotional development, and both physical and mental health.

At the very front and center of this new conversation needs to be the power of a strategy that leads to guided self-talk. Why should we discuss guided self-talk for preschoolers when talking about lifelong health? In an article in the *American Journal of Education* titled "The Power of Inner Voice: Examining Self-Talk's Relationship with Academic Outcomes," Benjamin Uhrich and his colleagues (2023) say that:

> Self-talk is a unique and influential construct that should be of interest to academics and practitioners across the disciplines of psychology and education. Self-talk is ubiquitous in human beings and plays a role in virtually all learning functions. . . . [It's a] free-flowing internal dialogue that guides our behavior and future thoughts, for better or for worse.

We agree that the power of self-talk should be at the forefront of this new conversation for academics and practitioners across the fields of education and psychology. However, both we as authors and the psychologists with whom we have collaborated with for over a decade do not agree that self-talk has to be totally free-flowing, for better or for worse. This book is the outcome of a long-term conversation between preschool practitioners and psychologists on how preschoolers can be taught to guide their own self-talk, for the better thinking, behavior, and lifelong health of our next generation.

The Evidence-Based Underpinnings of Metacognition and Problem Solving

The greatest sign of success for a teacher is to be able to say, "The children are now working as if I did not exist."

—Maria Montessori

In the introduction (page 1), we recognized how things are different since COVID-19 and that preschoolers were among the hardest hit. Cognitive neuroscientist and former educator Janet N. Zadina (2023) eloquently puts this perception into words in her essay about neuroeducation, the brain, and instruction, titled "Connecting the Mind, Brain, and Heart for the Ideal Classroom Learning Environment:"

> The pandemic exacerbated the mental health issues of faculty and students, creating a mental health crisis that impairs learning. . . . Mental health issues are escalating. Teachers report across educational social media that students are lacking focus, have trouble paying attention, and are engaging more frequently in problematic behavior. . . . As teachers around the world have said to me, "Our students are not the same as before." We must recapture them.

While this may sound daunting, the good news is that there are evidence-based pathways to recapturing our students. Preschool teachers, administrators, and researchers like Zadina (2023) and the National Scientific Council on the Developing Child (2020) all agree that one of the most effective ways to recapture preschoolers is to teach whole child education, or in other words, connect hearts, minds, and brains. However, many preschool teachers and school administrators wonder, "How can we connect the hearts, minds, and brains of all preschoolers today, in such a short timeframe, with everything else we have to teach them?"

If you are skeptical, and that would be completely understandable, we are confident these next two chapters will convince you that this is not only possible, but it is also accomplished in a way that is evidenced-based, brain-based, and practical. This chapter shows the evidence-based pedagogies that make it possible to do all this connecting of preschoolers hearts, minds, and brains with just one metacognitive strategy. The next chapter shows how this one metacognitive strategy has also been designed to align with how the human brain works and develops. In so doing, connecting preschoolers' hearts, minds, and brains can be taught to flow naturally, but also in a way that is structured, guided, logical, and adaptive, all at the same time.

The Importance of Developing Metacognitive Problem Solvers

All this is perhaps best explained by CASEL researchers, who report that SEL is the process of learning to "integrate thinking, feeling, and behaving to achieve important life tasks" (Zins et al., 2007, p. 194). Connecting or integrating the hearts, minds, and brains of our youngest students through evidence-based pedagogies, and in alignment with neuroscience, may sound more complex than it does practical. To simplify this process, it can help to get really specific with what skills we are actually talking about integrating and connecting to each other.

In an article written by Amy Sippl (2023), a board-certified behavior analyst, she pinpoints with great specificity the skills entailed in problem solving that need to be connected:

> Problem-solving is the capacity to identify and describe a problem and generate solutions to fix it. Problem-solving involves other executive functioning behaviors as well, including attentional control, planning, and task initiation. Individuals might use time management, emotional control, or organization skills to solve problems as well. Over time, learners can observe their behavior, use working memory, and self-monitor behaviors to influence how we solve future issues.

The following is a breakdown of the various skills Sippl (2023) identifies and their alignment to the hearts, minds, and brains of preschoolers:

- **Hearts:** SEL competencies (*self-awareness*—observe and self-monitor behavior, and *self-management*—display attentional and emotional control)
- **Minds:** Higher-order critical thinking skills (*identify*, *describe*, and *generate*)
- **Brains:** Executive functions (such as *planning*, *organizational skills*, and *using working memory*).

When it comes to understanding the similarities and differences between these skills, it can get very nuanced, especially when trying to figure out the difference between SEL competencies and executive functioning. To that end, a report in the *International Journal of Child Care and Education Policy* titled "Fostering Socio-Emotional Learning Through Early Childhood Intervention" (Mondi, Giovanelli, & Reynolds, 2021) explains these distinctions well:

> SEL skills are often grounded in skills related to cognition, learning, and memory. Among the most significant contributors to SEL are executive functioning (EF) skills, which include the cognitive processes necessary for planning, organizing, and problem-solving. . .Thus, EF and SEL competencies, (including self-management, as identified by CASEL's framework) can be conceptualized as distinct but related, and at times overlapping, constructs.

Understanding the nuanced differences is complex, and therefore, knowing how to connect these skills can be even more complex. That said, how can we expect preschoolers to be aware of and manage connecting all of these skills, especially when just trying to connect two snap blocks can lead to tantrums and breakdowns?

Without structured SELf-questioning, preschoolers are too often left to their own devices. Leaving preschoolers without a strategy to help them figure out what thinking, SEL, and executive function skills to use when and in what sequence is not as effective as providing them with a strategy that does all that for them. According to the evidence-based SEL curriculum SDM/SPS for grades K–1 (Butler et al., 2011):

> The cornerstone of SDM/SPS, as with any life skills, character education, or social-emotional learning program, is to provide students with a problem-solving and decision-making strategy they can internalize to use in a variety of everyday and challenging situations they encounter. (p. 4)

With the metacognitive strategy of structured SELf-questioning, preschoolers finally have a strategy they can use not only for social-emotional problem solving and decision making but also for academic problem solving. Therefore, with the metacognitive strategy of structured SELf-questioning, preschoolers have one strategy that does all the connecting of hearts and minds for them. (Remember, we will get deeper into the brain connections in the next chapter.)

A Bird's Eye View of the Metacognitive Strategy of Structured SELf-Questioning

The coauthors of the K–12-focused *The Metacognitive Student: How to Teach Academic, Social, and Emotional Intelligence in Every Content Area* (Cohen et al., 2021) designed the metacognitive strategy of structured SELf-questioning as a derivative of the evidence-based SEL curriculum SDM/SPS for grades K–1 (Butler et al., 2011). Maurice J. Elias, coauthor of *SDM/SPS*, himself described *The Metacognitive Student* as a "research-informed book… that derives from thorough, long-term practice" in the foreword he authored (Cohen et al., 2021, p. xv). The coauthors of this book, in conjunction with guidance from Elias, have slightly modified the derivative of *The Metacognitive Student* to be developmentally appropriate and highly effective for preschool (both preK and kindergarten).

Before diving into some of the specific, long-term practices and pedagogies derived from *SDM/SPS*, let's take a bird's eye view of this derivative we call *structured SELf-questioning.* Graphic organizers often provide the best visuals both for adult and student understanding of the concept. The examples of graphics organizers for structured SELf-questioning that follow in figure 1.1 (page 16) and figure 1.2 (page 17) were created by the coauthors of *The Metacognitive Student,* along with teachers at Campbell Elementary School in Metuchen, New Jersey (grades 1–4). While these graphic organizers are not developmentally appropriate and therefore not recommended for use with preschool students, they make grasping the concept of structured SELf-questioning much easier.

In these images, you can observe the use of steps aligned with open-ended questions to guide students' thinking step by step through academic, social, and emotional problem solving. We encourage you to adapt these as you see fit.

Of course, there is nothing wrong with a good old simple T-chart. To that end, another way we can take a step back and have a bird's eye view of the strategy is via figure 1.3 (page 18).

Select a Focus What is the problem?	**Gather Information** What do I know?
Brainstorm, Evaluate, Plan and Act How can I solve this problem? What is the best way to solve this problem? What do I do first, second, and so on?	**Reflect** Did it work? How do I know?

Source: ©2024 Campbell Elementary School, Metuchen, New Jersey. Adapted with permission.

Figure 1.1: Four-square graphic organizer most often used in academic and social problem solving.

*Visit **go.SolutionTree.com/instruction** for a free reproducible version of this figure.*

Source: ©2024 *Campbell Elementary School, Metuchen, New Jersey. Adapted with permission.*

Figure 1.2: Funnel used for social and emotional problem solving.

Visit ***go.SolutionTree.com/instruction*** *for a free reproducible version of this figure.*

Academic and Social Steps	Academic and Social SELf-Questions	Social and Emotional Steps	Social and Emotional SELf-Questions
Select a Focus 	What is the problem? What is the question? What is the task? What is important? What is the user's need?	Identify Feelings 	How do I feel? What am I feeling? How does he, she, or they feel?
Gather Information 	What do I know? What do I need to know? What is important? How does he, she, or they feel?	Gather Information 	What do I know? What is causing this feeling? What can I control? What is my goal?
Brainstorm 	What can I do? What strategies can I use? How can I solve this problem? What are possible solutions? What is similar, and what is different? What connections can I make?	Brainstorm 	What can I do? What strategies can I use?
Evaluate 	What is the best way to solve this problem? Does this make sense? What are possible consequences?	Evaluate 	Has this strategy helped me in the past? Which is best?
Plan and Act 	What do I do first, second, and so on? Is this working?	Plan and Act 	What do I do first, second, and so on? Is this working?
Reflect 	Did it work? How do I know?	Reflect 	Did it work? How do I know?

Source: Adapted from Cohen et al., 2021.

Figure 1.3: Structured SELf-question sets for academic and social problem solving and social and emotional problem solving.

This version (see figure 1.3) lists the common set of steps and step names on the left column of each T-chart and a list of SELf-questions (to be used like a drop-down menu) on the right column of each T-chart. The left-half T is the structured SELf-question set for academic and social problem solving. The right-half T is the structured SELf-question set for social and emotional problem solving.

While T-charts provide an easy-to-follow visual, there is a lot going on underneath the surface. For example, you may be wondering why we refer to this as *one* metacognitive strategy while also talking about two seemingly separate question sets (an academic and social SELf-question set and a social and emotional SELf-question set). Having two separate question sets that use the same structure for all problem solving is necessary because of the way the brain works.

From years of implementation, we learned a formative, valuable lesson from Martín Blank, wellness consultant and founder of School Wellbeing Solutions. Martín had been serving as Metuchen School District wellness consultant and trainer for a number of years. According to Martín (personal communication, November 10, 2020), resolving academic and social problems requires that we look outward, while becoming aware of and managing emotions involved in personal and social problems requires that we look inward. This is because solving emotional challenges calls for a different neural pathway or circuitry—a different habit of mind. To that end, note the following.

- The SELf-questions on the left side of figure 1.3—or the academic and social SELf-question set—prompt students to look outside of themselves, to gather information from sources outside themselves, to read text, to read the body language and facial expressions of others, to listen to other's words, feelings, perspectives, and ideas, and to notice what they see in the world around them.
- The questions on the right side of figure 1.3—or the social and emotional SELf-question set—are designed to prompt preschoolers to read their own thoughts, their own bodies, and their own feelings. Guiding one's own self-talk through emotional problem solving requires looking inward.

This breakdown explains why the first step names are not identical. As a whole, each step, step name, and SELf-question is fateful in terms of the direction it will lead a student's thinking. We will talk more later in the chapter about step names and SELf-questions and how they have been carefully designed to direct students' thinking in a logical sequence to take the cognitive and metacognitive weight off the shoulders of three-, four-, and five-year-olds engaged in problem solving.

There are numerous and powerful evidence-based pedagogies and brain-based components underlying this one strategy. Now that we have an overview, we can dive deeper into the numerous evidence-based pedagogies that serve as the foundation of the one metacognitive strategy.

The Evidence Base of the Metacognitive Strategy of Structured SELf-Questioning

In the introduction of *SDM/SPS*, Butler and colleagues (2011) provide an evidence-based road map to developing independent social-emotional problem solvers. Turns out, this evidence-based SEL road map can also be used as a road map for developing independent academic problem solvers. With this exciting discovery, we have the means to develop students as academic, social, and emotional problem solvers simultaneously.

In this section, we show seven of the evidence-based SEL pedagogies the coauthors of this book and *The Metacognitive Student* (Cohen et al., 2021) all use. However, before you read the list, we want to assure you that this list of pedagogies does not need to be learned separately or in addition to anything. The evidence-based pedagogies that follow have already been baked into the structure and strategy itself. Any teacher could successfully use structured SELf-questioning without even reading this chapter. With that in mind, the purpose of this chapter is to promote your awareness of these evidence-based pedagogies to deepen your understanding of why and how one strategy can teach academic, social, and emotional problem solving simultaneously.

- **Evidence-based pedagogy 1:** Introducing an overall strategy for guided self-talk
- **Evidence-based pedagogy 2:** Using a *prompt or name* for the skill
- **Evidence-based pedagogy 3:** Linking cognitive (thinking) and social-emotional processes
- **Evidence-based pedagogy 4:** Asking questions through a facilitative approach
- **Evidence-based pedagogy 5:** *Integrating* social and emotional cognitive processes [the multistep problem-solving strategy] *into the academic work* of students
- **Evidence-based pedagogy 6:** *Teaching each element* [of the multistep problem-solving strategy] *as a separate skill*
- **Evidence-based pedagogy 7:** *Practicing* [the multistep problem-solving strategy] in the context of a variety of hypothetical, age appropriate, and open-ended choice and conflict situations (Butler et al., 2011)

Now, we are finally ready to take a closer look at how structured SELf-questioning adapts evidence-based best practices and synthesizes them all into one practical metacognitive strategy.

Evidence-Based Pedagogy 1: Introducing an Overall Strategy for Guided Self-Talk

In this book's introduction (page 1), we cited research on the power of self-talk and the benefits of harnessing such power through teaching preschoolers to *guide* that self-talk instead of leaving it to flow too freely. In order to provide an overview of structured SELf-questioning as an overall strategy for *guided* self-talk, we need to first take a step back and focus on the overall structure. First and foremost, the reason the coauthors of *The Metacognitive Student* (Cohen et al., 2021), in conjunction with the coauthors of this book, created one structure was based on a recommendation from *SDM/SPS*: "Giving students cognitive choices is good exercise for their intellect, as well as for their social-emotional and character development. Activities in SDM/SPS curricula accomplish this goal by structuring the initial questions teachers ask, both verbally and in written formats" (Butler et al., 2011, p. 17). Based on this long-term practice recommendation, we established one common structure, or one common set of problem-solving steps, that could be used to solve any problem (academic, social, or emotional).

Introducing one common set of steps for all problem solving as a guide for self-talk has almost limitless benefits for students and teachers, as well as parents. By establishing one common structure, or set of steps and step names, we've made the process much more efficient than the more common methods other educators have been following for decades, which involve teaching a different and separate set of steps and step names for every discipline. With one common set of steps and names, teachers no longer have to take the time to teach one set of steps and step names for solving mathematics problems, another similar set to teach the scientific method, another for solving social conflict, yet another for inquiry or engineering, and so on. With just one set of steps to learn and apply for problem solving, students are capable of:

- Making better use of working memory
- Logically sequencing the multiple steps of multistep problem solving
- Mastering application of the structure more efficiently
- Transferring the structure across academic, social, and emotional contexts with ease
- Deepening learning

Finally, since cohesion between home and school can benefit student learning, having one set of steps and step names for problem solving that work both at school and at home accelerates internalization and makes the transfer, practice, and reinforcement of learning from inside school to outside school easier for everyone.

Evidence-Based Pedagogy 2: Teaching for Internalization Through Step Names

Next came a way to help preschoolers internalize this overall strategy to guide self-talk through multistep problem solving across academic content and social and emotional contexts. In *SDM/SPS* (Butler et al., 2011), there is guidance on teaching skills that includes "using a prompt or name for the skill. . .Skill learning is increased when the skill has a name" (p. 13). To that end, the coauthors of *The Metacognitive Student* (Cohen et al., 2021) developed the one common set of steps with common step names. We have seen success with other school districts adopting the step names in this book. To demonstrate this in great detail, each chapter of this book provides numerous examples of scenarios of students using the step names to help guide their thinking from the entire spectrum of preschool classroom settings and placements. We have also seen success with districts collaboratively developing their own step names.

As discussed earlier in this chapter, figure 1.3 (page 18) shows two structured SELf-question sets: one for academic and social problem solving and one for social and emotional problem solving. Notice that the two sets are identical except for the starting action, which differentiates between selecting a focus and identifying feelings. From this point, the structured progression is the same in both SELf-question sets; only the SELf-questions associated with each prompt change. To that end, we do recommend that you focus your introduction of the overall strategy of structured SELf-questioning on the social and emotional SELf-question set first (before introducing the academic and social SELf-question set) as part of your morning routines. In so doing, preschoolers are less likely to get confused. Most importantly, once students master the strategy to help calm their own emotions, students are in a better emotional state for thinking and learning, so best to focus on emotional problem solving right away; it will pay major dividends.

Evidence-Based Pedagogy 3: Linking Cognitive and Social-Emotional Processes

The third evidence-based recommendation of *SDM/SPS* recommends "linking cognitive and social-emotional processes" (Butler et al., 2011, p. 6). The coauthors understood this to mean that the social-emotional cognitive processes involved in social and emotional decision making and problem solving (heart) should be connected with critical thinking skills found throughout preschool academic state standards (mind). We find it easier to say that hearts, minds, and brains can be connected most effectively and efficiently through "linking thinking skills."

Figure 1.4 shows how the critical thinking skills found throughout the social-emotional cognitive processes from *SDM/SPS* (the second column) are directly linked with the most common academic critical thinking skills found throughout academic problem-solving processes and national academic state standards (the third column). In the first column, you will see that the step names are also linked to the cognitive verbs that are aligned to each step within the problem-solving processes.

Figure 1.4 provides a bird's eye view of how all the critical thinking skills connect across academic, social, and emotional processes. But again, we would like to reiterate an important note here and remind you that you may choose your own step names to best fit your classroom, personal preferences, or already existing curricula. You are, of course, also invited to consider adopting the step names as we use them in this book. There is a great deal of flexibility when it comes to the names you give the steps or separate skills. However, we strongly recommend fidelity to the sequence of the steps and fidelity to the SELf-questions within the chart. The sequence of the steps and SELf-questions have been tested over many years with preschool students, and the students have shown over time that they can successfully internalize the SELf-questions and transfer them across contexts with ease.

Teaching students the one common sequence of thinking skills along with aligned SELf-questions is where connections between the heart and mind really begin to take off and occur without effort.

Academic and Social and Social and Emotional SELf-Question Set Steps	Critical Thinking Skills of SDM/SPS (Butler et al., 2011)	Cognitive Verbs Found in Common Core State Standards (CCSS; and number of times they appear in K–12)
Select a Focus or Identify Feelings	*Identifying* issues or problems and putting them into words	Identify (35)
Gather Information	*Determining* goals	Determine (80)
Brainstorm	*Generating* alternative solutions	Create (41) Develop (71)
Evaluate	*Selecting* the best solution	Evaluate (36)
Plan and Act	*Envisioning* what can happen and *planning* the details	Solve (111)
Reflect	*Noticing* what happened and *using the information* for future problem solving	Interpret (78) Reflect (26)

Source for standard: National Governors Association Center for Best Practices (NGA) & Council of Chief State School Officers (CCSSO), 2010.

Figure 1.4: Linking thinking skills.

Evidence-Based Pedagogy 4: The Facilitative Approach Involves Asking

With thinking skills inherent in the multiple steps sequenced and aligned, the next focus is the role questioning plays. As we have found from decades of practice, not all questions are equal. To that end, the main derivative of the evidence-based recommendations from *SDM/SPS* can be summarized simply as a shift from structured teacher-driven questioning to structured SELf-questioning. According to the evidence-based pedagogy recommended by Butler and colleagues (2011), when a student is stuck:

> The main role of the teacher is not to solve students' problems or to make their decisions for them. Instead, teachers are facilitators of students' decision-making and problem-solving skills. . . . *The facilitative approach involves asking questions rather than telling*. However, questions are not all the same. (pp. 16–17)

The metacognitive strategy of structured SELf-questioning modifies the facilitative approach from a teacher-generated questioning approach to an approach that utilizes purposeful student-generated self-questions.

Teacher-generated questioning engages the teacher in doing most of the critical thinking, while structured SELf-questioning engages the student in doing all of the critical thinking and problem solving. Teacher-generated questions send an unintended, covert, subtle message to students as they begin their educational career: "When stuck, stop and wait for the teacher to help you figure out how to get unstuck." SELf-questions used from the very beginning of students' educational careers send an intentional, overt, powerful message: "When stuck, I ask myself questions to help me figure out how to get myself unstuck." Certainly, teacher-generated questions can lead a student to the kind of thinking needed to get unstuck. But what happens when that same student gets stuck, and the teacher is not there by their side to prompt them?

You may have found what we found to be the case all too often at Moss School; when stuck on a word, early readers often stop reading rather than trying to independently problem solve, or they may just skip over the word or make it up incorrectly, negatively impacting comprehension. Instead, with structured SELf-questioning, students of all ages are trained on how to prompt their own thinking, step by step, to get unstuck. As an intended byproduct within the design of structured SELf-questioning, preschoolers develop greater perseverance because they develop the habits of mind, behaviors, and character traits of independent problem solvers that do not give up at the first sign of struggle.

Evidence-Based Pedagogy 5: Integrating Social and Emotional Cognitive Processes Into the Academic Work of Students

You've likely already noticed that the *S*, *E*, and *L* of SELf-questioning are capitalized. The reason the strategy is called *structured SELf-questioning* as opposed to *structured self-questioning* is that each step has questions that can be used without modification for academic learning in any content area as well as SEL. For example, if a preschooler were stuck on a word while trying to read, a teacher might ask an open-ended question like, "*What do you know* about the sounds these letters make? *Can you identify* any picture clues that might help us figure out the unknown word?" Or, a student could learn to ask themselves when stuck reading, "Can I find any picture clues?"

Now imagine preschoolers, when stuck on a word, asking themselves, "What do I know?" and "What can I do?" This subtle difference means students can transfer the guide they use to think through problem solving in reading to any problem they come across at school and in life without the need for additional instruction. Perhaps the most impactful difference between teacher-driven questions and structured SELf-questioning is that SELf-questions make connecting preschoolers' hearts, minds, and brains automatic. The SELf-questions students ask themselves are easily transferred and applied not only across different academic content areas (such as mathematics, science, reading, and social studies) but also across social and emotional contexts (such as for peer mediation and collaborative problem solving).

Evidence-Based Pedagogies 6 and 7: Teaching Each Element as a Separate Skill and Practicing the Strategy

The sixth evidence-based pedagogy in the road map to developing all preschoolers as metacognitive problem solvers is to teach each step of the structure one at a time "as a separate skill" (Butler et al., 2011, p. 4). The seventh evidence-based pedagogy is to have students practice each step as a separate skill before trying to put all the pieces of the puzzle together all at once. To take this evidence-based approach to teaching social and emotional problem solving and translate that into an evidence-based approach to teaching academic problem solving, a gradual release of responsibility approach is adopted (Fisher & Frey, 2021). Figure 1.5 shows the evidence-based pedagogy we recommend for each phase of a gradual release approach.

I Do	We Do	You Do
Teacher models how to use one SELf-question using first person, or *I* format, via a think aloud.	Teacher asks students one SELf-question using second person, or *you* format.	Students tasked to ask themselves one SELf-question using first person, or *I* format.

Figure 1.5: Facilitating structured SELf-questioning through gradual release of responsibility.

Note that in later chapters, the I do phase of gradual release is split into two components—(1) I do, you watch and (2) I do, you help—but both involve the teacher using SELf-questions in first person format.

The following are examples of how each phase of the gradual release approach looks and sounds when teaching one step of the strategy at a time.

- **I do (teachers model the use of internal mediators):** The teacher conducts a think aloud in a whole group for all students to hear and see what thinking metacognitively looks and sounds like. The teacher plans an inner dialogue in advance and selects a real or hypothetical situation in which one SELf-question can be asked and answered by the teacher. For example, the teacher tells a story about spilling coffee on her clothes before coming to work one morning. She asks herself a SELf-question from the Evaluate step, *What is the best way to solve this problem?* The teacher is encouraged to use thinking dispositions to demonstrate what it looks like to ask herself a question and literally take a step back and have a think about her thinking. The teacher may also look up and put her hand to her chin to further demonstrate thinking dispositions and answers her SELf-question out loud, saying, "Since I don't want my shirt to stain, but I also don't want to be late to work, one thing I can do is run to the dry cleaners on my way to work, pick up my cleaned clothes, and drop off my stained shirt to be cleaned."
- **We do (teachers provide external mediators):** Preschool teachers and instructional assistants ask their students a SELf-question in *you* format (second person). For example, when a teacher sees that a student is stuck on a word while writing, the teacher asks, "What can you do?" In Butler and colleagues' (2011) words, "Pedagogy recommends that teachers first try to ask open-ended questions. . . . Giving students cognitive choices is good exercise for the intellect, as well as for the social-emotional and character development . . . curricula accomplish this goal by structuring the initial questions teachers ask, both verbally and in written format, to be open-ended" (p. 17).

- **You do (students use internal mediators):** To facilitate this transition, preschool teachers and support staff ask students to ask themselves a SELf-question in the first person. For example, after a month or so of the adults asking students during morning routine, "How do you feel?" the teacher posts on the SMART Board, "How do I feel?" The teacher then asks students to ask themselves the SELf-question, gives them think or wait time, and has students respond individually, in a full sentence, offering a variety of choices for student responses (verbally, using an augmentative or alternative communication [AAC] device, coming up to the SMART Board, giving a touch screen response to emoji or a zone of regulation, or so on).

The gradual release approach, as described here, is how, eventually and over time, the onus of responsibility for guiding one's own self-talk adaptively through multistep problem solving (across academic, social, and emotional situations) can be put on the shoulders of three-, four-, and five-year-olds.

Asking students to practice one SELf-question at a time serves as a great vehicle with which to deliver instruction via a gradual release approach within students' zone of proximal development (Vygotsky, 1978; often referred to as *productive struggle* [Blackburn, 2018]) in the first half of the school year. Over time, as students demonstrate efficacy with utilizing one SELf-question from each of the first five steps (which usually occurs by the spring, if not sooner, of the first school year of implementation), teachers can begin providing practice opportunities that ask students to use all the steps needed to solve a problem from start to finish without any prompting. Chapters 3–7 provide detailed examples of planned practice opportunities in every preschool classroom setting.

Every day provides both planned and unplanned opportunities for students to practice their metacognitive problem-solving strategies. Throughout the day and throughout the curricula, teachers are encouraged to use teachable moments as a means to provide both practice opportunities and low-level interventions for students needing support with academic, social, or emotional problem solving. Of course, we also recommend best practices for providing feedback and specific praise on student performance. As the researchers found in *SDM/SPS*, "It is through this process of practice and feedback that skills become internalized, over a period of months, not days" (Butler et al., 2011, p. 2). Even if students are not successful, it is always a good time to ask students to ask themselves a SELf-question from the Reflect step to further develop students' strategy application as well as their metacognition. This type of review approach solidifies the learning further (Butler et al., 2011). Once students have internalized the logically sequenced steps and just one SELf-question for each step, preschoolers know exactly what they can do to be a metacognitive problem solver.

That's really all it takes to develop your preschoolers as the CEOs of their own brains, releasing them into their own development as more autonomous critical thinkers, problem solvers, and decision makers across academic, social, and emotional situations.

Conclusion

A study on the impact of constructive self-talk on classroom successes titled "The Power of Inner Voice: Examining Self-Talk's Relationship with Academic Outcomes" (Uhrich et al., 2023) published by the *American Journal of Education,* reports substantial benefits for K–12 as well as college students. Uhrich and colleagues (2023) conclude that "self-talk is a unique and influential construct that should be of interest to academics and practitioners across the disciplines of psychology and education" (p. 31) and further state that "interventions that promote adaptive self-talk in the context of the school setting have the potential to be transformative" (p. 60). This finding confirms what practitioners of structured SELf-questioning already know: constructive, adaptive self-talk can be a game changer for student success.

It is one thing to teach students a step-by-step procedure to follow in order to solve a specific, siloed problem. That is perhaps the most common practice today when we teach mathematics. We too often teach students how to follow the procedure without adaptation and avoid cognitive choices. While this can help students learn how to solve mathematics problems in isolation, this does not teach them how to think like mathematicians, and this focus on procedural knowledge does not develop adaptive thinkers. But when open-ended, easily transferable SELf-questions are added into the structure for problem solving, students transform from procedure followers to adaptive thinkers and interdisciplinary problem solvers. Structured SELf-questioning is one strategy teachers can use in mathematics, science, or in any other academic subject to teach preschoolers how to structure, sequence, and guide their self-talk while also developing them as adaptive thinkers and problem solvers.

Parent Corner

There are numerous ways to encourage your parents' and caregivers' support of their children's application of structured SELf-questioning at home, including the following.

- Provide printouts of the steps and SELf-questions from chapter 1 (page 13) and from the Solution Tree website (visit **go.SolutionTree.com/instruction**) to post around the home, such as on the refrigerator.
- Use a back-to-school night or similar event to explain how you plan to sprinkle on the SELf-questioning strategy in your classroom.
- Encourage them to read this book, which we wrote to be teacher and parent friendly (although they probably don't need to read the practical guide chapters, as those were written specifically for preschool teachers).
- Have them search and visit *The Metacognitive Preschooler* on social media platforms such as Instagram, X, and Facebook to support understanding of the SELf-questioning strategy and how to apply it at home.
- Encourage them to download the free parent app called *SELF-Q* from the smartphone's app store (search "selfq education"; be sure to pick the app for educational purposes). This app is user-friendly, easily accessible, free, and used by parents (using gradual release of responsibility, as described earlier in this chapter) to guide their children's self-talk through academic, social, and emotional challenges that occur on a daily basis at home.

2 The Brain-Based Underpinnings of Emotional Structured SELf-Questioning

Given the personal and societal problems inherent in less-than-optimal frontal lobe development, it is crucial for educators to promote the evolution of neuronal networks (e.g., by actively teaching children, as well as modeling, how to calm down and achieve self-control over their behaviors).

—Carol A. Kusche & Mark T. Greenberg

At this point, some of you may be asking or saying to yourself, "This is great. I already do something very similar, but what about when students are too upset to do all this structured, logical, linked thinking? What if they're too upset to take a step back and think about anything?" This is a key question, especially post COVID-19, for far too many teachers today.

In December of 2023, *Edutopia* reporters Paige Tutt, Andrew Boryga, and Sarah Gonser (2023) published the site's annual article covering the most common themes and conversations of the Edutopia channels from the past year. One common theme from the article was a perceived lack of return to normalcy since COVID-19 by teachers across grade levels and across the United States. The following are quotes from teachers from the article describing the conditions for students and teachers post COVID-19 (Tutt et al., 2023).

- "Disequilibration."
- "The cadence just isn't there."
- "Dysregulation."
- "The thing we're dealing with most is behavior. We have these kids who are just so dysregulated, they become the priority, and you can't teach."
- "I have been teaching forever, and I love how you are articulating the dysregulation I see every day. Our kids need more help than we have training or knowledge or resources for. Still keep trying for genuine connections, but I wonder if I can realistically keep up this level of sustained effort."
- "Kids' behaviors are bigger, more intense, more disruptive than ever before. . . . And what I'm seeing is a lot of desperation among teachers. They're exhausted."

This book has already chronicled many of the challenges educators of all age groups and content areas face when it comes to adding curriculum and instruction on top of emotional coping skills. According to the Tutt and colleagues (2023), "To meet the incredible needs among students," teacher training sessions are now focused on going "back to what we know about the brain and how it works, focusing on creating classrooms based on safety, connection, and problem-solving." Fortunately, the metacognitive strategy of structured SELf-questioning accomplishes all of that and more.

This chapter shows you in great detail how structured SELf-questioning was designed to teach all preschoolers emotional self-regulation (or the SEL competencies of *self-awareness*, *self-management*, and the executive functions thereof); promote safer classroom environments (less aggressive behaviors like kicking, throwing chairs, and so on); make connections to hearts, minds, and brains; and develop independent, adaptive problem solvers with ease, efficiency, and effectiveness. In so doing, your preschoolers will learn and apply one strategy to calm their own emotions so that they are in an emotional state conducive to learning.

Doesn't that sound wonderful? This is not only key to a safer, calmer classroom environment with less disruption and less need for adult intervention, but this development is also key to helping any student's brain be more emotionally ready for academic and social learning, critical thinking, and problem solving.

Yes, this chapter talks about neuroscience, but please do not be intimidated. Neuroscience is not rocket science, and we will make the neuroscience talk as user-friendly as possible. We are confident you will find this chapter to be digestible and helpful in understanding structured SELf-questioning even better. We are also confident that you will find, as we have, that understanding the underpinnings of how the brain works to process emotions, think critically, and make thoughtful decisions is valuable to us as adults to better understand ourselves. With a deeper understanding of our own brains, we are more empowered to teach preschoolers how to maximize their own brains. In other words, we hope this chapter makes you an even stronger CEO of your own brain.

The Importance of Developing Emotional Problem Solving

According to Sippl (2023), teaching emotional problem solving to students with diverse needs provides additional challenges:

> Not all diverse learners develop adequate problem-solving. Learners with a history of behavioral and learning challenges may not always use good problem-solving skills to manage stressful situations. Some students use challenging behaviors like talking back, arguing, property destruction, and aggression when presented with challenging tasks. Others might shut down, check out, or struggle to follow directions when encountering new or unknown situations.
>
> Without a step-by-step model for problem-solving, including identifying a problem and choosing a replacement behavior to solve it, many of our children and students use challenging behaviors instead.

Preschool teachers in every classroom know that if a student gets frustrated with an academic challenge or social conflict with a classmate, that student can get emotional. As a result, thinking and skill applications can completely break down. When upset, preschool students do not think well. Neither do most adults, for that matter. The ability to identify emotions and self-calm, therefore, has always been the key to success for any student, any professional, and, indeed, any person. So, for preschoolers to be able to think metacognitively about academic or social problem solving, they must first think metacognitively about their feelings and be able to cope with their feelings effectively. As stated clearly in the previous quote by Sippl (2023), to do that, they need a step-by-step model for problem solving.

In light of day-to-day stressors, it is crucial that educators teach students self-awareness and self-management so they can learn adequately. The good news is that structured SELf-questioning provides both an evidence- and brain-based pathway. Carol A. Kusche and Mark T. Greenberg (2006), coauthors of the chapter "Brain Development and Social Emotional Learning: An Introduction for Educators" in *The Educator's Guide to Emotional Intelligence and Academic Achievement*, posit that there are not only invaluable lessons about the importance of teaching all preschoolers self-awareness, self-management, and the executive function skills inherent in self-control but also of how to do so. Kusche and Greenberg (2006), who we cite frequently in this chapter as their work remains seminal for the purpose of this chapter, perhaps summarize the proverbial big idea best when they say, "Children benefit greatly when specific models of bodily self-control, which are used during times of emotional arousal, are taught and mastered, followed by more advanced forms of verbally mediated self-control" (p. 26).

While we must admit bias, we firmly believe and have observed that structured SELf-questioning is the most effective and efficient way to teach three-, four-, and five-year-olds a verbally self-mediated form of self-control (self-awareness and self-management). A major reason for this confidence, beyond years and years of our professional and personal experience and observation, is due to how well-aligned structured SELf-questioning is with how the brain functions to develop awareness and management of one's own emotions.

The remainder of this chapter takes a bird's eye view of how the preschooler's brain works and how the steps and SELf-questions have been designed to help students guide their self-talk to verbally mediate mental self-control. In other words, we will show you how structured SELf-questioning empowers preschoolers to be the CEOs of their own brains.

A Bird's Eye View of the Brain

In its most basic sense, the brain has three main parts: (1) stem, (2) limbic system, and (3) cortex. The brain stem is the first part of the brain to develop, and everything that occurs in the brain stem (primarily the maintenance of the body) occurs unconsciously. No SELf-question is designed to direct students' conscious thinking to the brain stem because no conscious thinking occurs there. The second part of the brain to develop is the limbic system, which is responsible for the initial processing and storage of emotions (Aggleton, 1992). The limbic system houses the amygdala, which many of you may have heard is where the fight-or-flight instinct occurs. The third and last part of the brain to develop is the cortex.

The cortex is divided into two hemispheres, the right and left. The cortex is the part of the brain that structured SELf-questioning specifically targets because of all the powerful thinking and processing that occurs there, including:

- secondary processing of emotions at a more refined level. . .
- greater (socialized) control over the more instinctual, automatic responses of the mammalian brain. . .
- allows us to accumulate and combine information over time to form schemas or templates about the external world. . .
- contains "association areas" in which sensory data from different modalities can be integrated. . .
- allows for complex verbal and nonverbal intelligence (Kusche & Greenberg, 2006, p. 21)

The preceding might sound like a neuroscientist's way of saying, "This is where the connecting of hearts and minds occurs in the brain." Since the goal is to get preschoolers to connect their hearts, minds, and brains, this is the exact place we designed the structured SELf-questions to direct preschoolers' thinking. The big idea is to create a flow or stream of neural circuitry that maximizes every student's brainpower and development from the earliest of ages by drawing up a road map of neural circuitry that flows through the cortex and maximizes processing. That is how and why the metacognitive strategy of structured SELf-questioning was designed.

The Role of the Preschool Teacher in Developing Preschoolers as CEOs of Their Own Brains

Kusche and Greenberg (2006) state that there are areas within the cortex that "specialize social, emotional and attentional processing" (p. 21) and that "teachers play powerful and crucial roles in . . . brain growth and integration . . . [and the teacher] has a crucial impact on learning and brain development" (p. 31).

How does this occur exactly? According to Kusche and Greenberg (2006), by:

> providing optimal, balanced stimulation. . . . [In so doing,] a very important positive foundation will be laid for the later achievement of such things as self-control, internal motivation and paying attention. This will also result in a good foundation in regard to early brain development. (p. 30)

That is a lot of great-sounding stuff to the ears of most preschool teachers. It's why taking a gradual release of responsibility approach and teaching one SELf-question at a time works so effectively. In so doing, preschool teachers can utilize a brain-based approach to achieve great gains in student self-control and the foundations of early brain development.

Furthermore, the cortex includes countless other functions that are highly conducive to the development of both social and emotional self-control. The cortex contains the neocerebellum, which Kusche and Greenberg (2006) describe as a "structure for facilitating semantic connections between words and for higher level processing of social intelligence" (p. 21). SELf-questions like "How does he, she, or they feel?" have a direct correlation to the development of social intelligence and empathy. In addition to the neocerebellum, the cortex includes the frontal lobes, which are also essential to processing and thinking. Kusche and Greenberg (2006) indicate that the frontal lobes allow for "higher level processing of functions such as planning, anticipation, attention, concentration, insight, moral conscience, sense of identity, empathy, and altruism" (p. 21).

More great stuff. One example of how SELf-questions can direct neural activity to the frontal lobes to prompt planning and anticipation include the SELf-question, "What can I do first, second, and so on?" and the function of insight can be prompted by the SELf-questions, "Did it work?" and "How do I know?"

From this overview or bird's eye view of the brain, we can see how SELf-questions can direct neural circuitry, or preschoolers' brain activity, to the parts of the brain that are the highest functioning for the type of thinking that is being targeted for a specific step in the social and emotional problem-solving process. In the next section, you will see how the sequence of the SELf-questions prompts students' thinking to trailblaze the kind of neural circuitry optimal for the development of emotional self-awareness and self-management. With practice, students' neural circuitry can be wired in ways that empower them to maximize their brain power.

Optimizing Neural Circuitry Through Rewiring

Perhaps the best metaphor for rewiring neural circuitry is to imagine a person attempting to traverse a forest that has never been traversed before. At first, the traveler will find it difficult to find the way ahead and have to spend a great deal of time clearing out obstacles. But with each pass, the path becomes clearer. Likewise, the more students use the sequence of SELf-questions from the emotional question set (refer to figure 1.3, page 18), the more the neural pathways lead brain functioning from their amygdala to the prefrontal cortex and across the right and left hemispheres of the brain. With practice self-prompting or self-cueing (SELf-Qing) their own brains—the more and more iterations a preschooler has with the emotional SELf-question set—the easier that path can be followed, and the more likely the child's pattern of thinking will become to follow this path or neural circuit.

Growth occurs when the pathway becomes clear and easy to traverse. Mastery occurs when the pathway becomes the natural path that the preschooler's brain follows, almost unconsciously, because the path has become a true habit of mind. When this occurs, we say that we have created the optimal *brainstream* for self-awareness, self-management, social awareness, and responsible decision making on a day-to-day basis. Ultimately, the end result is the development of optimal brain functioning through developing the neural circuitry conducive to preschoolers becoming the CEOs of their own brains.

Side-Stepping the Amygdala Through Structured SELf-Questioning

The first step of laying the foundation—in other words, the first step into the forest—begins by redirecting or side-stepping neural activity away from the amygdala (so to speak) within the limbic system by prompting thinking up into the cortex. When a student is clearly upset or has a strong emotional reaction or occurrence, asking the simple question, "How do you feel?" can have a powerful effect on neural circuitry. When a student asks themself the question, "How do I feel?" the emotional impact is even greater as it further facilitates the development of self-awareness and, in turn, leads to self-management.

According to psychologist, emotional intelligence expert, and science journalist Daniel Goleman (2022), there is a road map to neural circuitry, and a great deal of positive developments arise when this road map is set:

> My model of emotional intelligence is grounded in how the brain operates to create the four domains of emotional intelligence: self-awareness, self-management, empathy and social skills. Each of these abilities rests in differing sets of neural circuitry. . . . For instance, the self-mastery domain includes the ability to stay emotionally balanced. This, in turn, rests on a neural dynamic where the amygdala, perceiving a threat, can drive circuitry in the right side of the prefrontal cortex when we are having an emotional hijack. But the left side of the prefrontal cortex has circuits that "just say no" to disruptive emotional impulses.

When educators ask students, "How are you feeling?" they act as an external mediator to redirect thinking out of and away from the limbic system up into the right or left prefrontal lobe, where more complex processing of emotions can occur. When students can recognize a strong emotion and ask themselves, "How am I feeling?" they can side-step their thinking around the amygdala, literally puppeteering their own brains. When students do this over and over, as we stated previously, the more activity in those prefrontal lobes occurs—and the more activity in the prefrontal lobes, the better. As explained by Goleman (2022), the more activity in the prefrontal lobes, the better because "Research at the University of Wisconsin shows that people who are resilient—who recover quickly from such upsets, have up to thirty times more activity in these left prefrontal circuits than do those who are slow to recover."

Once neural activity has been puppeteered away from the amygdala and into the prefrontal cortex, the preschooler is ready to be asked, "What are you feeling?" or ask themself: "What am I feeling?" from the Identify Feelings step feature in figure 1.3 (page 18). This question promotes the concept of what Kusche and Greenberg (2006) call *interhemispheric* or *horizontal communication*, with the resulting horizontal communication. *Horizontal communication* is "made possible by the corpus callosum, a bundle of nerve cells that traverse the two sides" (p. 26), which allows information to travel from the right to the left hemisphere and from the left to the right hemisphere. Kusche and Greenberg (2006) stress the importance of horizontal or interhemispheric communication because:

> To verbally label our emotional experiences, and thus become aware of them, information from the right [hemisphere] must be transmitted to the left [hemisphere]. . . . To be truly aware of our emotional experiences, we must use horizontal interhemispheric communication between the left and right hemispheres. (pp. 27–28)

When anyone asks themselves, "What am I feeling?" interhemispheric communication is prompted because neural activity shifts from the right side of the brain, where emotions are sensed, to the left side of the brain, where linguistic processing occurs. To that end, both emotional SELf-questions—"How am I feeling?" and "What am I feeling?"—are carefully designed and sequenced to set a neural pathway out, or away from, the amygdala, to the right prefrontal cortex and to the left prefrontal cortex, trailblazing the neural pathways conducive to producing emotionally aware and emotionally expressive preschoolers. As Kusche and Greenberg (2006) further explain:

> The way in which interhemispheric structuralization occurs depends heavily on environmental input during development. Verbal identification and labeling of feelings should powerfully assist with managing these feelings, controlling behavior and improving interhemispheric integration. Thus, the use of emotion recognition cues . . . (mediated by the right hemisphere) in conjunction with the verbal labels (mediated by the left) during the process of emotional experience should improve the development of interhemispheric communication. (pp. 29–30)

In other words, using the environmental input (teachers asking "How are you feeling?" or "What are you feeling?") and emotion recognition cues (the SELf-questions "How am I feeling?" and "What am I feeling?") leads to enhanced brain functioning, development, and learning of the emotional competencies of self-awareness and self-management. In short, Kusche and Greenberg (2006) state that "the capacity to automatically use inner speech . . . allows for verbal thought to serve as a mediator for behavioral self-control" (p. 25).

This leads us to another aspect of brain science—linguistic accuracy—that structured SELf-questioning taps into through neural circuitry to develop preschoolers' awareness and management of their own emotions and brains.

Prompting Linguistic Accuracy

Let's continue to traverse the forest of neural circuitry to further empower students to be the CEOs of their own brains. Now that we have used the SELf-questions, "What am I feeling?" and "How am I feeling?" to direct thinking into the right or left prefrontal lobes, we can use more of the emotional structured SELf-question set steps and SELf-questions that correlate with the Identify Feelings and Gather Information steps to prompt more accurate, granular, interhemispheric communication for linguistic accuracy.

For the purposes of emotional problem solving, we focus more heavily on the questions that elicit emotional information. Examples of these questions may include "How do I feel?" "What am I feeling?" and "What is causing this feeling?" Figure 2.1 (page 36) represents the steps and possible SELf-questions.

Step Name	Examples of Structured SELf-Questions
Identify Feelings	"How do I feel?" "What am I feeling?" "How does he, she, or they feel?"
Gather Information	"What do I know?" "What is causing this feeling?" "What can I control?" "What is my goal?"

Figure 2.1: Example steps and SELf-questions for linguistic accuracy.

Emotional SELf-questioning prompts linguistic accuracy. Linguistic accuracy is facilitated via the interhemispheric or horizontal communication between the left and right hemispheres of the cortex, which we mentioned earlier. Communication between the hemispheres is essential for many purposes, including the linguistic processing of emotions.

To illustrate, Kusche and Greenberg (2006) indicate that the left hemisphere "specializes in linguistic communication (e.g., expressive and receptive language)" (p. 26). The linguistic processing of the left hemisphere has advantages when compared to the nonverbal processing of the right hemisphere. Kusche and Greenberg (2006) state that "emotions and language are both important for different purposes, and to function in an integrated and optimal way, it is important to coordinate both systems of communication" (p. 27).

Here is where structured SELf-questioning serves as a coordinated system of self-prompts or self-cues that function in an integrated and optimal way. The sequence of SELf-questions encourages brains to communicate nonverbal recognition of emotions (conducted by the right hemisphere) to the left hemisphere, where linguistic processing can occur. The SELf-questions "How do I feel?" "What am I feeling?" and "What is causing this feeling?" result in linguistic processing by the left hemisphere to interpret emotions received by the right hemisphere.

The trailblazing neural circuitry that crosses hemispheres and results in linguistic processing allows for even more powerful brain activity to occur in the preschoolers' brains, namely, *metaconsciousness*. Kusche and Greenberg (2006) state:

> Once the communication networks that cross the bridge have been created, nonverbal data emanating (emotions) from the right hemisphere can travel across the bridge to the left hemisphere, where linguistic processing allows for metaconsciousness of internal responses to the external environment (e.g., emotional awareness.). . .(i.e., the ability to observe and analyze one's own thoughts), which in turn, provides increased ability for self-control, allows for sequential thinking, and provides greater specificity and accuracy. (p. 27)

In this same resource, Kusche & Greenberg (2006) also cite the work of Nathan A. Fox (expert on early childhood experiences and the brain) and Richard Davidson (professor of psychology and psychiatry; 1984) who write:

> Once the communication networks that cross the bridge have been created, nonverbal data emanating from City R can travel across the bridge to City L, where linguistic processing allows for metaconscioussness of internal responses to the external environment (e.g., emotional awareness). Information from City L, on the other hand, can travel across the bridge to City R to help clarify, influence, and control processing. (p. 27)

In essence, metaconsciousness allows for "the ability to observe and analyze one's own thoughts, which, in turn, provides increased ability for self-control" (Fox & Davidson, 1984, p. 27). In addition to metaconsciousness, linguistic processing empowers sequential thinking for increased specificity and accuracy (Kusche & Greenberg, 2006). Put one more way, all the linguistic processing prompted by structured SELf-questioning can lead to metaconsciousness, which allows us to analyze our own thoughts and increases our ability to self-manage or self-control our emotions and thoughts. Metaconsciousness also allows for the sequential thinking needed to successfully solve multistep problems and make decisions (topics for the next section).

Further, the specificity and accuracy allotted by linguistic processing may allow for detailed verbal thinking, which builds further on the power of interhemispheric communication to promote emotional granularity and improved self-management. "Information from the left hemisphere travels across the bridge to the right hemisphere to help clarify, influence, and control emotional processing" and, in turn, facilitate self-control (Kusche & Greenberg, 2006, p. 27). This interhemispheric communication is facilitated by the structured SELf-questions (for example, "How do I feel?" and "What am I feeling?"), as the response requires a label (such as *happy*, *mad*, and *silly*) or explanation (such as, "My fists feel tight"), which requires linguistic accuracy. Nonlinguistic emotional information from the right hemisphere is processed by the left hemisphere using linguistic accuracy. Kusche and Greenberg (2006) indicate that:

> Nonlinguistic information (such as an emotional signal) that is processed preconsciously by the right hemisphere will not reach conscious awareness until we verbally "think" about it with the left hemisphere. And to verbally label our emotional experiences, and thus be consciously aware of them, information from the right must be transferred to the left via the corpus callosum. (p. 27)

Structured SELf-questioning ("How do I feel?" and "What am I feeling?") self-prompts this horizontal crossing of the bridge from preconscious processing in the right hemisphere to metaconscious processing in the left hemisphere by encouraging us to use linguistic accuracy to label our emotions or feelings. According to Kusche and Greenberg (2006), this horizontal communication "powerfully assists with managing these feelings, controlling behavior, and improving interhemispheric integration" (p. 29). Put simply, linguistic accuracy, when used to answer SELf-questions, facilitates self-awareness.

It is important to note that Kusche and Greenberg (2006) report that "the way in which interhemispheric structuralization occurs depends heavily on environmental input during development" (p. 29). They further indicate that "encouraging children to talk about emotional experiences (both at the time that they are occurring and in recollection) should further strengthen cortical integration" (Kusche & Greenberg, 2006, p. 30). As teachers, we can provide environmental input via the implementation of the metacognitive strategy of structured SELf-questioning, which often utilizes facial expressions, visual cues, and verbal labels. Through structured SELf-questioning, students are encouraged to use linguistic accuracy to express and manage emotions. By doing so, we can help students traverse the forest to promote horizontal communication between hemispheres. With the self-awareness gathered using linguistic accuracy prompted by structured SELf-questioning, we can subsequently use the metacognitive strategy for processing and thinking purposes by posing the next questions within the structured SELf-questioning steps.

Emotional SELf-Questions and Higher-Order Processing and Thinking

We continue to encourage students to be the CEOs of their own brains by further establishing a path in the forest of neural circuitry by using structured SELf-questioning via subsequent SELf-questions to prompt processing and thinking. Thus far, we have used the SELf-questions in the first two steps of the social and emotional SELf-question set to direct thinking away from the limbic system and into the prefrontal lobes and promote interhemispheric communication for self-awareness, self-control, and linguistic accuracy. Next, we can use the structured SELf-question set to prompt those higher-order critical thinking skills inherent in multistep problem solving and decision making. The SELf-questions for the Brainstorm, Evaluate, Plan and Act, and Reflect steps have been designed to prompt emotional processing and critical thinking. Examples of these SELf-questions include those listed in figure 2.2.

Step Name	Examples of Structured SELf-Questions
Brainstorm	"What can I do?" "What strategies can I use?"
Evaluate	"Has this strategy helped me in the past?"
Plan and Act	"What do I do first, second, and so on?" "Is this working?"
Reflect	"Did it work?" "How do I know?"

Figure 2.2: Example steps and SELf-questions for processing and thinking.

All of these questions prompt activity through the cortex to assist in processing and thinking. Processing and thinking for problem solving and decision making may require complex verbal and nonverbal intelligence, which is made possible due to *association areas* in the cortex that integrate sensory data from different modalities through tertiary processing (Kusche & Greenberg, 2006). Similar to interhemispheric communication, we can provide environmental input through structured SELf-questioning to strengthen these neural pathways to promote secondary and tertiary processing of the cortex.

Social and emotional SELf-questions (for example, Brainstorm step SELf-questions "What can I do?" and "What strategies can I use?" and Reflect step SELf-questions "Did it work?" and "How do I know?") promote critical thinking and processing. Such complex processing, as reported by Kusche and Greenberg (2006), also "allows us to better understand what has happened and to make appropriate plans for further action" (p. 24). This type of processing and thinking can be self-prompted using SELf-questions within the Plan and Act step (for example, "What do I do first, second, and so on?" and "Is this working?"). Kusche and Greenberg (2006) also report that "the frontal lobes play an important role in processing complex information, sustaining attention to relevant versus irrelevant stimuli, and integrating incoming information with prior knowledge" (p. 21). They indicate that attention and concentration are facilitated by "adequate frontal lobe organization and functioning" (Kusche & Greenberg, 2006, p. 21).

Attention is essential when problem solving and making decisions. Renowned author and education expert Robert Sylwester (1995) indicates that "a well functioning attentional system must fulfill several tasks, including . . . the ability to shift attention rapidly as a result of new information" (as cited in Kusche & Greenberg, 2006, p. 22). We find that being able to process and think about new information by shifting attention is crucial during academic, social, and emotional problem solving and decision making. In regard to emotional problem solving, we must consider the Reflect step and SELf-question, "Did it work?" Not every self-management strategy elicited by the SELf-question, "What can I do?" will be successful; therefore, the answer to the SELf-question, "Did it work?" will sometimes be *no*. This new information must be considered, and attention must shift to brainstorm alternative self-management strategies.

Based on information gathered by researchers Wayne C. Drevets and Marcus E. Raichle (1998), when students regulate their emotions, their ability to use cognitive processes, such as concentration, is impacted. By using structured SELf-questioning, we can facilitate students' ability to more readily regulate their emotions by solving emotional problems, making the prefrontal cortex available for processing and thinking. Once their brains are available for processing and thinking, we can further facilitate the use of such cognitive processes by using SELf-questions (for example, "What is the best way to solve this problem?" "What do I do first, second, and so on?" "Did it work?" and "How do I know?") for social, emotional, and academic problem solving and decision making.

When using structured SELf-questioning to facilitate processing and thinking by strengthening neural circuitry, we must consider the *5 to 7 shift* (Elias & Arnold, 2006; Luria, 1976; White, 1970). Reflecting on the work of A. R. Luria (1976) and Sheldon H. White (1970), Kusche and Greenberg (2006) indicate that between the ages of five and seven, children may "show dramatic changes in functioning" which is "sometimes termed the '5 to 7 shift'" (p. 25). According to Kusche and Greenberg (2006), children demonstrate "better regulation of impulses and action tendencies, greater independence, improved planning skills, and ability to assume greater responsibility" due to "pathways of vertical control from the frontal lobes" as a result of the "5 to 7 shift" (p. 25). Kusche and Greenberg (2006) further indicate that after successfully experiencing the 5 to 7 shift, a child can use the following sequence.

1. Experience a feeling.
2. Verbally process that feeling or information.
3. Create a plan to respond to that feeling or information.
4. Act on the plan.

The structured SELf-questions can be used to elicit processing and thinking during each step within this sequence. Figure 2.3 includes examples of SELf-questions that correlate and may be used to self-prompt each step of the 5 to 7 shift.

5 to 7 Shift	Structured SELf-Questions
Experience a feeling	"What am I feeling?"
Verbally process that feeling or information	"How do I feel?"
Create a plan to respond to that feeling or information	"What can I do?" "What strategies can I use?" "What is the best way to solve this problem?"
Act on the plan	"What do I do first, second, and so on?" "Did it work?" "How do I know?"

Figure 2.3: Examples of 5 to 7 shift steps and facilitating SELf-questions.

The 5 to 7 shift explains to some degree why structured SELf-questioning is so effective in kindergarten and first grade, but we find it is never too early to build the foundations for success by teaching three- and four-year-olds structured SELf-questioning. According to Kusche and Greenberg (2006), "It is crucial for educators to promote the evolution of neuronal networks" (p. 26). Every time we provide the environmental input of structured SELf-questioning, we continue to traverse the forest of neural circuitry to lay the groundwork for social-emotional success and encourage students to be the CEOs of their own brains.

Conclusion

Structured SELf-questioning is unique because it has the power to connect hearts (the CASEL SEL competencies), minds (critical thinking skills), and brains (executive functioning) all together into one superpowered brainstream. This chapter mapped out how the superpowered brainstream that structured SELf-questioning creates is aligned with brain functioning. Each SELf-question modeled for or posed to students capitalizes on how the brain functions and facilitates the development of neural pathways. The structure, or sequence of steps, of structured SELf-questioning and the SELf-questions (such as "How do I feel?" and "What am I feeling?") by design lead neural pathways toward the brain parts best suited for the brain functioning needed at that step or phase in problem solving. We believe that structured SELf-questioning is an essential strategy that can not only help students navigate a variety of social, emotional, and academic situations but also help them navigate their own brains to maximize their thinking and learning.

Parent Corner

Here is a script that you can use to try and explain to parents and caregivers the connection between hearts, minds, and brains in a digestible manner:

> *The social and emotional SELf-questioning set elicits executive functioning skills inherent in the SEL competencies of self-awareness and self-management. When combined with the academic and social SELf-questioning set (which promote social awareness and responsible decision making), the two sets combine to provide one strategy that promotes the critical thinking skills inherent in SEL competencies and executive functioning. The chart I've provided emphasizes how the structured SELf-questions align with important thinking skills, social-emotional learning competencies, and executive functions.*

Along with adapting this script, it can also be helpful to provide parents and caregivers the reproducible "SELf-Questioning 101: A Parent and Caregiver's Guide to the Process" (page 42), which includes the SELf-questioning step names, SELf-questions, executive functioning skills elicited, and CASEL SEL competencies facilitated. We recommend using this script and reproducible chart with parents and caregivers at back-to-school nights, parent orientations, and similar events to give them an overview of the strategy and its power. Finally, in order to deepen their understanding, we recommend you model the SELf-questions within adult academic and social situations and adult social and emotional situations via think alouds at these parent sessions to facilitate their understanding of the strategy so they can be better partners and support their child's internalization and transfer from school to home.

SELf-Questioning 101: A Parent and Caregiver's Guide to the Process

The following chart outlines the SELf-questioning structure your child will learn to utilize at school. We encourage you to use this framework with your child at home.

Academic and Social Step Names	Academic and Social SELf-Questions	Social and Emotional Step Names	Social and Emotional SELf-Questions	Executive Function Skills	CASEL Social-Emotional Learning Competency
Select a Focus	What is the problem? What is the question? What is the task? What is important? What is the user's need?	Identify Feelings	How do I feel? What am I feeling? How does he, she, or they feel?	Self-monitoring	Self-awareness Social awareness
Gather Information	What do I know? What do I need to know? What is important? How does he, she, or they feel?	Gather Information	What do I know? What is causing this feeling? What can I control? What is my goal?	Goal setting Impulse control	Self-awareness Self-management
Brainstorm	What can I do? What strategies can I use? How can I solve this problem? What are possible solutions? What is similar, and what is different? What connections can I make?	Brainstorm	What can I do? What strategies can I use?	Flexibility Emotional control	Self-management Responsible decision making

Academic and Social Step Names	Academic and Social SELf-Questions	Social and Emotional Step Names	Social and Emotional SELf-Questions	Executive Function Skills	CASEL Social-Emotional Learning Competency
Evaluate	What is the best way to solve this problem? Does this make sense? What are possible consequences?	Evaluate	Has this strategy helped me in the past?	Prioritizing Self-regulation Emotional control Use of working memory Coping flexibility	Self-awareness Self-management Responsible decision making
Plan and Act	What do I do first, second, and so on? Is this working?	Plan and Act	What do I do first, second, and so on? Is this working?	Planning Organization Time management Task initiation Problem solving	Self-awareness Self-management Responsible decision making
Reflect	Did it work? How do I know?	Reflect	Did it work? How do I know?	Self-monitoring Self-correcting	Self-awareness Responsible decision making Social awareness

Source: Adapted from CASEL. (n.d.). What is the CASEL framework? *Accessed at https://casel.org/fundamentals-of-sel/what-is-the-casel-framework on September 27, 2023.*

3 A Practical Guide to Emotional Recognition and Self-Expression

If your emotional abilities aren't in hand, if you don't have self-awareness, if you are not able to manage your distressing emotions, if you can't have empathy and have effective relationships, then no matter how smart you are, you are not going to get very far.

—Daniel Goleman

If I were to ask you, "How do you feel?" what emotion might come to mind? Maybe you might think *exhausted* or *overwhelmed*. Maybe you would think *calm* or *confident*. Regardless of your response, you would demonstrate self-awareness by recognizing your emotion as well as verbal thinking by labeling that emotion. If we were having this conversation aloud in person, you would also demonstrate self-expression of an emotion by telling me how you feel. This one simple question can require and elicit many skills.

We routinely ask others how they feel; however, we seldom pose this question to ourselves. The less common, yet more meaningful, question is for us to ask ourselves, "How do I feel?" When students begin asking themselves this question—one of the foundational SELf-questions—a transformation may occur. The ability to accurately identify and coherently express emotions allows students to demonstrate self-awareness, which in turn provides them with the opportunity to be self-managed, socially aware, and responsible decision makers with positive relationship skills. Now *that* is a powerful question.

When students have not yet developed self-awareness, self-expression of emotions may be frustrating and unsuccessful for both teacher and student. Regardless of the grade level or subject area being taught, we are asking students to try new, possibly difficult things all school day long, which can lead to a variety of feelings, including anger, sadness, and frustration. When students have not yet developed self-awareness, these feelings may be amplified.

Take Emily's student, Shawn, who was working on increasing his speech clarity. When Emily asked Shawn to attempt something he perceived as challenging, such as the production of target speech sounds, Shawn frequently expressed frustration by turning away from her, crossing his arms, saying "No!" in a stern voice, stomping around the classroom, grunting, and ultimately leaving the table to play with another activity. Through his body language, shouting, and grunting, Shawn was expressing frustration; however, he wasn't expressing it functionally. Emily suspected that with each elicitation of a target sound,

Shawn became more and more dysregulated until he finally used inappropriate means to express and manage his emotions. Shawn most likely was not asking himself, "How do I feel?" His yet-to-be-developed self-awareness skills—specifically, emotional recognition and functional self-expression—thus negatively impacted the productivity of his speech sessions.

This chapter describes how educators can help preschoolers develop self-awareness through emotional recognition and self-expression of emotion. It discusses the importance of accurate recognition and expression of emotion and describes how teachers can use the metacognitive strategy of structured SELf-questioning to facilitate this competency in students. It is important to note that the ultimate goal of structured SELf-questioning is for students to *internalize* the strategy. This means that students will no longer need to rely on a teacher asking them how they feel to demonstrate emotional recognition and self-expression; rather, they will demonstrate the verbal thinking necessary to recognize an emotion and, in turn, express that emotion all by themselves.

The Importance of Teaching a Metacognitive Strategy for Emotional Recognition and Self-Expression

Think about a time when you told your students to clean up, and one student screamed and refused to leave the play area. Now, think about another time when your class was headed to the playground, and one student sprinted down the hallway toward the exit. Such students present with an underdeveloped self-awareness competency that results in difficulty recognizing and expressing their emotions—in these cases, sadness due to transitioning away from a preferred activity and excitement due to transitioning to a preferred activity. As a result, students instead turn to behavior to communicate. Teaching structured SELf-questioning helps students develop the self-awareness they need to respond appropriately both inside and outside the classroom.

Self-awareness is defined as "the abilities to understand one's own emotions, thoughts, and values and how they influence behavior across contexts" (CASEL, n.d.). We find that self-awareness and the ability to recognize one's own emotions, in particular, can be considered the foundation of self-management, social awareness, relationship skills, and responsible decision making. Cohen and colleagues (2021) write that the identification and regulation of emotions allows students to be "truly in an emotional state that is conducive to maximizing their mental capacities—specifically, the critical-thinking and problem-solving skills that will guide them toward coping successfully and flexibly when faced with stressful situations and making responsible decisions" (p. 114).

Emotional recognition (self-awareness) serves as a foundational skill as it facilitates accurate identification and application of coping strategies (self-management). Furthermore, this self-awareness and self-management maximize a student's ability to use critical thinking, which facilitates responsible decision making and problem solving—skills that can be used to promote social awareness and relationship skills.

Besides assisting in identifying one's emotions, CASEL (n.d.) indicates that self-awareness is necessary for an individual to demonstrate the following skills:

- Integrating personal and social identities
- Identifying personal, cultural, and linguistic assets
- Demonstrating honesty and integrity
- Linking feelings, values, and thoughts
- Examining prejudices and biases
- Experiencing self-efficacy
- Having a growth mindset
- Developing interests and a sense of purpose
- Recognizing one's own strengths and limitations with a well-grounded sense of confidence and purpose

The capacity for self-awareness underpins many critical life skills and is evidently necessary for optimal mental health. We cannot stress its importance enough.

Self-awareness encompasses not only the ability to recognize one's emotions but also effectively express those emotions. *Self-expression of an emotion* can be defined as any way an individual functionally expresses their emotion to another person. Students' effective expression of emotions can serve many purposes.

First, when students functionally express their emotions and have their emotions honored by another person, their view of themselves as an individual and as a part of a social group improves. Self-expression of an emotion may allow students to feel "prosocial toward themselves" and develop positive relationships with others (Elias & Arnold, 2006, p. 33). According to Elias and Arnold (2006), when students demonstrate self-expression and, in turn, feel heard by teachers and their peers, they feel:

> Valued, cared for, appreciated, supported, respected, and part of a social group. This, along with empathy from their teachers and peers, motivates children to value, care for, appreciate, and feel prosocial toward themselves, the environment, the social groups to which they belong, other people, and their world. (p. 33)

Second, an individual's ability to demonstrate emotional recognition and self-expression promotes positive interpersonal relationships by increasing a communication partner's understanding of the individual's feelings and behaviors. For example, imagine pulling your preschool students Carlos and Tiffany to work on answering questions about a story. As you open the book and begin reading, Tiffany turns away from her peer and begins to cry. You and Carlos feel concerned and confused. Carlos may also feel offended that his friend appears not to want to read a story with him. If Tiffany were to demonstrate self-awareness and recognize that she feels distraught because that story reminds her of her grandmother, and in turn, demonstrate self-expression of that emotion, this act of self-awareness would result in understanding and a positive interpersonal interaction between students and staff.

Third, self-expression of a recognized emotion may facilitate a student's self-management skills, as their response allows for more accurate modeling. For example, following a student's self-expression of anger, a teacher can model possible self-management strategies specific to that emotion. We review self-management more thoroughly in the next chapter. For now, our focus is on emotional recognition and expression of emotions. However, before teachers can effectively teach the expression of emotions, they need to help students accurately identify what they are feeling.

When reflecting on self-awareness (namely, emotional recognition and self-expression), we must refer to SELf-questions within our social and emotional SELf-question set introduced in chapter 2 (page 29). Figure 3.1 includes some SELf-questions within our social and emotional SELf-questioning set as well as the correlated CASEL (n.d.) competencies that SELf-questions within each step may elicit.

CASEL Competency	Step Name	SELf-Questions
Self-Awareness	Identify Feelings	"How do I feel?" "What am I feeling?"
Self-Awareness Self-Management	Gather Information	"What do I know? What is causing this feeling?" "What can I control?" "What is my goal?"
Self-Management Responsible Decision Making	Brainstorm	"What can I do?" "What strategies can I use?"
Self-Awareness Self-Management Responsible Decision Making	Evaluate	"Has this strategy helped me in the past?"
Self-Awareness Self-Management Responsible Decision Making	Plan and Act	"What do I do first, second, and so on?" "Is this working?"
Self-Awareness Responsible Decision Making	Reflect	"Did it work?" "How do I know?"

Source: Adapted from CASEL, n.d.; Cohen et al., 2021.

Figure 3.1: Social and emotional structured SELf-questions and possible correlating SEL competencies.

It is important to note that the competencies of relationship skills and social awareness are not reflected in figure 3.1. Emotional recognition is primarily concerned with an individual's internal world (namely, internal reactions to internal and external stimuli). Relationship skills and social awareness are primarily concerned with an individual's external world (for example, the use of internal skills to promote interaction with and awareness of others). Still, with the understanding that all five SEL competencies are interrelated, it is clear that a level of self-awareness is absolutely necessary to answer some, if not all, of the SELf-questions.

To that end, Identify Feelings is the first step in the problem-solving process (Butler et al., 2011; Cohen et al., 2021), and the foundational skill of self-awareness can be targeted via the first set of SELf-questions, "How do I feel?" and "What am I feeling?" (This chapter does not reflect on the third SELf-question within the Identify Feelings step, "How does he, she, or they feel?" as this SELf-question pertains to social awareness.) Each of these SELf-questions encourages students to recognize their emotions. When educators ask or model these SELf-questions, they encourage students to express their emotions. If appropriate for your learner, you can venture into the Gather Information step by asking or modeling the SELf-questions, "What do I know?" "What is causing this feeling?" "What can I control?" and (or) "What is my goal?" For the purposes of emotional recognition and self-expression of an emotion, we focus on the SELf-questions for the Identify Feelings step in figure 3.1.

Structured SELf-questioning follows a sequence for the purpose of teaching the metacognitive strategy to students. However, a student's development of skills across competencies may be simultaneous or independent. For example, a student may recognize an emotion and respond to it by implementing ineffective self-management strategies instead of functionally expressing the emotion. Consider Emily's student, Shawn. Even though his actions were inappropriate and ineffective, Shawn used vocalizations, body language, and behavior (such as grunting, turning away, or leaving the activity) to express and attempt to manage his frustration. He may also have been able to express that he was feeling angry if he were asked, "How do you feel?" but he did not yet possess the emotional granularity to express that he wasn't simply angry that Emily was asking him to do something difficult; rather, he was truly frustrated because it was difficult for him to do.

Shawn needed to better identify his emotions through emotional recognition as well as better express his emotions through functional communication. Likewise, he needed to implement more appropriate and effective self-management strategies, such as taking a deep breath and going to an acceptable area to rest. The following sections discuss the importance of both emotional recognition and self-expression of emotions in developing self-awareness.

Emotional Recognition

Emotional recognition allows us to recognize emotions we experience. Kelly Mahler (n.d.) reflects on the important role interoception plays in this, stating, "Interoception is a sense that allows us to notice internal body signals like a growling stomach, racing heart, tense muscles, or full bladder. When we notice these body signals, our body uses them as clues to our emotions." For example, if we feel pressure in our bladder, we recognize this internal sensation and know we need to use the bathroom. If our stomach rumbles, we recognize this internal sensation and know we feel hungry (C. Mandel, personal communication, January 27, 2023).

We have to learn to recognize interoceptive information, connect this information to a feeling, and regulate it (C. Mandel, personal communication, January 27, 2023). If someone were to tell you, "I have butterflies in my stomach!" how would you assume he feels? Maybe you'd assumed he feels excited, as this is a common expression used when someone is experiencing excitement. However, consider a similar flutter we may feel in our stomachs when feeling nervous. People often refer to these flutters as nerves. For some people, excitement and fear may both elicit similar interoceptive information that presents in the stomach. We find that how we label the emotion often depends on internal information we experience in that moment, knowledge from previous experiences, and external information we gather from context or the environment in real time.

To depict the influence of previous experiences, contextual and environmental information, and interoceptive information, consider the following examples. First, think of that moment when you had completed setting up your classroom last year. Think of the tabletop toys you tucked neatly on shelves, the colorful carpet you laid in one corner of the room for circle time, and the row of empty cubbies you topped with each student's name. Think back to the first time you met those students you grew to love. You will likely feel those flutters in your stomach. You may interpret this interoceptive information, consider the positive relationships you formed with your previous students, pair this knowledge with the contextual information of a new school year and the environmental information of a clean classroom, and recognize the emotion of *excitement*.

Next, think of that moment just before an administrative observation. All of your students are sitting at circle, ready to start the school day. You look at the clock: two minutes until an administrator comes through the classroom door. You begin your greetings and ask the students how they feel. You look at the clock: one minute until administration comes through the door. One student gets up and finds his way to the blocks center. You hear what might as well be ten pounds of wooden bricks hit the floor right in the middle of the morning meeting, and your heart drops as your personal goal for the year is to increase classroom management. At that precise moment, the door begins to open. You feel those same flutters in your stomach, but this time, you interpret this interoceptive information, consider the goal of classroom management, pair this knowledge with the contextual information of a student not following directions and a looming observation, and recognize the emotion of *nervousness*.

Once you have identified your emotion correctly, the next step is to further develop self-awareness through effective and functional self-expression of that emotion. The following section discusses self-expression of an emotion through communication.

Self-Expression of an Emotion

Have you ever seen one of your students smile, cheer, and jump with excitement when you introduced a new center? Students who do this are using total communication to express their emotion. As cited by ASHA (n.d.), examples of total communication may include verbal speech, gestures, facial expressions, pictures, sounds, and sign language. Consider a time when one of your students performed a skill you were targeting. You may have felt your chest swell with pride. You may have smiled while you told your student, "You did it! I am so proud of you!" and enveloped him in a hug. Through your facial expression of a smile, your words telling him you felt proud, and your body language of a hug, you used total communication to demonstrate self-expression of an emotion—*pride*.

Self-expression of an emotion may not be considered functional if the student has not yet recognized the emotion. Rather, expression without emotional recognition is simply a reaction to stimuli. For example, consider a student who pushes a friend after she takes his toy. This student may have been using his limbic system instead of his cortex to respond to the situation and express his emotion. Although he is responding to and expressing the emotion through his behavior, he is not displaying functional self-expression of the emotion.

The aim when teaching the metacognitive strategy of structured SELf-questioning to promote self-awareness is to enable students to both recognize and communicate their emotions in developmentally appropriate ways. In the following section, we discuss approaches educators can use to teach structured SELf-questioning as well as facilitate student independence through internalization of the SELf-question set to promote self-awareness.

How to Teach a Metacognitive Strategy for Emotional Recognition and Self-Expression

Recall the vignette earlier in the chapter about Emily's student, Shawn, who struggled to recognize, express, and manage his emotions during speech sessions. This occurred at the start of his schooling; therefore, his exposure to the metacognitive strategy of structured SELf-questioning was just beginning. Emily and her fellow teachers continued to use structured SELf-questioning to facilitate his social-emotional learning. Over a short period of time, he learned to ask himself, "How do I feel?" and then express his emotions to staff and peers. With increased self-awareness, Shawn actively worked toward producing his target sounds regardless of the perceived difficulty.

Throughout a speech session with Shawn, he will most likely both accurately produce and struggle to produce targeted sounds. When Shawn is presented with a challenging sound, you will likely see him take a deep breath, stand up from the table, and jump on a huge bean bag. You'll hear Emily say, "When you're ready, come back, and we'll try again." Within seconds, Shawn will come back to the table and actively work on producing the targeted sound.

Shawn has internalized structured SELf-questioning, and the positive impact is apparent. He now demonstrates the ability to use verbal thinking to ask himself how he is feeling, recognize the emotion in his body, identify that he does not need to express it in the therapeutic environment he shares with Emily, and implement functional strategies to manage that emotion. Shawn's independent and internalized use of structured SELf-questioning has not only allowed Emily and him to develop a positive rapport but has also resulted in productive therapy sessions and increased student success in and out of the therapeutic environment.

As an educator, the importance of facilitating students' self-awareness and self-expression is clear, but teaching these skills may feel like just another thing to add to your already overflowing plate of expectations and tasks. Fortunately, you can increase your students' self-awareness and self-expression within the current context of your classroom using structured SELf-questioning. Furthermore, as your students' self-awareness and self-expression increase, so will their engagement in learning, resulting in a still-full but more manageable plate.

The following sections focus on how to teach the SELf-questions for the first step (Identify Feelings) from the social and emotional structured SELf-questioning set to facilitate learners' self-awareness through emotional recognition and self-expression.

Using the Two Questions

The SELf-questions for developing self-awareness through emotional recognition are as follows.

- How do I feel?
- What am I feeling?

In your practice, it is important to use your discretion when using one or both of these SELf-questions. For some students, consistent use of one SELf-question may facilitate their ability to access the SELf-question independently; therefore, using one instead of both SELf-questions is more effective. For some students, using both SELf-questions provides multiple language models and increases their emotional granularity as the use of both SELf-questions may encourage them to gather additional and different information about their feelings. For example, the SELf-questions "How do I feel?" and "What am I feeling?" may elicit a response of an emotions word; however, the SELf-question "What am I feeling?" may also elicit a response regarding interoceptive information, which could lead to increased self-awareness.

To clarify, let's look at an example of when the SELf-question "What am I feeling?" elicited interoceptive information from students. During a summer program, Katie was conducting a listening lesson that was tied to the academic standard *1.1.6: Use movement/dance to convey meaning around a theme or to show feelings* (Teaching Strategies, n.d.a). She presented students with songs from different music genres during their music and movement routine. While the students listened to a song, she asked them, "What are you feeling?" These preschool students demonstrated emotional recognition and self-expression of emotions as well as interoceptive awareness by providing specific information regarding not only what they were feeling but also where they were feeling it. Some students felt the music in their throats, while others felt it in their chests. They reflected on interoceptive information without even knowing that word existed. We all know our students, even those as young as preschool age, are capable of learning all types of content. Structured SELf-questioning provides them with the opportunity to learn about their own emotions, which will set them up for academic, social, emotional, and personal success. I encourage you to use one or both of the SELf-questions that facilitate self-awareness depending on what you feel is best for each of your learners.

The following sections introduce several methods or approaches (self-talk, parallel talk, and total communication) you can apply while modeling structured SELf-questioning during your preschool classroom daily routines as well as during structured or unstructured activities to teach emotional recognition and self-expression.

Modeling Using Self-Talk and Parallel Talk

If we want our students to demonstrate self-awareness, we must lead by example. We all know preschoolers see and hear everything. It's why you, as their teacher, may know about most things going on in your students' homes, whether their parents tell you or not. To teach emotional recognition and self-expression, we can capitalize on students always listening by modeling the first SELf-question within the structured SELf-questioning set ("How do I feel?") as well as variations of possible responses (for example, "I feel . . .") throughout the entire school day. Many sound approaches to modeling exist (such as Fey, 1986), but we like how authors Rhea Paul, Courtenay Norbury, and Carolyn Gosse (2018) describe it as a process during which the student:

> listens as the model provides numerous examples of the structure being taught. . . . Through listening, the child is expected to induce and later produce the target structure [without the requirement of immediate imitation. Modeling] implicitly requires the child to find a pattern in the model's talk that is similar across all the stimuli presented. (p. 69)

There is a reason why modeling is so effective. Kusche and Greenberg (2006) state that *mirror neurons* are "nerve cells that fire in response to observations of behaviors in others as if the individual were actually performing them" (p. 24). In short, they allow modeling to be a powerful teaching strategy. An example of the target structure modeled for self-awareness and self-expression is "How do I feel?" followed by "I feel ____________." Teachers and other staff can model structured SELf-questions for self-awareness ("How do I feel?" and "What am I feeling?") and meaningful responses all throughout the day so that students will recognize the pattern of the structured SELf-questions and internalize them.

Note that you may feel like modeling all day long can be overwhelming; however, it is not something you have to do all on your own. We find that when other adults working or interacting with students utilize the strategy, student development of emotional recognition and self-expression accelerates. This may include staff such as teachers, paraprofessionals, related service providers, school nurses, and administrators. We believe that frequent and consistent exposure to structured SELf-questioning demonstrated by all stakeholders across settings allows students more opportunities to internalize this metacognitive strategy.

Modeling Using Self-Talk

What is *self-talk*? According to Paul and colleagues (2018), "In self-talk we describe our own actions" (p. 71). Self-talk can also be referred to as *self-directed speech* (Kapa & Mettler, 2021). According to researchers Aisling Mulvihill, Annemaree Carroll, Paul E. Dux, and Natasha Matthews (2020), self-directed speech can be used "to describe any speech directed at oneself (i.e., not social speech) that supports self-regulation, which includes both regulation of one's behaviors and cognitive processes" (as cited in Kapa & Mettler, 2021, p. 1317). We can use self-talk to recognize and express our own emotions by modeling the structured SELf-question, "How do I feel?" and the response, "I feel ______________." As Kapa and Mettler (2021) state, "Preschoolers are more likely to have overt rather than covert [self-directed] speech" (p. 1321). *Overt* and *covert* refer to the level of internalization of self-directed speech, with overt referring to language that "can be heard" and covert language meaning language that is "silent" or "fully internalized" (Lidstone et al., 2012, as cited in Kappa & Mettler, 2021, p. 1317). The act of self-talk is much like a think aloud, "when you say out loud what you are thinking" (Lopes et al., 2022). Like self-talk, think alouds facilitate comprehension and problem-solving skills by using modeling to encourage thinking things through (Lopes et al., 2022). Think alouds are most likely common practice in your classroom. You may do them while reading a story or to problem solve during centers. If you are currently using think alouds, you are most likely already modeling self-talk.

Furthermore, by using the "I feel" response, we can strategically model as many feelings as possible that are applicable. This approach can teach students a diverse emotional vocabulary, something psychiatrist Lisa Feldman Barrett (2018) calls *emotional granularity*, which is necessary for the development of emotional recognition and literacy. Barrett (2018) offers an explanation to further describe the importance of emotional granularity:

> If you could distinguish finer meanings within "awesome" (happy, content, thrilled, relaxed, joyful, hopeful, inspired, prideful, adoring, grateful, blissful . . .), and fifty shades of "crappy" (angry, aggravated, alarmed, spiteful, grumpy, remorseful, gloomy, mortified, uneasy, dread-ridden, resentful, afraid, envious, woeful, melancholy . . .), your brain would have many more options for predicting, categorizing, and perceiving emotions, providing you with the tools for more flexible and useful responses. You could predict and categorize your sensations more efficiently and better suit your actions to your environment. (as cited in Cohen et al., 2021, p. 119)

By modeling granular identification and expression of emotions within our self-talk, we provide students with the opportunity to increase their emotional vocabulary. Imagine you are carrying a case of markers to a student's table but trip over a little chair. The case falls to the floor, spilling markers all over the floor. Your self-talk might include the following sequence of thoughts.

> *Oh no, I dropped all of the markers!*
>
> *What am I feeling? I am feeling that my teeth are clenched, and my shoulders are raised.*
>
> *How do I feel? I feel frustrated!*

To model the complete structured SELf-questioning set, you would continue to demonstrate self-management following your self-expression of the emotion *frustrated*. We discuss self-management in the next chapter.

Modeling Using Parallel Talk

Parallel talk is a process during which "we provide self-talk for the child" (Paul et al., 2018, p. 71). We can use parallel talk to model for students how they can recognize and express emotions by asking, "How do you feel?" and responding, "Your body is telling me you may feel ______________." In parallel talk, we assume the student's emotions. As teachers, we want to provide parallel talk that is meaningful and as accurate as possible. This means we must consider any previous knowledge of the student's emotional experiences, contextual and environmental information, and any additional information the student may give us using total communication. By encouraging students to identify and express their emotions to a more specific degree during parallel talk when appropriate, we facilitate their self-awareness skills and boost their likelihood of success with self-management of those emotions (Cohen et al., 2021).

Imagine you go into a classroom to pick up your student, Avery, for a session. When she sees you, she smiles and jumps up from her seat. You tell her it's time to go and begin walking to the door. She runs ahead of you. You see the door fly open and watch her race through it. You pick up your pace. As soon as you get to the classroom door, you see her just across the hall jumping at the closed door to your classroom. You approach her and squat down so you are at eye level with her. The following might be an example of your parallel talk.

> *You: "What are you feeling? I saw your feet moving quickly and jumping high. I see a big smile on your face and tight fists."*
>
> *You: "I wonder, how do you feel? Your body is telling me you may feel overjoyed!"*
>
> *Avery: "How do I feel? I feel overjoyed!"*

If the student were to express interoceptive or emotional information, you would also include that in your parallel talk. An example of how you could incorporate student-provided information into your parallel talk is as follows.

> *In response to "What are you feeling?" Avery told you, "I can't control my feet!" You honor this by acknowledging the response in your parallel talk.*
>
> *You: "What are you feeling? I hear you telling me your feet feel out of control. I saw them moving quickly and jumping high. I see a big smile on your face and tight fists."*
>
> *You: "I wonder, how do you feel? Your body is telling me you may feel overjoyed!"*
>
> *Avery: "How do I feel? I feel overjoyed!"*

If a student were not to express any information, as in the first part of the preceding example, we would model the SELf-question set and provide functional and appropriate responses based on assumed intent. We must remember that *behavior is communication*. In addition to student behavior, we can also use other modalities of total communication (for example, facial expressions or gestures) to assume their intent. For example, if a student is giggling and reaching her hands toward us, we can assume she feels happy. The following might be an example of your parallel talk.

You: "What are you feeling? I hear your mouth giggling and see your hands reaching toward me!"

You: "I wonder, how do you feel? Your body is telling me you may feel happy!"

Avery: "How do I feel? I feel happy!

Through self-talk and parallel talk, we can model SELf-questions and responses that facilitate students' emotional recognition and self-expression. Next, we explore how we can use total communication to interpret students' emotions to facilitate their emotional recognition as well as their ability to demonstrate self-expression of emotions.

Using Total Communication for Emotional Recognition and Self-Expression

As previously noted, total communication may include verbal speech, gestures, facial expressions, pictures, sounds, and sign language (ASHA, n.d.) *Augmentative and alternative communication* (AAC) is a communicative modality within total communication. Any way we communicate without using our voices is considered AAC. According to ASHA (n.d.), AAC is "augmentative when used to supplement existing speech" and "alternative when used in place of speech that is absent or not functional." Examples of AAC include sign language, gestures, and pictures. We can *use* total communication, including AAC, during self-talk to model emotional recognition and self-expression of emotions to facilitate self-awareness skills. We can *interpret* a student's use of total communication, including AAC, during parallel talk to model how they can demonstrate emotional recognition and self-expression of emotions to facilitate self-awareness skills. Ultimately, this means we are going to use any and all communicative tools we can to teach emotional recognition and self-expression of emotions.

In addition to using these tools during our self-talk and parallel talk, we can honor them during a student's functional and non-functional expression of emotion. A student may use non-functional communication to express emotions via inappropriate self-management strategies before they have access to functional communication to demonstrate self-expression. What might this look like? It may look like Shawn grunting and stomping away from a therapeutic activity when angry. It may look like a boy throwing a chair when frustrated. It may look like a girl running down the hallway when excited. These examples include students using total communication via their behaviors, body language, and vocalizations to express their emotions. We may be able to understand the emotions they are expressing; however, the modality they used to express those emotions was not functional. So, what can we do? We can interpret, assume, and recognize the emotions they are experiencing based on their use of total communication. We can then use total communication to model how they can functionally express their emotions.

In addition to possibly facilitating students' self-expression, our use of total communication during self- and parallel talk may also facilitate their receptive language or their understanding. Modeling using total communication to express our feelings and their feelings provides models of SELf-questions and emotional vocabulary responses within context using multiple modes of communication. As a result, such modeling provides students with ample opportunities to understand SELf-questions and vocabulary through a variety of modalities.

We all know students benefit from multimodality teaching and that not all students learn the same way. According to Elias and Arnold (2006), "Educational experiences marked by instruction that uses different modalities are most likely to reach all children and allow them to build their skills and feel that the classroom environment is suited to their preferred way of learning" (p. 8). Like any material that is being taught, we must teach emotional recognition and self-expression of emotions through different modalities to ensure all students have the opportunity to effectively access and use these skills to the best of their current ability.

We can use total communication to model emotional recognition and self-expression of an emotion during self-talk by using AAC (facial expressions, body language, vocalizations, and pictures or symbols) while modeling and responding to the SELf-question set. You can see an example of total communication modalities you may use and what that expression may look like based on the emotion of *angry* in table 3.1.

Table 3.1: Tools to Model and Express Anger

Tool (Modality)	Example
Facial expression	Exaggerated frown; gritted teeth with eyebrows pointing in and down
Body language	Body leaned in or turned away; arms crossed
Vocalization	Grunting

In addition to the modalities in table 3.1, you will use functional communication via speech, sign language, and picture symbols to express that you feel angry. While twisting your face into an exaggerated frown (facial expression), you lean your body in (body language), and grunt (vocalization) before asking yourself aloud, "How do I feel?" You look up and to the side while facing your palms upward (facial expression and body language or gesture to express contemplation). You say, "I feel," while patting your chest (gesture), "*angry*!" while signing *angry* (sign language), then pointing to a picture or symbol representing angry.

Table 3.2 (page 58) is how you might use AAC during total communication when modeling self-talk to express the emotion *silly*. In addition to the modalities in table 3.2, you will use functional communication via speech, sign language, and picture symbols to express that you feel silly. While opening your mouth into a big smile (facial expression), you lean your body in, bob your head, and reach toward the student (body language). You let out a loud laugh (vocalization) before asking yourself aloud, "How do I feel?" You look up and to the side while facing your palms upward (facial expression and body language or gesture to express contemplation). You say, "I feel," while patting your chest (gesture), "*silly*!" while signing *silly* (sign language), then pointing to a picture or symbol representing silly.

Table 3.2: Tools to Model and Express Silliness

Tool (Modality)	Example
Facial expression	Exaggerated smile
Body language	Body leaned in or swaying with head bobbing; arms reaching out to the student
Vocalization	Laughing; making silly noises

We can use similar tools via total communication to model emotional recognition and self-expression of an emotion when providing parallel talk for a student. Prior to providing parallel talk to students, interpret their use of total communication to assume the emotions they are experiencing. Our use of modalities will be completely dependent on the assumed emotions. We can use total communication to model emotional recognition and self-expression of the assumed emotions during parallel talk by using AAC (facial expression, body language, vocalizations, and picture or symbol) while modeling and responding to the SELf-question set.

Table 3.3 includes examples of how we may interpret a student's use of total communication to assume the emotion that student is experiencing (scared) as well as what total communication modalities may be used while modeling self-expression based on the assumed emotion.

Table 3.3: Tools to Model and Express Fear

Tool (Modality)	Example
Facial expression	Wide eyes; frown; eyes looking around
Body language	Shoulders hunched; head down; hands covering face
Vocalization	High-pitch vocalization

You interpret the student's facial expression, body language, and vocalizations and consider the environmental and contextual information that the student is entering an unfamiliar room. You also use your previous knowledge of how the student appeared to feel scared entering a new classroom on the first day of school. While mirroring these modalities, you also use functional communication via speech, sign language, and picture symbols to express that the student may be feeling scared. While frowning (facial expression) and putting your hands on your face (body language), you say aloud, "I wonder, how do you feel? I see your eyes are big, and you're looking around to gather information. I see your hands are covering your face, and I heard you go [repeat high-pitch vocalization]." You look up and to the side while facing your palms upward (facial expression and body language or gesture to express contemplation). You say, "I think your body is telling me that you feel scared," while signing *scared* (sign language), then pointing to a picture or symbol representing scared.

Table 3.4 shows how you might use AAC during total communication when modeling parallel talk to a student expressing the emotion *tired.*

Table 3.4: Tools to Model and Express Tiredness

Tool (Modality)	Example
Facial expression	Eyes closing
Body language	Head on table; laying down; stretching arms and body
Vocalization	Yawning

You interpret the student's facial expression, body language, and vocalizations and consider the environmental and contextual information that the student just got back from playing outside and that it is near the end of the school day. While mirroring these modalities, you also use functional communication via speech, sign language, and picture symbols to express that he may be feeling tired. While slightly closing your eyes (facial expression) and stretching your arms (body language), you say aloud, "I wonder, how do you feel? I see your eyes are almost closed. I see your hands are covering your face. I heard you yawn." You look up and to the side while facing your palms upward (facial expression and body language or gesture to express contemplation). You say, "I think your body is telling me that you feel tired," while signing *tired* (sign language), then pointing to a picture or symbol representing tired.

Knowing When Not to Teach SELf-Questions

If a student screams and throws a chair after a friend takes something from them, we can assume that student feels furious. When a student is dysregulated, we should not ask SELf-questions and expect a response. Any perceived demands or excessive input may only further escalate the dysregulation. Dysregulation makes it more challenging for anyone to learn; therefore, when students are dysregulated, this is not the time to directly teach them self-awareness skills. Kusche and Greenberg (2006) indicate that this is partially because the prefrontal cortex that regulates emotion is located closely to the part of the brain responsible for regulating cognitive processes. They further indicate that "these two areas appear to be mutually inhibitory. . . . When one of these areas is active, functioning of the other is compromised" (Kusche & Greenberg, 2006, p. 22).

This means that when students are focused on regulating their emotions, they are not ready to learn. It is clear that this is not when we should place demands on them to learn directly. Instead, we can simply expose them to the SELf-questions of the Identify Feelings step by modeling through parallel talk.

The following is an example of what your parallel talk might look like when modeling for the student who threw a chair and screamed after a friend took something away—once the student is no longer screaming. It is important to note that a student experiencing dysregulation may benefit from the pronoun *I* instead of *you* as this more closely aligns with the targeted internal language of the SELf-question set.

"What am I feeling*? I heard my mouth yell loudly and felt my arms throw a chair."*

"How do I feel? I feel furious!"

Scenarios for Emotional Recognition and Expression

The following sections offer three example scenarios for interactions between teachers and students that are focused on emotional recognition and expression to facilitate self-awareness. Note that the scope of these scenarios goes beyond the scope of this chapter, as each includes its own utilization and range of steps within the metacognitive strategy for SELf-questioning, as illustrated in figure 1.3 (page 18).

Scenario 1: Preschool Arrival, Morning Meeting, and Daily Activities

Program: Integrated preschool

Objective: Identify feelings.

Standard: 0.3.1 "Recognize and describe a wide range of feelings, including sadness, anger, fear, and happiness" (Teaching Strategies, n.d.a, p. 3).

Teacher: Mrs. Herold

In Mrs. Herold's integrated preschool setting, teachers embed emotional recognition and expression at the end of morning meetings. Teachers have students do this by turning and talking to each other. At the beginning of the year, this is first modeled by teachers through a teacher-led discussion, and eventually it becomes a student-led discussion. The following is an example of a teacher-led turn and talk to promote self-awareness.

IDENTIFY FEELINGS

SELf-Question: How do I feel?

At the end of the morning meeting, Mrs. Herold says, "Now, it is time for our turn and talk activity. Today, I will be asking all of you, 'How are you feeling?'" She gives the students a few seconds to check in with their feelings before asking, "Anthony, how are you feeling?"

"I feel sad," states Anthony.

GATHER INFORMATION

SELf-Question: What is causing this feeling?

Mrs. Herold models the next step in our structured SELf-questions by stating, "What is causing this feeling?" Anthony states that before arriving at school, his little sister took his favorite toy. Mrs. Herold validates his feelings by stating, "I understand. It is upsetting when someone takes your favorite toy."

BRAINSTORM

SELf-Question: What can I do?

Mrs. Herold continues, " Hmmm. What can you do when you feel sad? You can take belly breaths." This opens up the conversation for other students to offer their ideas! Encourage this! Aria suggests, "You can ask for a hug." Hannah suggests, "You can count to ten." Victor adds, "You can take a break." These are coping strategies for students to learn, have modeled for them, and practice throughout the classroom. Anthony says, "I can take a break!"

EVALUATE

SELf-Question: Has this strategy helped me in the past?

Mrs. Herold adds, "What's the best way to solve this problem?" Anthony thinks for a few seconds and says, "I think I want to take a break." Mrs. Herold asks, "Has taking a break helped you in the past when you felt sad?" Anthony thinks for a few seconds and says, "Yes!"

PLAN AND ACT

SELf-Question: What do I do first, second, and so on?

Mrs. Herold and Anthony make a plan. She adds, "What do you do first?" Anthony says, "First, I can finish circle time; then, I can take a break in the break area."

REFLECT

SELf-Question: Did it work?

After the morning meeting, Anthony walks over to the break area next to Mrs. Herold's desk. This is where he will find a soft place to sit and tools to calm his body, such as sensory toys, books about feelings, and calming visuals. After a few minutes, Anthony makes his way over to center time. The teacher continues, "Anthony, I see you are ready to play. Did it work?" Anthony exclaims, "Yes, I am ready to play!"

Scenario 2: Students With Special Needs or Differing Abilities

Program: Preschool disabilities

Objective: Respond to emotional cues.

Standard: 0.3.1 "Recognize and describe a wide range of feelings, including sadness, anger, fear, and happiness" (Teaching Strategies, n.d.a, p. 3).

Teacher: Ms. Young

Ms. Young pulls two three-year-old students, Shannon and Raul, for small-group instruction. Shannon has a diagnosis of oppositional defiant disorder, and Raul has a diagnosis of autism spectrum disorder. Both students are verbal and use core boards to enhance their spoken language.

IDENTIFY FEELINGS

SELf-Question: How do I feel?

The teacher places a mirror in front of herself and the two students. She models asking herself and the students the SELf-question, "How do I feel?" Ms. Young answers, "I feel tired." She then poses the SELf-question to the students. Shannon says, "Happy," and Raul points to *silly* on the core board.

GATHER INFORMATION

SELf-Question: What do I know?

Ms. Young looks at herself in the mirror and points to her mouth, which is opened wide. She models asking the SELf-question, "What do I know?" She models pointing to the words *mouth* and *open* on the core board. She then states, "I know that my mouth is opened wide, and I am yawning," before posing the SELf-question to the students. Shannon points to her mouth, which is upturned into a smile, and Raul sticks out his tongue and says, "Goo-goo ga-ga," which makes Shannon laugh and say, "You are so silly, Raul!"

BRAINSTORM

SELf-Question: What can I do?

Ms. Young first models using a think aloud and self-talk by stating, "What can I do when I am yawning at school? I can go to the calming corner and take out the blanket to relax my body." She then asks the students the structured SELf-question, "What can you do?" Shannon again states that she is happy and asks Raul if she can hug him. Raul says she can. The students hug. Raul starts to tickle Shannon. Ms. Young tells the students, "Shannon, your body is feeling happy, and you gave Raul a hug. Raul, your body is feeling silly. You tickled Shannon to make her laugh."

REFLECT

SELf-Question: Did it work?

Ms. Young follows through with her think aloud and self-talk. She leads the students to the calming corner. She takes the blanket and puts it over her legs. She asks the SELf-question aloud, "Did it work?" She answers, "Yes! It worked. I was feeling tired, and the blanket helped me feel relaxed."

Ms. Young asks Shannon, "Did it work?" Shannon says, "I am happy, so I gave him a hug!" The teacher smiles and validates Shannon's feelings. "Yes. Your strategy worked. When you feel happy, you can hug a friend." She turns to Raul and asks, "Did it work?" Raul sticks out his tongue again and begins to tickle Ms. Young. The teacher smiles and validates Raul's feelings. She models, "You see. Your strategy worked, Raul. You are feeling silly, so you can tickle."

Scenario 3: Expression of Emotion Using Multimodal Communication

Program: Preschool disabilities

Objective: Show curiosity and motivation.

Standard: 0.2.1 "Make independent choices and plans from a broad range of diverse interest centers" (Teaching Strategies, n.d.a, p. 2).

Teacher: Ms. L

The preschool class is learning about pets. The discovery center includes pretend foods different pets may eat. The dramatic play center features a veterinarian's office equipped with play tools and uniforms. The blocks center consists of building materials and pictures of a variety of places a pet may live or enjoy (for example, a dog house, cage, and playpen). Each area of the classroom includes static boards that offer picture symbols with written words of core (high-frequency words) and fringe (topic-specific words) vocabulary. In addition to speech and picture symbols, Ms. L uses facial expressions, gestures, and body language while implementing structured SELf-questioning, as the use of multiple modes of communication is implemented to promote the student's receptive, expressive, and pragmatic language skills.

IDENTIFY FEELINGS

SELf-Question: What am I feeling?

During circle time, Ms. L asks each student, "What pet do you like best?" while presenting them with a field of three pictures. The three pictures are of a dog, cat, and bird (picture symbols). She turns toward Amelia to ask this question (body language to express turn). While asking this question, she points to the *what* symbol on the core board (picture symbol). Ms. L subsequently points to the student (gesture for *you*).

Throughout the entire exchange, Ms. L smiles (facial expression expressing interest and excitement) and leans in (body language expressing interest, excitement, and waiting). Amelia smiles, leans in, looks at the pictures, points to the bird, and says, "Bird!" in a high-pitched voice. She begins to stomp her feet while smiling and holding her hands together.

Ms. L models parallel talk using total communication by saying, "Amelia, what are you feeling?" as she leans in (body language to express interest), points to Amelia (gesture for *you*), tilts her head to the side (body language to express waiting), and points to the symbol for *what* on a core board (picture symbol). Amelia begins to stomp her feet again while smiling and holding her hands. Ms. L says, "I heard you say, 'Bird!' I see a big smile on your face and that you are holding your hands. I see and hear your feet stomping." Ms. L mirrors Amelia's expression through her production of *bird*, facial expression of a smile, and body language of holding her hands together and stomping her feet.

Ms. L says, "Your body is telling me you may feel excited!" as she smiles (facial expression), points to Amelia (gesture for *you*), demonstrates American Sign Language by signing *excited* (gesture), and points to a corresponding picture symbol for *excited* (picture symbol). Following this model, Ms. L holds the picture symbol for *excited* out to Amelia and tilts her head to the side (body language expressing waiting). This expectant waiting provides Amelia with the opportunity to express the emotion. Amelia touches the *excited* symbol. Ms. L continues her parallel talk with the singular first person pronoun *I* to closely align with the student's possible internal language. Ms. L smiles (facial expression for excitement and praise) and says, "How do I feel? I feel excited!" while pointing to herself (gesture for *I*), signing *excited* (gesture), and pointing to a corresponding picture symbol for *excited*.

GATHER INFORMATION

SELf-Question: What do I know?

Ms. L goes on to introduce centers to the class. She says, "I know some of my friends feel excited about birds! What do I know? I know we have bird food in the discovery center, a bird in dramatic play, and a picture of a birdhouse in the blocks center." Ms. L says this while smiling (facial expression), pointing to herself and each center (gesture for *I* and gesture to bring attention to center options), signing *excited* (gesture), and pointing to picture symbols for *what*, *excited*, and each center (picture symbols). Additionally, when she poses the SELf-question, "What do I know?" she looks up and to the side (facial expression and body language for contemplation) and faces her palms upward (gesture to signal question).

Amelia's smile widens as she turns to look at all of the centers. Ms. L continues her parallel talk with the singular first person pronoun *I* to closely align with the student's possible internal language. Ms. L goes on to say, "What do I know? I know I can look at the centers to gather information. I know I am smiling!" while smiling (facial expression) and pointing to herself (gesture for *I*), then to each of the centers (gesture).

BRAINSTORM

SELf-Question: What can I do?

Ms. L continues her parallel talk with the singular first person pronoun *I* to closely align with the student's possible internal language. Ms. L states, "When I feel excited about playing with birds, what can I do? I can pick a center!" while pointing to herself (gesture for *I*), signing *excited* (gesture), signing *bird* (gesture), pointing to the *what* symbol on the core board (picture symbol), and leaning in (body language to express interest and waiting).

Ms. L presents Amelia with picture symbols on the board representing each center as well as Amelia's picture for her to place under the center she chooses. Amelia takes her picture, stands up, and puts her picture under dramatic play. She stares at the board and her selection. She turns to look at the discovery center. She takes her picture and moves it to the discovery center. She then takes her picture and puts it back at dramatic play. While Amelia makes these selections, she is smiling. Ms. L says, "I feel so excited about playing with birds at centers! I feel curious about the centers. I feel a little confused about what center to choose. What can I do? I can pick one center to play at first, then come back and pick another center to play at next." As she answers the SELf-question, she demonstrates facial expressions for excitement, curiosity, and confusion followed by contemplation (facial expressions).

Ms. L also points to herself (gesture for *I*), signs *excited, curious,* and *confused* (gestures), points to *excited, curious,* and *confused* picture symbols (picture symbols), and points to the *what* symbol on the core board (picture symbol). Amelia plays at the discovery center, where she finds a sensory bin filled with bird seed. In the bird seed, there are toy birds, cats, and dogs, along with foods they like to eat (bugs, fish, and bones). She enjoys feeding the different animals. She goes toward the centers board and takes her picture off the discovery center.

Ms. L waits about ten seconds to provide Amelia with the opportunity to switch centers and independently implement the plan created using the SELf-questions. Ms. L says, "I feel so excited about playing with birds at centers! I feel curious about the centers. I feel a little confused about what center to choose. First, I chose to play at the discovery center. What can I do? I can pick another center to play at now." Repeating the plan created prior to playing at centers, Ms. L uses the same modes of communication previously used (facial expressions, sign language, gestures, and picture symbols). Amelia puts her picture at the blocks center. Amelia goes to the blocks center, where she uses a variety of materials to build a town of bird houses.

REFLECT

SELf-Question: Did it work?

Ms. L continues her parallel talk with the singular first person pronoun *I* to closely align with the student's possible internal language. Ms. L approaches Amelia. She says, "I felt excited about playing with birds at centers. I felt curious about the centers. I felt confused about which center to pick. What did I do? First, I played at the discovery center; then, I played at the blocks center. Did it work? Yes or no?"

Ms. L points to herself (gesture for *I*), points to picture symbols for *excited, curious,* and *confused* (picture symbols), signs *excited, curious,* and *confused* (gestures), points to the picture symbol for what on a core board (picture symbol), points to the center picture symbols (picture symbols), signs *yes* and *no* while nodding and shaking her head (body language), and leans in (body language to express waiting). Amelia smiles, says "Yes," signs *yes,* and nods her head. Ms. L. says, "Yes! It did," while signing *yes* (gesture) and smiling (facial expression).

Throughout these steps (Identify Feelings, Gather Information, Brainstorm, and Reflect), Ms. L uses multiple modes of communication. She uses speech to ask and answer the structured SELf-questions, makes statements to describe Amelia's expression of emotions, expresses emotions, makes a plan, reflects on a plan, and makes statements about centers. She also uses picture symbols, gestures, facial expressions, body language, and American Sign Language.

The use of multiple modes of communication promotes the student's comprehension of the structured SELf-questions, statements, emotions vocabulary, the planning process, and reflection, and it also promotes the recognition of emotions and how they present in the body, which facilitates receptive language skills. It promotes the student's ability to ask and answer the structured SELf-questions, make statements, use emotions vocabulary, make plans, reflect on plans, describe emotions and how they present in the body, and express emotions, which facilitates expressive language skills. Additionally, it promotes the student's ability to interact with others, participate in exchanges, and take turns, which facilitates pragmatic language skills.

Conclusion

We can facilitate self-awareness in our students by targeting their ability to recognize and self-express emotions through the metacognitive strategy of structured SELf-questioning using just two structured SELf-questions ("How do I feel" and "What am I feeling?"). We encourage you to use all modalities of communication that are functional to express your emotions for modeling self-talk. We encourage you to interpret all modalities of communication that a student uses that are functional as well as not functional to assume the intent or expression of an emotion for modeling parallel talk purposes. In doing so, you may promote the social-emotional learning of your students and set them up for academic, social, and emotional success.

Now that we know what the foundational skill of self-awareness is, why self-awareness is important, and how it can be targeted using structured SELf-questioning, we now move forward to self-management and provide a practical guide as to when all of this teaching can occur into an already full school day.

Parent Corner

We have learned what structured SELf-questioning looks like in the classroom, but what about at home? Parents and caregivers and the relationship they share with the student play an important role in facilitating social-emotional success. Furthermore, we understand that when many people in the student's life use the strategy, it allows for a multitude of opportunities to learn the metacognitive strategy. You can equip parents and caregivers with the skills to implement this valuable strategy by providing them with the reproducible tools that follow: "SELf-Questioning 101: Self-Awareness Key Concepts" (page 67), "SELf-Questioning 101: Teaching Self-Awareness to Your Child" (page 69), and "SELf-Questioning 101: Using Self-Talk and Parallel Talk With Your Child" (page 70). Use these reproducible tools with parents and caregivers to summarize important key terms, explain the use of self-talk and parallel talk via total communication to model structured SELf-questions, and provide meaningful examples of what the implementation of structured SELf-questioning to facilitate self-awareness may look like in the home environment.

SELf-Questioning 101: Self-Awareness Key Concepts

Self-awareness may be composed of emotional recognition and self-expression of an emotion. You can facilitate emotional recognition and self-expression of an emotion (self-awareness) by modeling structured SELf-questions using self-talk and parallel talk. To promote self-awareness in your child, let's learn about these important key terms.

Key Term	Description

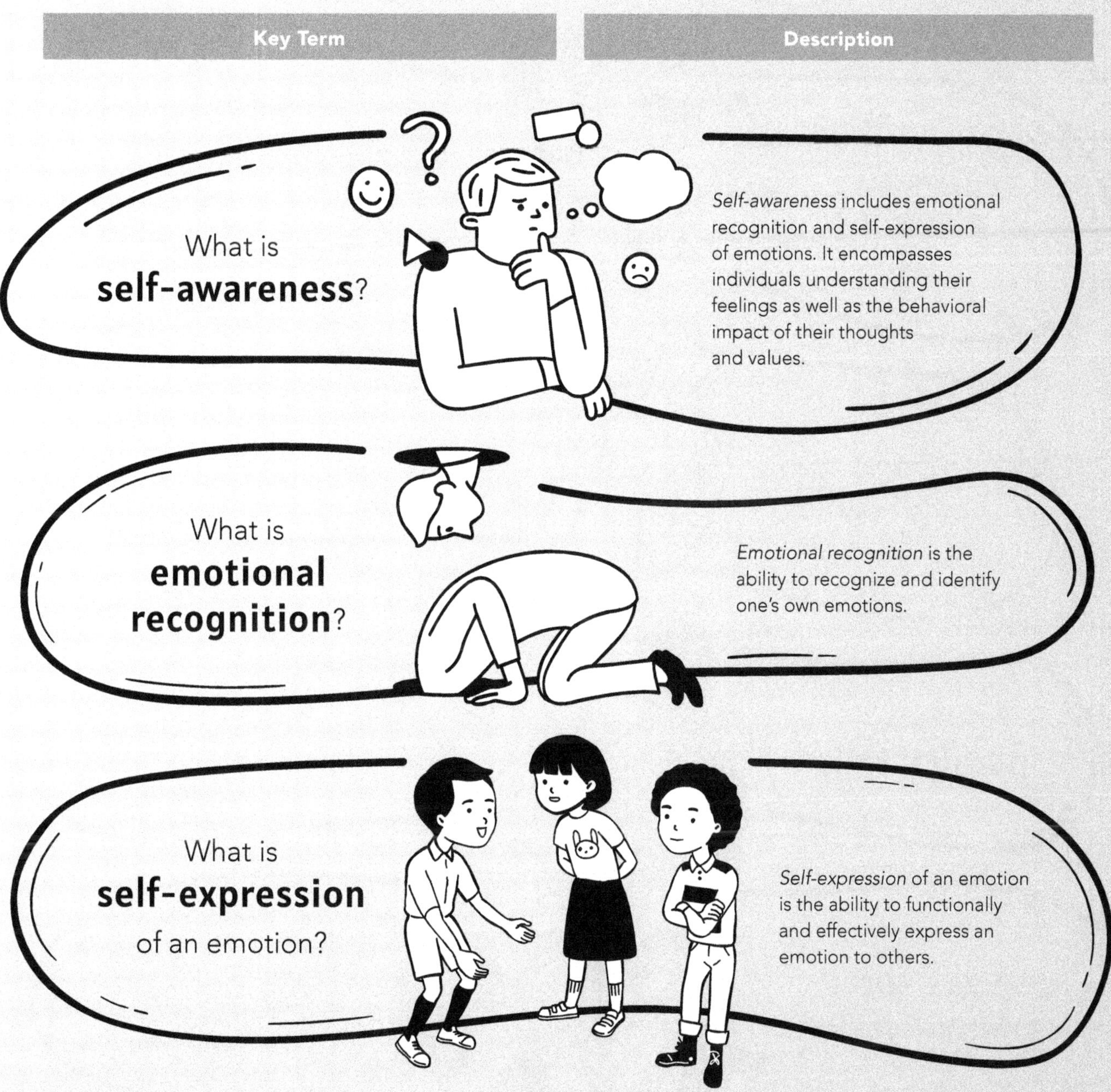

page 1 of 2

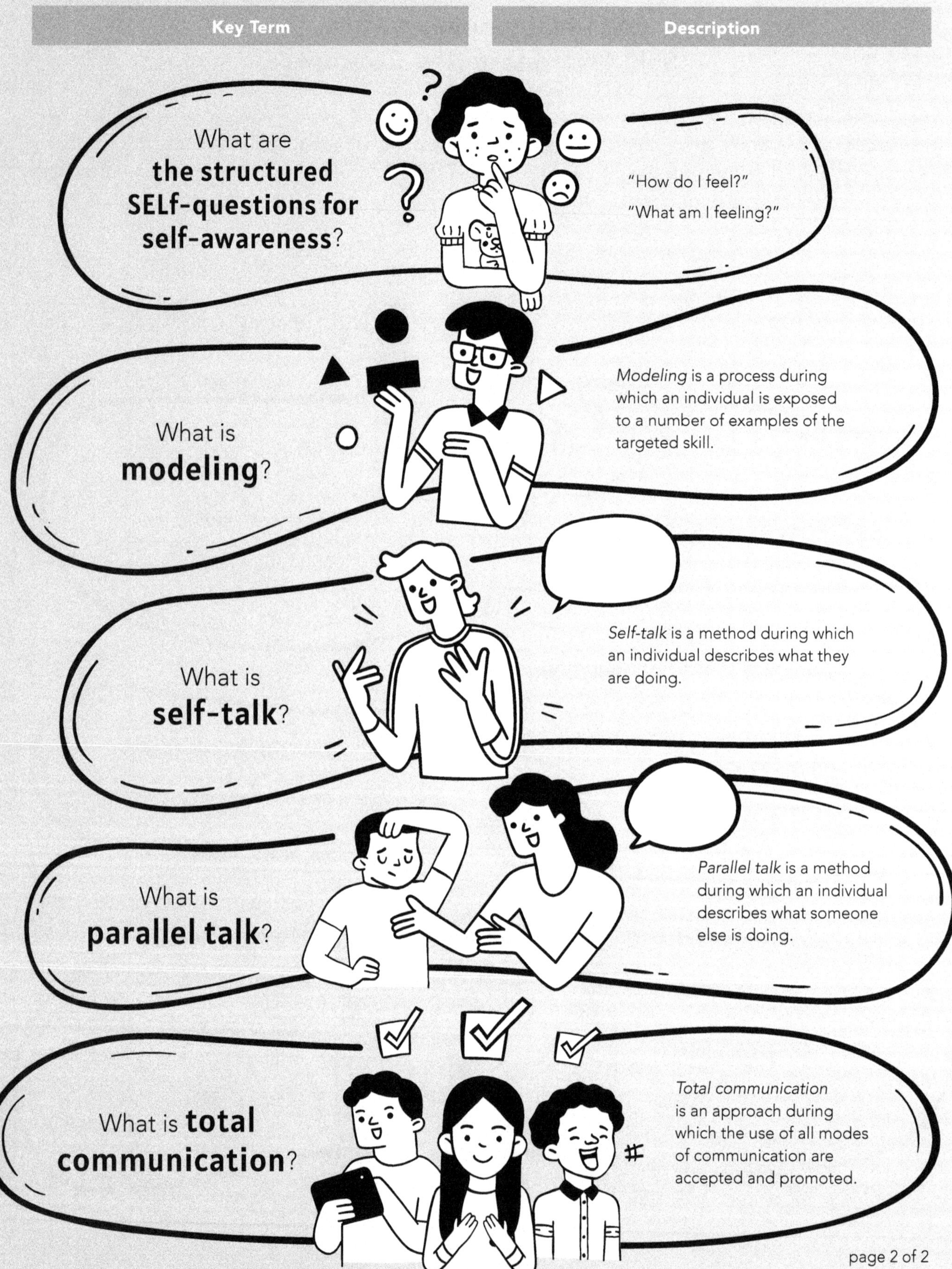

Key Term
Description
What are **the structured SELf-questions for self-awareness**?
"How do I feel?"
"What am I feeling?"
What is **modeling**?
Modeling is a process during which an individual is exposed to a number of examples of the targeted skill.
What is **self-talk**?
Self-talk is a method during which an individual describes what they are doing.
What is **parallel talk**?
Parallel talk is a method during which an individual describes what someone else is doing.
What is **total communication**?
Total communication is an approach during which the use of all modes of communication are accepted and promoted.

SELf-Questioning 101: Teaching Self-Awareness to Your Child

We teach self-awareness by using structured SELf-questions ("How do I feel?" and "What am I feeling?") in the Identify Feelings step to facilitate emotional recognition and self-expression of emotions through modeling self-talk and parallel talk using total communication. See the following chart for more information on how to implement structured SELf-questioning to promote self-awareness using self-talk and parallel talk at home.

How to Implement Using Structured SELf-Questioning	
How to model self-talk of structured self-questions using total communication	Throughout the day, model the use of the SELf-questions for your child by recognizing and expressing your own emotions using multiple modes of communication. 
How to model parallel talk of structured SELf-questions using total communication	Throughout the day, assume your child's intent and model the use of the SELf-questions for your child by recognizing and expressing their emotions using multiple modes of communication.   

SELf-Questioning 101: Using Self-Talk and Parallel Talk With Your Child

At school, we model the use of the structured SELf-questions "How do I feel?" and "What am I feeling?" to promote your child's self-awareness. You may enhance your child's self-awareness by using these structured SELf-questions at home. See the following chart for examples of self-talk and parallel talk models of structured SELf-questioning using total communication that may be used at home to teach self-awareness.

Method	Situation	Model of Self-Talk or Parallel Talk	Examples of Total Communication
Model self-talk of structured SELf-questions using total communication to express *happiness.*	You receive a phone call from your cousin.	"My phone is ringing! It is my cousin Janet calling us!" "What am I feeling?" "I feel my mouth smiling!" "How do I feel?" "I feel happy!"	Use an exaggerated facial expression to express happiness. Use facial expression, body language, and gesture to express contemplation of SELf-questions by looking up and to the side while facing your palms upward.
Model self-talk of structured SELf-questions using total communication to express *anger.*	You drop your plate of dinner all over the floor.	"I just dropped my dinner all over the floor!" "What am I feeling?" "I feel my teeth clenching, and my stomach turning." "How do I feel?" "I feel angry!"	Use an exaggerated facial expression to express anger. Use facial expression, body language, and gesture to express contemplation of SELf-questions by looking up and to the side while facing your palms upward.
Model parallel talk of structured SELf-questions using total communication to express assumed *excitement.*	You approach the gate to the park, and your child begins to laugh and smile.	"We are at the park!" "What are you feeling?" "I see you are smiling, and I hear you laughing." "How do you feel?" "Your body is telling me you feel excited!"	Use an exaggerated facial expression to express excitement. Use facial expression, body language, and gesture to express contemplation of SELf-questions by looking up and to the side while facing your palms upward.
Model parallel talk of structured SELf-questions using total communication to express assumed *sadness.*	The toy your child is playing with breaks. They lay on the floor and begin to cry.	"Your toy broke." "What are you feeling?" "I see you laying on the floor, and I hear you crying." "How do you feel?" "Your body is telling me you feel sad."	Use an exaggerated facial expression to express sadness. Use facial expression, body language, and gesture to express contemplation of SELf-questions by looking up and to the side while facing your palms upward.

A Practical Guide to Emotional Self-Management and Emotional Regulation

4

We must remember that one day our children are going to follow our example instead of our advice.

—Carolina King

In the previous chapter, we wrote about how students develop the skill of identifying their own emotions (their self-awareness) by answering the question "How do I feel?" or "What am I feeling?" It is important for students to learn the SEL competency of self-awareness so they can implement corresponding coping strategies to manage identified emotions successfully. Just by naming a feeling, students sidestep their thinking from the amygdala back to the prefrontal cortex and begin the process of regulating (see chapter 2, page 29). The more granularly that students can identify their emotions, the more successful they will be at implementing the appropriate strategy for that feeling.

To be granular with the language we use to label our emotions is to be able to make very subtle distinctions between the emotions that we are feeling. For example, the difference between *nervous* and *anxious* is granular, and the ability to accurately identify the difference between such closely related feelings directly impacts the way we self-manage. Research by Sheila L. Macrine and Jennifer M. B. Fugate (2022) finds that "individuals who use emotion words in a granular manner are less prone to maladaptive behaviors" (p. 317). This only adds to the importance of teaching a wide variety of feelings language as we delve into the teaching of self-awareness.

Self-awareness can often be developed simultaneously and independently of self-management. However, accurate and intuitive identification of one's thoughts and emotions can lead to more accurate self-management, which is our focus in this chapter. Research shows that it is essential for teachers to have knowledge of brain research and student development as it can provide them with a different perspective on how students learn and aid in the use of appropriate and specific strategies to support student learning (McBrien & Brandt, 1997). Banu Özkan and Mehmet Nur Tuğluk (2022) expand on this research further by stating that through our understanding of the preschool brain, as educators, we can make more informed decisions around everything from the classroom environment to interventions for students.

This chapter shows how structured SELf-questioning can provide a scaffold that aids in the development of students' independent self-management skills through a gradual release of responsibility and an embedded approach as illustrated in figure 4.1.

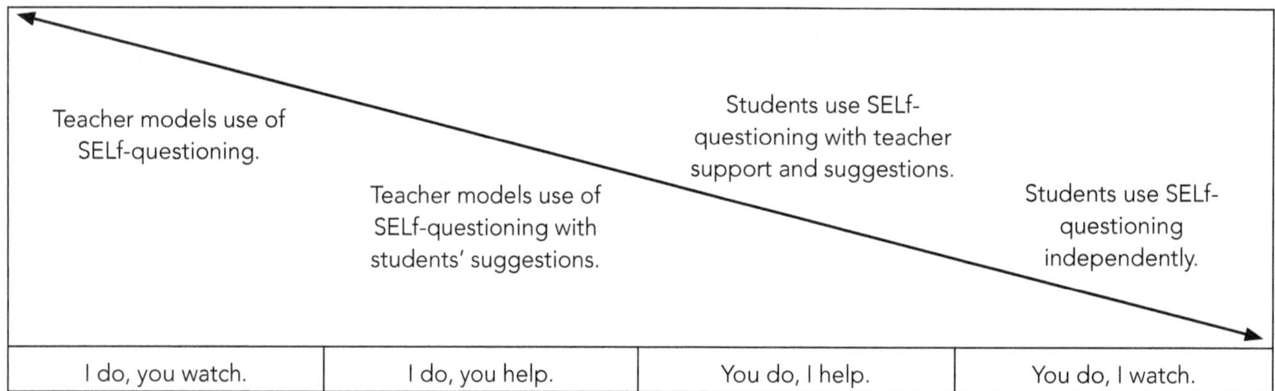

Source: Adapted from Fisher & Frey, 2021; Pearson & Gallagher, 1983.

Figure 4.1: Gradual release of responsibility applied to SELf-question sets.

We include guidance for teaching in the form of least to most direct teaching while providing scenarios, activities, modifications, and accommodations. This chapter also lays out how the scaffolded approach of structured SELf-questioning aids in the development of students' ability to self-manage. CASEL (n.d.) defines *self-management* as the ability to successfully self-regulate one's emotions, thoughts, and behaviors. This includes traits such as identifying and using stress-management strategies, exhibiting self-discipline and self-motivation, and setting personal and collective goals (CASEL, n.d.).

This chapter also provides examples and starting points for teaching self-management strategies while modeling and implementing structured SELf-questioning. It demonstrates how teachers can use one structured set of SELf-questions to collaborate with educational professionals, specialists, and stakeholders in the cohesive implementation of these questions for the purpose of consistency and continuity. When everyone in a student's life is on the same page and can implement structured SELf-questioning with fidelity, students will not only be surrounded by models for this strategy at every turn but also see that they are in an environment that supports their emotional regulation and management while building positive relationships between teachers and students.

The Importance of Teaching a Metacognitive Strategy for Emotional Regulation

Now that we have an operational definition of self-management, let's talk more about what it looks like in the preschool classroom. In a classroom that fosters the development of self-management, you may find students utilizing a break area in the room before taking on a challenging transition. It may look like a student asking a teacher for help or, less observable, a student walking away from a frustrating situation to self-calm before coming back to try again. A classroom that fosters self-management takes the time to pause an activity to pursue a teachable moment, such as a teacher observing students feeling tired on a Friday afternoon and taking a collective movement break before continuing to the next activity.

Conversely, a classroom with an absence of self-management may have a higher level of student behaviors occurring, like students who are escalating quickly and not using more communicative or productive strategies to have their needs met. A classroom with an absence of self-management may also be reflected in the teacher: less patience, more likely to unintentionally reinforce inappropriate behaviors, and so on. A classroom with a general absence of self-management is just a classroom lacking the right tools and support!

As a first-year teacher, many moons ago, I (all cases of *I* in this chapter refer to Katie) worked with a student who had such a lack of understanding of his emotions that it was expressed physically through hitting, throwing, and spitting. After I began implementing structured SELf-questioning with my student, the rate at which he acquired awareness of his feelings, what was causing them, and how to manage them with the right teaching and modeling was nothing short of extraordinary. I will never forget the moment his parents came to our parent-teacher conference and thanked me for taking the time to understand his needs and meet him where he was at the moment we met.

This story, in addition to structured SELf-questioning to teach self-awareness and self-management, is supported by the research of Matthew Lieberman (2009), who finds that just by labeling our feelings, we begin to engage in emotional self-management. Lieberman (2009) goes on to state that beginning in preschool, "students improve in their ability and tendency to use emotional words to describe their feelings, [and] they evidence fewer emotional outbursts" (p. 7). Making strides in the right direction as a teacher to support students' emotional self-management using the metacognitive strategy structured SELf-questioning not only sets up students as individuals for great success in managing their emotions but also the classroom as a whole, as students work together to support each other by asking themselves and each other these questions.

Imagine, for a moment, that you have walked through the door of a preschool classroom just before dismissal. The class sings its goodbye song, and students practice their departure, saying "goodbye" to each of their friends and teachers with a wave. As students make their way to their cubbies to grab their jackets and backpacks, you notice that a student, Parth, is struggling to get his arm through the strap to pull on his backpack.

The teacher approaches the student, asking, "How are you feeling?" Parth states that he is frustrated. The teacher follows up by stating, "What can I do when I feel frustrated? I can ask for help." This simple think aloud models for the student how he can use the phrase *I need help* as one strategy in response to the question, "What can I do?" Parth says, "I need help," back to his teacher. The teacher helps with the strap, and Parth joins his classmates to line up at the door.

Unbeknownst to you, this interaction has been going on for weeks. The teachers have repeatedly practiced stepping in before the student becomes frustrated, teaching the appropriate phrase for this moment, helping, and then moving right out the door. Now, almost a month later, the teachers have begun waiting a little longer to help students and instead model different ways students can put on their backpacks independently.

Imagine you return to the same classroom a week later. On that day, you notice Parth showing emerging perseverance, starting with placing his backpack on the table and trying the left strap first. It doesn't work. He tries again with the right strap, but again, no luck. Finally, Parth turns to his teacher and states, "I need help!" in the most confident voice you have ever heard. Of course, the teacher goes over to help.

You return again to the classroom, this time three months later. You notice Parth will now try three different strategies for getting his backpack on before stating, "I need help with the right strap." With time, consistency, perseverance, and patience, he has developed the skills he needs—indeed, the skills we need as adults—to display not just emotional self-management but increased confidence. This example provides one way teachers can gradually release responsibility to students by modeling the structured SELf-question, "What can I do?" paired with a strategy, which will (based on student need) be, over time, faded out until students are independently demonstrating the use of this structured SELf-question.

With the consistent modeling of the structured SELf-questions "How do I feel?" and "What can I do?" students gain confidence and control over how to manage the answer to the structured SELf-question, "What is causing this feeling?"

How to Teach Structured SELf-Questioning for Emotional Self-Management

Managing our emotions is challenging as an adult sometimes; imagine being a child who has a brain still developing in all areas, including in how it responds to its own behaviors and emotions. Structured SELf-questioning for emotional self-management is a metacognitive strategy that I wish the adults in my life had taken the time to model as I was growing up. Having an easy-to-access, functional way to manage emotions is something that I knew I grew up lacking, resulting in a lack of emotional and behavioral control. That is one reason we take the time to pace our teaching of structured SELf-questioning for emotional self-management: to set up students for current and future success. Taking a deeper look inside ourselves to discover how we think about our thinking by asking ourselves the questions, "What is causing this feeling?" and "What can I do?" requires practice and repetition even for the more seasoned user of the metacognitive strategy of structured SELf-questioning. Having an understanding as a teacher of how to implement this strategy in curriculum instruction, guided activities, direct teaching, and through your natural environment takes student learning to a whole new level, immersing them in the world of structured SELf-questioning without adding too much to the workload a teacher already bears.

To support you in this effort, the following sections review vital concepts and strategies for teaching SELf-questions effectively.

Emotional Regulation

We begin teaching structured SELf-questioning with the understanding that teaching and learning self-management strategies is not a one-size-fits-all approach. As we know, everyone feels their feelings differently. What supports students need to manage their feelings will also vary, especially as students become more adept in their emotional recognition (self-awareness). We recommend that you focus on teaching structured SELf-questions because they remain constant as students discover how to answer the questions "What is causing this feeling?" and "What can I do?" in response to their emotions.

It is also essential to know that we should teach and model these questions while students are *not* in crisis. When students are in crisis or under stress, their brains are not in a place where they will be able to learn or process any questions we may be asking. You need to teach self-management strategies *before* any behavior or a moment of stress occurs. We also encourage you not to focus too much on escaping negative feelings. All feelings have a purpose. Maybe the solution is for the student to sit with the negative emotion they are feeling with a teacher as a guide for support and a guide for emotional self-management and guided self-talk through the questions. That is OK! Structured SELf-questioning has the flexibility to meet all students where they are currently and provides a scaffold for future growth.

Steps to Structured SELf-Questioning

When teaching emotional self-management through the lens of structured SELf-questioning, the first step (and first metacognitive trait) is understanding how the student is feeling and raising awareness of the feeling. Students in the preschool classroom consistently face new challenges, as many students are stepping into the classroom for the first time. The teacher plays a pivotal role in modeling structured SELf-questioning from the moment students step through the door. This means that first, the teacher serves as a direct model for the implementation of the metacognitive strategy of structured SELf-questioning to facilitate the student's understanding of the questions "How do I feel?" and "What am I feeling?" as it directly relates to the student's self-awareness. (See chapter 3, page 45, for more about these questions.) As discussed at the beginning of this chapter, we are now also ready to begin teaching the structured SELf-questions that enhance and support the development of students' self-management.

In the preschool classroom, it is common for our students to become tired during a full day of school. Preschool can be a long day for a three- or four-year-old! Feeling tired or spent can present itself in many ways. For our student Adam, tiredness shows itself as putting his head on the table or beginning to play rough with toys in centers.

For the teacher serving as a model for the use of these structured SELf-questions, it is important to observe Adam and guide him when these small behaviors begin to occur. By using a think aloud (as described in the previous chapter) to model these questions aloud, they become part of a student's repertoire of self-talk, allowing for independent use of the structured SELf-question set over time. Figure 4.2 (page 76) dives into different ways a teacher can model and support the teaching of our first structured self-question. Notice how this approach utilizes gradual release of responsibility, as illustrated in figure 4.1 (page 72).

Step	Structured SELf-Questions	Example Response
Identify Feelings	**I do, you watch:** Teacher models asking using parallel talk with *I* pronoun, stating, "How do I feel?" "What am I feeling?"	Teacher models using parallel talk with *I* pronoun, stating, "I feel tired."
	I do, you help: Teacher states, "How do I feel? "What am I feeling?"	Teacher provides student with choices; student states, "I am feeling tired."
	You do, I help: Teacher prompts, "How do you feel? What are you feeling?"	Student states, "I feel tired."
	You do, I watch: Student asks self the question (out loud or to self)	Student independently tries strategy.

Figure 4.2: Emotional structured SELf-questioning.

The teacher, serving as a model and guide, may enter the center where Adam is playing with his peers, talking aloud with the blocks, stating, "How do I feel? I may be starting to feel tired." The teacher then begins the gradual release approach by fading their direct support over time for Adam as his self-awareness grows through his use of the structured SELf-question, "How do I feel?"

To begin teaching the structured SELf-questions that enhance and support the development of students' self-management, students must learn how to gather information about what they are feeling. This supports students' self-management by teaching the student to become more aware of what could be *causing* this feeling by asking the question, "What is causing this feeling?" Other questions that can be asked when gathering information include "What can I control?" and "What is my goal?"

It is at a teacher's discretion with regard to which question to ask at the moment based on the student's circumstances; however, we recommend that you choose one question to ask or model at the moment. The modeling of different questions through different situations not only supports students' mastery over the learning of these questions but also supports their coping flexibility (which we will talk about later in the chapter).

Let's go back to Adam. We know that Adam may be feeling tired at centers based on his rough play with the blocks, which his teacher has observed over time as something that he frequently does when he is tired. Now that Adam has identified his feeling, we can teach him through modeling and self-talk about how to gather information using structured SELf-questioning (see figure 4.3).

Step	Structured SELf-Questions	Example Response
Gather Information	**I do, you watch:** Teacher models asking using parallel talk with *I* pronoun, stating, "What is causing this feeling?"	Teacher models using parallel talk with *I* pronoun, stating, "Maybe I did not sleep last night?"
	I do, you help: Teacher asks, "What is causing this feeling?"	Teacher redirects student to a visual, with choices. The student puts an X through an image of a bed.
	You do, I help: Teacher prompts student with the question, "What is causing this feeling?"	The student states, "I did not sleep."
	You do, I watch: Student asks self the question (out loud or to self).	Student independently expresses to the teacher, stating, "I did not sleep last night."

Figure 4.3: Gradual release example for structured SELf-question Gather Information step.

At this time, Adam may be ready to begin the brainstorming process, which will help him decide what strategy will help manage what he is feeling by asking the question, "What strategies can I use?" or "What can I do?" as illustrated in figure 4.4 (page 78).

As we can see demonstrated through this model, Adam's teacher can support him in many ways based on the level of support that he needs in the moment and as he attains an understanding of each structured SELf-question, such as what it is asking and what the expected outcome is. Through this scaffolded approach, the importance of structured SElf-questions leaps off the page. Over time, teachers will see students independently managing with just a watchful eye, increasing student independence and decreasing teacher direct support. If you ask me, this is the dream!

Modeling (and Then More Modeling)

Through continued modeling of our own emotions, we not only practice our self-awareness but also create an environment where students can visually see how they can safely express what they feel. We can impact our students' learning every day through the behaviors that we make acceptable in the classroom. By using self-talk and modeling how we feel, what we can do, and even what we can do when that first strategy doesn't work, we teach students aloud how to think about their thinking.

Step	Structured SELf-Questions	Example Response
Brainstorm	**I do, you watch:** Teacher models asking a SELf-questions through the use of parallel talk with *I* pronoun, stating, "What can I do? What strategies can I use?"	Teacher models using parallel talk with *I* pronoun, stating, "I can use a weighted blanket."
	I do, you help: Teacher asks, "What can I do? What strategies can I use?"	Teacher provides student with choices. The student selects a choice.
	You do, I help: Teacher prompts student with the questions, "What can I do? What strategies can I use?"	Student responds to the teacher with a strategy.
	You do, I watch: Student asks self the questions (out loud or to self).	Student independently executes an appropriate strategy.

Figure 4.4: Gradual release example for brainstorming.

One place to start with this modeling is at your morning meeting. As you officially start your day with all of your students at your morning meeting spot, start with modeling a think aloud.

- **Identify Feelings:** The teacher states, "How am I feeling? I am feeling excited!"
- **Gather Information:** The teacher states, "What is causing this feeling? We are learning about something new!"
- **Brainstorm:** The teacher states, "What can I do when I feel excited about learning? I can give my friends a thumbs-up," modeling a thumbs-up for the students.

Modeling emotional self-management consistently in one area of your daily routine gives you the opportunity to become familiar with the questions, have the strategy become a norm in your classroom routine, and physically demonstrate the expectation for students. Vary the questions and strategies that you are modeling through your morning meeting and the time of day you choose to consistently model this metacognitive strategy. Vary the feelings you model, the feelings' causes, and different strategies for brainstorming. I like to consider myself an award-winning actress when teaching in my classroom. Every day is a performance and an opportunity to make preschoolers excited about what I am there to teach them. It is important to remember, however, how sometimes the little moments (like the SMART Board not working or not being able to find the materials you need for a small group) are all opportunities to model structured SELf-questions as well as the overarching teaching goals in the classroom.

Here is one way I may contrive a situation in my classroom to create a moment where I can model structured SELf-questioning. I take a sip from my water bottle while students are eating and drop the water bottle on the floor. The lid flies off, the water bursts everywhere, and now I am soaked (along with the floor around me). I inhale deeply, thinking aloud, "How do I feel? I feel so frustrated that my water bottle fell, and I spilled this water everywhere! Ugh!" I continue to model deep breathing before saying, "What can I do? First, I can clean up all this water, then I can change my clothes." I go and grab towels and then start cleaning.

In this way, even as teachers, we react as if we are students and model how we are still constantly learning about the world around us and how to react to it. After all, we know our students are watching every move we make in the classroom; why not take advantage of these moments to model the metacognitive strategy of structured SELf-questioning so that we can further set them up for success in and out of the classroom? Consider Yohan Jo and colleagues' (2016) research on social learning through behavioral modeling, in which they point out that when students observe the model of expected behavior, not only do their inappropriate behaviors decrease but also their motivation and self-efficacy increase. In some classrooms and for some students, teachers are the only positive role models, especially for those students who are still learning or being exposed to structured SELf-questioning for the first time. How we, as teachers, conduct our behavior directly impacts students' confidence and comfort in feeling their feelings and managing them effectively.

We only sometimes have a glimpse into our students' lives outside of school. By giving them an intrinsic strategy that does not need tangible tools or direct support from another strategy after it is learned, we empower students with access to a skill they can use no matter their circumstances.

Coregulation

As teachers, we are tasked with creating and sustaining an environment where students feel safe and comfortable expressing their emotions and asking for what they need to manage their emotions. When our youngest students face their biggest feelings, they should be met only with adults who can calm their situation. This is how we begin *coregulation*, which is "the interactive process by which caring adults (1) provide warm supportive relationships, (2) promote self-regulation through coaching, modeling, and feedback" (U.S. Department of Health and Human Services, n.d.). The use of coregulation as both a starting point (for students who are currently in a state where they cannot manage their big emotions without teacher intervention) or as a model to guide students (through their feelings at the moment) provides students with the support they need at the moment while giving teachers the opportunity to turn chaos into a teachable moment for modeling the structured SELf-questions, "How do I feel?" and "What can I do?" while building trusting relationships with students.

In neurobiology, we understand that students enter fight, flight, and freeze mode when facing a big emotion (Aggleton, 1992). That means students are not thinking with their rational brains. As adults, if we were to enter this situation matching a student's energy (escalated, anxious, or tense), our response would have the potential to create chaos and escalate an already heightened situation. Instead, we can bring our calm to the situation, immediately setting the tone for how the management of this feeling begins.

Coregulation can occur for any feeling, not just big feelings. It takes modeling one step further as you are one-to-one with that student, setting the tone for how to regulate. We are not just modeling *for* students; we are modeling *with* them. Let's walk through the process.

It's morning arrival, and all of your students except one are in the classroom. Suddenly, you begin to hear the sounds of Sophia making her entrance into the building. You hear Sophia's feet moving slowly as she stomps up each individual step. You hear her scream, "I don't like school!" as she trudges down the hallway with her hood over her eyes and fists gripping her backpack straps.

You are standing outside the classroom door waiting like you do every time a student is late at arrival—waiting to make your greeting. But today, you do so differently. You wait quietly, watching Sophia make her way toward you.

Sophia stops just inches in front of you and leans her head into your arm. You slowly wrap one arm around her loosely and begin to breathe, modeling a think aloud with the SELf-question, "How am I feeling? I may be feeling frustrated." Slowly and thoughtfully, you breathe. Again, thinking aloud, "What can I do when I am feeling frustrated? I can breathe with my teacher."

After a minute, Sophia begins to breathe again, too. Her grip on her backpack straps relaxes, and her hands fall to her side. Together, you wait just a little longer, not speaking any words but communicating just the same. Sophia then pulls away from you and walks into the classroom independently, ready to begin her day.

It's in moments like this one that you have the opportunity to connect and build a relationship with your students that often is not naturally as present for some students as it might be for others. Moments like this come with consistency: consistency in modeling, consistency in sharing your peace, and consistency in taking these moments as opportunities to build lasting relationships. Will coregulating with your students at first look messy? Of course! Feelings can be messy, especially when your students are learning some of the first effective strategies they have had modeled for them as they enter your classroom.

Direct Teaching of Self-Management

In addition to the preceding strategies, we can teach structured SELf-questioning by embedding it into day-to-day activities. Through direct teaching, we address the structure of SELf-questions directly through targeted lesson planning, contrived situations, and even preplanned teachable moments.

The teaching of self-management can help students to develop a mind-to-body connection. Breathing is one strategy that you may most often associate with self-management. Breathing may seem like a strategy that can only be done one way, but there are many fun ways to practice and teach breathing.

Picture this: your students have just returned from the playground and are sweaty and overstimulated. You know that you are scheduled to begin your next whole-group activity in five minutes, but your students are not yet in a place where they are calm and ready to learn. It's one of those moments where you either regain control or lose it. So you begin to buzz like a bumblebee on your way to the carpet. Slowly breathe in, and on your exhale, buzz like a bee. Modeling self-talk, ask yourself out loud, "What other sounds can we make? We practice taking a deep breath in and letting it out slowly."

Invite students to join you on the carpet. Modeling placing your hand on your belly while you breathe in, one student volunteers, "We can hum!" You respond, "Yes! We can hum as we breathe out! Let's try it!" Model for the class how the exhale is slow, and the sound is quiet. Soon, each student in the class will be focused on making a sound in their exhale that they can just barely hear, too. Before you know it, your students will begin to build a repertoire of exhales that work best for them. With practice, students can transition to this mindful moment independently on the carpet without direct prompting, understanding it is a necessary part of the routine that brings the class back to the center as a group, calm and ready to learn.

Want to extend this activity? Incorporate different nature sounds into your practice. "Today, we will breathe like the waves. *How does your body feel* when you breathe with the waves?"

Activities like this continue to support and develop self-awareness and emotional granularity while also creating a safe and appropriate strategy for managing emotions by giving students a tool to access when brainstorming and asking themselves the structured SELf-question, "What can I do?"

Self-management is like a muscle. You don't go to the gym once and walk out with a six-pack. It takes time, consistency, patience, and different workouts over time to build the results you are looking for. As reinforced in chapter 2 (page 29), the importance of opportunities built in throughout the day for students through teachable moments is essential to support students' brain-based learning of metacognitive skills. Other activity ideas include the following.

- **Name the feeling:** During this activity, the teacher provides students with a mirror, either with handheld mirrors or by standing in front of a larger mirror. The teacher and students talk about feelings, with students taking turns pulling a card with the name of a feeling. The teacher can support students in reading the feeling name as needed. As the teacher and students read the emotion, they make the face of how that emotion looks for them in the mirror. The teacher asks the structured SELf-question using self-talk, stating, "How do I feel?

I feel ______________!" or by opening the question to students as a guide, asking, "How do you feel?" This continues and fosters the development of students' self-awareness. The teacher can expand this activity by asking and prompting more structured SELf-questions as students expand their knowledge of the questions.

- **Mindfulness:** Mindfulness activities led by the teacher may include the following.
    - Highlight one different deep breathing approach a day at the end of the morning meeting or circle time.
    - Have a mindfulness break in the middle of the day after lunch. During these breaks, highlight different ways we can use our senses to be mindful. Play the sound of a bubbling creek. The teacher can model structured SELf-questions during this activity: "Let's close our eyes. Think about what you hear. *How do I feel?* I feel calm. The sound of the water reminds me of the waves at the beach."
    - Have a Mindfulness Monday where the teacher picks one student's name from the popsicle jar with names, and that student shares their favorite mindfulness strategy they have learned so far or taught themself with the class.
- **Physical exercise:** We love movement breaks! Use physical exercise to practice building a repertoire of strategies for answering the structured SELf-question, "What can I do?" For example, a teacher might lead a yoga activity as follows by modeling stretches for students.
    - Teacher: "OK, my friends! Today, we are going to practice stretching our body using yoga!" Having chart paper of a visual on the SMART Board, the teacher should ask students, "How do you feel?" Have students record how they are feeling before the yoga activity begins. This "recording" may look like teacher dictation, a drawing (such as a feelings face or more detailed drawing), emergent writing, or spoken words.
    - Teacher: "I am feeling a little tired today. What is causing this feeling? I did not get a lot of sleep last night. What can I do when I feel tired? I can try some yoga!"
    - Teacher: "Let's practice some yoga poses that will help wake up our body!" The teacher leads students through two or three poses to maintain interest.
    - Teacher: "Did it work?" Students can assess this strategy by giving the teacher a thumbs-up or thumbs-down, recording it on a piece of paper with yoga on it where they can circle yoga or put an X through yoga.

It is OK if strategies do not work; for many, such strategies help students build their toolbox of strategies that they have learned through teacher modeling and can access independently with practice. This can come in handy later on, for example, if you were to establish a yoga poses practice area of the classroom where students can access them if they need them as a strategy.

- **Time in nature:** Time in nature can be achieved in many ways. According to the research of Trent University psychologist Lisa Nisbet, "There is mounting evidence, from dozens and dozens of researchers, that nature has benefits for both physical and psychological human wellbeing" (as cited in Weir, 2020). For example, take your writing time outside or give students a clipboard to take with them on a nature walk, tallying how many trees they see outside. Or, grab the classic *It Looked Like Spilt Milk* by Charles Shaw to read outside on a cloudy day, inviting students to lay in the grass and observe the clouds. Another great story is *Green Green: A Community Gardening Story* by Marie Lamba. This story takes place in the heart of a city and demonstrates how, no matter what your location, you can be surrounded by nature. This may even lead to an inquiry into gardening and nature in your community!

The direct teaching of self-awareness and self-management through the use of activities that support structured SELf-questioning is an essential step in supporting student growth and the development of these skills. Through this exposure to different strategies for self-management and modeling, we ultimately reinforce students' learning by acknowledging their emotions and their existence and teaching them different places that their emotions can go. These learning experiences provide students with concrete learning opportunities filled with the repetition of these SELf-questions, which in turn allows students to develop strong neural pathways in the brain that make it possible for students to internalize these SELf-questions and access them easier under stress (McBrien & Brandt, 1997). The more time we spend teaching students to think about their thinking through the use of structured SELf-questioning, the more readily they will be able to access the calm within them.

Coping Flexibility

While our structured SELf-questioning strategy is meant to be adaptable to any situation and environment, the specific strategies preschoolers under duress might come up with while using SELf-questioning will vary. This makes the ability to be flexible in having solutions to problems a vital component of self-management. In this context, *coping flexibility* is defined as:

> The ability to produce and implement a new coping strategy in place of an ineffective coping strategy. Specifically, coping flexibility includes two processes: evaluation coping and adaptive coping. Evaluation coping refers to sensitivity to feedback about the efficacy of a coping strategy, and adaptive coping involves the willingness to implement alternative coping strategies. (Kato, 2015, p. 138)

This is an important skill to teach as students begin to develop their repertoire of coping strategies, as it helps students learn what they can do and where. For example, I can use a weighted blanket in the classroom but not on the playground. I can close my eyes and meditate in my bedroom, but not while driving. Students' ability to have flexibility in how they cope develops naturally as you begin to teach them how to evaluate their behavior. This teaching dives us into our next problem-solving step, Evaluate, and the structured SELf-question, "What is the best way to solve this problem?" (see figure 4.5).

Step	Structured SELf-Questions
Evaluate	"What is the best way to solve this problem?" "Does this make sense?" "What are possible consequences?" "Has this strategy helped me in the past?" "Which is best?"

Figure 4.5: Emotional structured SELf-questions for evaluating.

Imagine yourself at a school assembly, a big gymnasium filled with three- to five-year-olds. A friendly musician invites students to grab an instrument and move their bodies to the rhythm, exploring the tempo. However, you have one student, Alec, who has a challenging time in loud environments. You ask Alec, "How are you feeling?" and he responds, "Scared!" He begins plugging his ears. You respond to Alec, validating his feelings ("I see you, and I hear you are feeling scared.") and modeling how to gather information ("It is very loud in here, and I see you are plugging your ears."). You then ask Alec, still on the floor with his ears plugged, "What can we do when something is too loud?" Alec screams, "Turn it down!"

This is a great strategy, but it won't work for the circumstance. So, you model for Alec how to evaluate the situation, stating, "Asking to turn down the music is a great strategy, but we have all our friends here enjoying the music. What else can we do? We could try these headphones." You then hand Alec headphones (a strategy you have practiced as a class). Alec is receptive to putting on the headphones and placing them on his head.

This example has so many components, including teacher modeling and support for the student's independent expression of feelings and strategies and demonstrating the importance of practicing strategies with your students so that you can maximize these teachable moments. When modeling and teaching students to evaluate their emotions, we put students in the driver's seat of their behavior. Becoming comfortable with expressing and managing emotions takes time and consistency (recall the example of going to the gym and achieving a six pack). Evaluation will come when the time is ready, and when students are ready, you will be ready.

Scenarios for Self-Management and Emotional Regulation

The following sections offer three categories of example scenarios for interactions between teachers and students that are focused on emotional self-management and emotional regulation: (1) general classroom management, (2) behavioral interventions in the classroom, and (3) self-management and receptive, expressive, and pragmatic language skills. Note that the scope of these scenarios each includes its own utilization and range of steps within the metacognitive strategy for SELf-questioning, as illustrated in figure 1.3 (page 18).

General Classroom Management

There are too many aspects of classroom management to cover in a single chapter (or book), but the following three scenarios focus on specific contexts for the use of metacognitive structured SELf-questioning with preschoolers, with students with special needs or differing abilities, and for managing transitions and downtime.

Scenario 1: Academic Lessons and Classroom Management

Program: Integrated preschool

Objective: Regulate and own emotions and behaviors.

Standard: 0.2.2 "Demonstrate self-help skills (e.g., clean up, pour juice, use soap when washing hands, put away belongings)" (Teaching Strategies, n.d.a, p. 2).

Teacher: Mrs. Herold

In Mrs. Herold's integrated preschool classroom, teachers use self-talk as a form of classroom management to promote independence and confidence. Teachers explain self-talk to students as kind words and positive affirmations all people say to themselves to help with a challenge. In Mrs. Herold's class, students use phrases like "I am smart," "I will try," and "I can do it." They use these phrases when a challenge arises to promote student independence and give them a chance to try something first before asking for assistance. Consequently, this helps manage the classroom by lessening the need for teacher assistance with all challenges. In the following scenario, Mrs. Herold uses self-talk to help with classroom management.

IDENTIFY FEELINGS

SELf-Question: How do I feel?

During whole-group instruction, Mrs. Herold's class is working on counting to twenty. Mrs. Herold models how to use self-talk during a challenging situation.

Mrs. Herold states to her class, "How do I feel? I feel nervous!"

GATHER INFORMATION

SELf-Question: What is causing this feeling?

As students watch, Mrs. Herold adds, "Today's whole-group activity is counting to twenty, but I am not sure how to do that!"

BRAINSTORM

SELf-Question: What can I do?

She continues, "What can I do when I feel nervous? I know that when I feel nervous, I can take belly breaths, count to ten, or I can use my self-talk!"

Antonio shouts, "What is self-talk?"

Mrs. Herold says, "Self-talk is kind words we say to ourselves to help us with a challenge. Our challenge today is counting to twenty. Before we try our challenge, we can use our self-talk and say, 'I am smart. I will try. I can do it!'"

EVALUATE

SELf-Question: What's the best way to solve this problem?

Mrs. Herold continues, "What's the best way to solve this problem? Let's try self-talk and see if it works!"

PLAN AND ACT

SELf-Question: What do I do first, second, and so on?

Mrs. Herold says, "What do I do first? First, I will use my self-talk, and then I will count to twenty."

Mrs. Herold encourages her students to join her and use self-talk. Together, they say aloud, "I am smart, I will try, I can do it!"

Mrs. Herold continues, "OK! I am ready to try counting to twenty." She moves deliberately from each number to the next until she gets to twenty and excitedly says, "I did it!" The class cheers.

REFLECT

SELf-Question: Did it work?

Mrs. Herold continues, "Did it work?"

The class states, " Yes!"

Mrs. Herold says, "It did, and now I feel proud because I used my self-talk to help myself through a challenge!"

Mrs. Herold continues modeling self-talk during challenging moments throughout the classroom, and in doing so, students start to internalize the skills and use self-talk during their own challenges.

Scenario 2: Students With Special Needs or Differing Abilities

Program: Preschool disabilities

Objective: Regulate own emotions and behaviors.

Standard: 0.3.3 "Channel impulses and negative feelings, such as anger (e.g., taking three deep breaths, using calm words, pulling self out of play to go to a 'safe spot' to relax, expressive activities)" (Teaching Strategies, n.d.a, p. 3).

Teacher: Mrs. Upshaw

Mrs. Upshaw is a preschool special education teacher who uses parallel talk in the classroom to support students' learning of structured SELf-questioning by talking in the first person to describe a student's situation and the aligned question to support them in the moment. Parallel talk to support the learning of structured SELf-questions for self-awareness and self-management are used throughout the day and embedded in the classroom routine to demonstrate consistency in usage across different settings to support both learning and generalization for all students, especially those who benefit from repetition to acquire skills.

IDENTIFY FEELINGS

SELf-Question: How do I feel?

Mrs. Upshaw states, "Circle time is over, it is time for a snack!" Students begin to transition to their cubby to retrieve their lunch box when Jamal cries out, "GRAAA! STUUU!" Mrs. Upshaw recognizes that Jamal is approximating "stuck" as he yanks at the lunchbox wedged in his backpack. Mrs. Upshaw walks over to Jamal, using a think aloud to model asking herself SELf-questions: "How do I feel? I feel frustrated!"

GATHER INFORMATION

SELf-Question: What is causing this feeling?

Mrs. Upshaw continues to model gathering information for Jamal by asking, "What is causing this feeling? My lunchbox is stuck." Jamal looks at his AAC device, where the teacher models selecting the icons for *frustrated*, *stuck*, and *lunchbox*.

BRAINSTORM

SELf-Question: What can I do?

As Jamal continues to yank on his lunchbox, Mrs. Upshaw continues to model using a think aloud, asking herself, "What can I do? I can ask for help!" Mrs. Upshaw selects the *help* icon on Jamal's AAC device, followed by providing immediate assistance to help him take his lunchbox out.

EVALUATE

SELf-Question: What is the best way to solve this problem?

Mrs. Upshaw begins to teach evaluating by modeling a simplified version of the question, "What strategies are supported by my circumstance?" by using self-talk while Jamal has his snack: "What can I do when I feel frustrated at school? I can ask for help." Jamal makes his way to his table, carrying his lunchbox.

REFLECT

SELf-Question: Did it work?

As Jamal takes a seat at the table, the teacher prompts Jamal with the question SELf-question, "Did it work?" to reflect. Jamal selects *lunchbox* on his AAC device and begins happily unzipping his lunchbox. Mrs. Upshaw models select *yes* on Jamal's AAC device.

Scenario 3: Transitions and Downtime

Program: Integrated preschool

Objective: Manage classroom rules, routines, and transitions with occasional reminders.

Standard: 0.2.3 "Move through classroom routines and activities with minimal teacher direction and transition easily from one activity to the next" (Teaching Strategies, n.d.a, p. 3).

Teacher: Mr. Tim

It is time for students to engage in a quiet activity following their lunch before entering the second half of their school day. At this time, students are expected to engage independently in an activity.

IDENTIFY FEELINGS

SELf-Question: How do I feel?

Student Natalie has finished her lunch and put her lunchbox back in her cubby. As Natalie looks around, she notices that all her other friends are still eating. Natalie sits inside her cubby stating, "I do not want next!"

Mr. Tim understands that downtime is challenging for Natalie. Over time, Mr. Tim has worked with Natalie to create an "independent activity bin" filled with closed-ended activities that Natalie highly prefers. Mr. Tim approaches Natalie and prompts her by stating, "Natalie, how are you feeling?" Natalie states, "I am really mad. I don't want to!"

GATHER INFORMATION

SELf-Question: What is causing this feeling?

Mr. Tim prompts Natalie for more information, asking, "What is causing this feeling?" Natalie points to "independent activity" on the class schedule. Mr. Tim models aloud, "I feel really mad because I do not want independent activities." Natalie nods her head *yes*, affirming Mr. Tim's statement.

BRAINSTORM

SELf-Question: What can I do?

Mr. Tim models using a think aloud. Pointing to his chin, he ponders aloud, stating, "What can I do? I can find my independent activity bin." Mr. Tim models taking out the bin and playing with Natalie's favorite puzzle at the table. As Natalie observes Mr. Tim, she states, "My bin," and takes out another puzzle. Mr. Tim encourages Natalie, stating, "I can take out a puzzle from my bin!"

Behavioral Interventions in the Classroom

In-class behavior interventions are perhaps more common in preschool than in any other educational environment. Numerous factors affect this, including that this is many students' first experience in the school setting outside of their home. The following two scenarios focus on the contexts for the use of metacognitive structured SELf-questioning with preschoolers and students with special needs or differing abilities.

Scenario 1: Behavior Interventions

Program: Integrated preschool

Objective: Regulate own emotions and behaviors.

Standard: 0.3.3 "Channel impulses and negative feelings, such as anger (e.g., taking three deep breaths, using calm words, pulling self out of play to go to a "safe spot" to relax, expressive activities)" (Teaching Strategies, n.d.a, p. 3).

Teacher: Mrs. Herold

Structured SELf-questioning can be used for behavioral interventions. In this scenario, a preschool student, Pedro, does not like the song that was chosen for music and movement. Before the introduction of structured SELf-questioning, Pedro would cry, scream, and hit when a song was played that he did not like. Here is how structured SELf-questioning is used to manage this behavior.

IDENTIFY FEELINGS

SELf-Question: How do I feel?

Mrs. Herold notices Pedro's expression change from excited to angry during music and movement. Pedro folds his arms and pouts. Mrs. Herold walks over to Pedro and prompts him by asking, "How do you feel?"

Pedro exclaims, "I feel angry!"

GATHER INFORMATION

SELf-Question: What is causing this feeling?

Mrs. Herold asks, "What is causing this feeling?"

Pedro responds, "I want 'Baby Shark!'"

Mrs. Herold adds, "OK, I hear you saying you are angry we aren't listening to 'Baby Shark.'"

BRAINSTORM

SELf-Question: What can we do?

Mrs. Herold guides Pedro to a strategy, asking, "What can you do when you feel angry? You can count to ten!"

Pedro repeats, "I can count to ten."

EVALUATE

SELf-Question: What strategies are supported by my circumstance?

Mrs. Herold models the question, "What strategies are supported by my circumstance?" by immediately trying the suggested strategy. Mrs. Herold begins counting from one to ten, and Pedro follows all the way to ten.

Mrs. Herold notices Pedro's arms relax and frown disappear. She adds, "I understand you want to listen to 'Baby Shark,' but today, we are listening to this song."

Pedro walks back to the carpet, noticing that the rest of his class is having fun with the song chosen for today.

REFLECT

SELf-Question: Did it work?

Pedro begins to dance with his friends.

Mrs. Herold states, "Your body is telling me you feel happy by dancing! Did it work?"

Pedro exclaims, "Yes! I feel better now!"

Scenario 2: Students With Special Needs or Differing Abilities

Program: Integrated preschool

Objective: Regulate own emotions and behaviors.

Standard: 0.2.2 "Demonstrate self-help skills (e.g., clean up, pour juice, use soap when washing hands, put away belongings)" (Teaching Strategies, n.d.a, p. 2).

Teacher: Ms. McKenna

Juan is a student in Ms. McKenna's class with a behavior intervention plan that targets the behavior of refusal, specifically refusal to participate in non-reinforcing activities (for example, sharing with peers, engaging in academic instruction with the teacher, and so on). Juan requires a fixed one-to-one schedule of reinforcement. This mean for every instruction followed, Juan receives reinforcement in the form of a high five.

IDENTIFY FEELINGS

SELf-Question: How do I feel?

Ms. McKenna is preparing to transition Juan to centers. Ms. McKenna states to Juan, "We can play at the block center or dramatic play. What is your choice?" Juan exclaims, "Dramatic play!" placing his picture at the dramatic play center. Ms. McKenna provides Juan with a high five, exclaiming, "Awesome choice! Let's go!"

As Juan approaches dramatic play, he observes Krish with his favorite toy ice cream cone. Juan falls to the floor screaming, "My ice cream, my ice cream!" Ms. McKenna prompts Juan with the structured SELf- question, "How are you feeling?" Juan grumbles and hits his fist to the ground. Ms. McKenna assumes Juan's communicative intent through his behavior, modeling the most plausible answer to the SELf-question: "It looks like you may be feeling sad."

GATHER INFORMATION

SELf-Question: What is causing this feeling?

Ms. McKenna continues to expand on this modeling, stating, "You may be feeling sad because Krish is playing with the ice cream cone."

BRAINSTORM

SELf-Question: What can I do?

As Juan continues to lay on the floor, Ms. McKenna uses self-talk to ask herself the question, "What can I do when a friend has something I want to play with?" Juan imitates Ms. McKenna, asking himself this question aloud.

EVALUATE

SELf-Question: What strategies are supported by my circumstance?

Juan lifts his head and begins to scan the dramatic play area. Ms. McKenna models asking aloud, "What strategies are supported by my circumstance?" Ms. McKenna thinks aloud as Juan continues to attend to her modeling, "I can offer my friend a different toy and ask to switch."

Juan jumps up off the floor and grabs a big toy birthday cake. Juan presents the cake to Krish, asking, "Switch with me?" Krish stares intensely at the cake and grabs it from him. In return, she hands him the ice cream. Ms. McKenna immediately provides Juan with a high five, reinforcing Juan's behavior and saying, "I love the way you asked your friend to switch toys." Ms. McKenna turns to Krish, stating, "Thank you for being a kind friend and sharing."

REFLECT

SELf-Question: Did it work?

As Juan pretends to eat his ice cream, Ms. McKenna models the use of the structured SELf-question for reflection, explaining, "You asked Krish to switch with you for the ice cream. Did it work?" Holding his ice cream proudly, Juan rejoices, "It worked! My ice cream!" as he holds his ice cream tight to his chest in an embrace.

Self-Management and Receptive, Expressive, and Pragmatic Language Skills

All individuals, preschoolers included, use their language skills to understand and use the metacognitive strategy of structured SELf-questioning. We believe preschoolers' developing language skills can be facilitated by structured SELf-questioning as the exchange elicits receptive, expressive, and pragmatic language skills. The following two scenarios focus on using academic and social problem-solving SELf-question sets and the ways in which language is used and facilitated to empower students to apply this strategy.

Scenario 1: Academic Problem Solving

Program: Integrated preschool

Objective: Demonstrate phonological awareness.

Standard: RF.PK.2b "Segment syllables in spoken words by clapping out the number of syllables" (Teaching Strategies, n.d.a, p. 15).

Teacher: Ms. Jeffries

The preschool class is working on phonological awareness through the segmentation of syllables. To emphasize and segment syllables, students are encouraged to produce, imitate, or listen to a word and clap for each syllable. To increase engagement and make this objective meaningful, Ms. Jeffries decides to use student names as the target words. She pulls a small group of two students. In addition to written names, her materials include static boards, which offer picture symbols with written words of core (high-frequency vocabulary words) and fringe (topic-specific vocabulary words) and a pacing board (a horizontal rectangle of paper with three to five dots or stickers). Ms. Jeffries uses verbal speech, picture symbols, facial expressions, gestures, and body language while implementing structured SELf-questioning. The use of multiple modes of communication are implemented to facilitate the students' receptive, expressive, and pragmatic language skills.

SELECT A FOCUS

SELf-Question: What is the task?

Ms. Jeffries invites Naomi and Eli to join her at the table for small group. She says, "We are going to learn about phonological awareness! What is phonological awareness? *Phonological awareness* is our awareness of sounds. Sounds make up words! Groups of sounds make up syllables."

Ms. Jeffries continues, "Let's learn about the syllables in our names. We can do this by clapping for each syllable in our name. What is the task? The task is to clap for each syllable in our name!" As Ms. Jeffries says this, she uses American Sign Language by signing *learn* and *name* (gestures) and points to the *what* symbol on the core board (picture symbol) as she poses the structured SELf-question, "What is the task?"

She uses *facial expressions* to express happiness, excitement, and eagerness. She uses *body language* by leaning in to express engagement.

GATHER INFORMATION

SELf-Question: What do I know?

Ms. Jeffries uses self-talk and says, "This is something new! What do I know? I know I am doing this with my teacher and friend. I know my name, my teacher's name, and my friend's name. I know I have my printed name and a pacing board to help if I need it."

Ms. Jeffries uses *facial expressions* to express excitement and curiosity. She uses a core board by touching the picture symbol for *what* when posting the SELf-question, "What do I know?" (picture symbol) and pointing to herself (gesture for first person singular *I*). She uses American Sign Language by signing *name* (gesture). She uses body language by leaning in to express engagement.

BRAINSTORM

SELf-Question: What can I do?

Ms. Jeffries uses self-talk and says, "I will learn about the syllables in my name first! What can I do? I can clap with each syllable as I say my name. Ms. [clap] Jeff-[clap]-ries [clap]. Ms. [clap] Jeff-[clap]-ries [clap]. Ms. [clap] Jeff-[clap]-ries [clap]."

Ms. Jeffries continues, "Each time I said my name, I clapped three times! What else can I do? I can try on the pacing board. Here I go! Ms. [touch first dot] Jeff-[touch second dot]-ries [touch third dot]. Ms. [touch first dot] Jeff-[touch second dot]-ries [touch third dot]. Ms. [touch first dot] Jeff-[touch second dot]-ries [touch third dot]."

Mrs. Jeffries uses facial expressions to express excitement, curiosity, and eagerness. She uses American Sign Language by signing *name* (gesture). She uses a core board by touching the picture symbol for *what* as she poses the question, "What can I do?" (picture symbol). She points to herself (gesture for *I*).

REFLECT

SELf-Question: Did it work?

Ms. Jeffries encourages Naomi to clap the syllables in her name. Naomi begins to say her name and clap. She says, "Nay-[clap]-omi (clap)."

Ms. Jeffries says, "I think we should have heard one more clap! Did clapping work?" while pointing to herself (gesture for *I*), holding up one finger (gesture for *one*), and signing *more* (gesture).

Naomi puts her head down, says "No," and shakes her head. Ms. Jeffries provides parallel talk (see Modeling Using Parallel Talk, page 54 in chapter 3) by saying, "I see your head is down. How do you feel? Your body is telling me you may feel sad that clapping didn't work. What else can you do?" Ms. Jeffries points to herself and to Naomi (gestures for first person singular *I* and second person singular *you*) and touches the picture symbol for *what* on the core board (picture symbol).

Naomi points to the pacing board and says, "We can use this!" Ms. Jeffries, Naomi, and Eli use the pacing board to segment the syllables in Naomi's name. Ms. Jeffries asks Naomi, "How many syllables did we touch on the pacing board?" Ms. Jeffries provides expectant waiting by leaning in (body language) and smiling (facial expression).

When Naomi doesn't respond, Ms. Jeffries presents her with a field of numbers, one through five. "Did we count three or four syllables?" she asks while pointing to the numbers three and four (picture symbols). Naomi says, "We counted three," while pointing to the number three.

Ms. Jeffries says, "Fantastic!" while offering a high five (gesture). She then encourages Eli to clap the number of syllables in his name. Eli claps and counts two syllables. "Wonderful work!" says Ms. Jeffries before she turns to Naomi (body language to express turn) and says, "What was the task?" while touching the *what* symbol on the core board (picture symbol).

Naomi says, "Counting syllables!"

Ms. Jeffries provides says, "You got it! Counting the syllables in our names. What did we know? We knew we were doing it together, we knew our names, and we knew that we could use our written name and a pacing board too! What did we do? We clapped. Naomi, did clapping work? No! What else did we do? We used the pacing board. Did it work? Yes or no?" While reviewing the structured SELf-questions, Ms. Jeffries smiles (facial expression) and touches the *what* picture symbol on the core board (picture symbol) while posing questions. She leans in (body language to express support and waiting). When Naomi does not respond, Ms. Jeffries asks again, "Did it work? Yes or no?" while pointing to picture symbols for *yes* and *no* (picture symbols) and signing *yes* and *no* (gestures).

Naomi says, "Yes!" while pointing to the picture symbol for *yes*. Ms. Jeffries then turns toward Eli (body language to express turn) and says, "What was the task? Counting the syllables in our names. What did we know? We knew we were doing it together, we knew our names, and we knew that we could use our written name and a pacing board too! What did we do? We clapped. Did it work?" While reviewing the SELf-questions, Ms. Jeffries continues to smile (facial expression) and touch the *what* picture symbol on the core board while posing questions. She also touches the picture symbols for *yes* and *no* on the core board following the presentation of the SELf-question, "Did it work?"

Ms. Jeffries leans in (body language to express support and waiting). Eli touches the symbol for *yes* and says, "Yes!"

Throughout these steps (Select a Focus, Gather Information, Brainstorm, and Reflect), Ms. Jeffries uses multiple modes of communication. She uses verbal speech to ask and answer the structured SELf-questions, explain tasks, describe material, provide praise, make a plan, reflect on a plan, make statements to describe Naomi's expression of emotions, and express emotions. She uses picture symbols, gestures, facial expressions, body language, and American Sign Language.

The use of multiple modes of communication promotes students' comprehension of the structured SELf-questions, tasks, descriptions, praise, the planning process, reflection, and emotions vocabulary as well as promotes the recognition of emotions and how they present in the body, which facilitates receptive language skills. It promotes students' abilities to ask and answer the structured SELf-questions, explain, describe material, describe emotions and how they present in the body, praise, make a plan, use emotions vocabulary, and express emotions, which facilitates expressive language skills. Additionally, it promotes the students' abilities to interact with others, participate in exchanges, provide praise, and take turns, which facilitates pragmatic language skills.

Scenario 2: Social Problem Solving

Program: Preschool disabilities

Objective: Participate cooperatively and constructively in group situations.

Standard: 0.4.5. "Express needs verbally or nonverbally to teacher and peers without being aggressive (e.g., "I don't like when you call me dummy. Stop!")" (Teaching Strategies, n.d.a, p. 4).

Teacher: Mr. Bryne

The preschool class is playing at centers as they engage in their study of roads. On this day, many of the students chose to play at the blocks center, as they had the opportunity to build roads with different types of building materials. Students who use AAC devices and students who do not are playing together in this center. Leonard, an AAC user, is creating a road with Shane, who is not. Shane is familiar with AAC, as his friends use it, but he primarily uses verbal speech to communicate.

As they are building their road, Shane places a toy car on top of it. Leonard looks at the car and quickly adds more blocks to the road to make it longer. Shane places another toy car on the road. Leonard looks at Shane and reaches for more blocks to add. Shane picks up the bucket of cars with the intention of adding many cars to the road. Leonard protests by vocalizing "uh-uh" and shaking his head. Shane does not appear to hear or understand Leonard's protest. Shane adds another car to the road. Leonard pats Shane's arm and vocalizes "uh-uh" while shaking his head. Engrossed in the selection of cars, Shane does not seem to notice that Leonard is attempting to gain his attention to protest. Mr. Bryne sees Leonard's facial expression of anger as his hands go to grab the bucket of cars. Mr. Bryne uses verbal speech, picture symbols, facial expressions, gestures, and body language while implementing structured SELf-questioning. The use of multiple modes of communication is implemented to facilitate the students' receptive, expressive, and pragmatic language skills.

IDENTIFY FEELINGS

SELf-Question: What am I feeling? How do I feel?

Mr. Bryne sits on the floor at blocks center and turns toward Leonard (body language). Mr. Bryne provides parallel talk and says, "I see your eyebrows are pinched in, and your teeth are clenched. What are you feeling?" while modeling the core words *I* and *what* on his AAC device and mirroring his facial expression of *anger* (symbols and facial expression).

Mr. Bryne navigates Leonard's AAC device to the adjectives page. He says, "Maybe you are feeling that your body is tight," while selecting the *tight* symbol and leaning in (body language to express interest and waiting). Leonard selects the *yes* symbol on his AAC device and nods his head.

Mr. Bryne asks, "How do you feel?" while selecting the symbols to compose this sentence. Mr. Bryne touches the message window to activate speech output. Leonard selects the *I* and *feel* symbols from the home page and navigates to his feelings page on his AAC device. He selects *angry* and makes an angry face. Mr. Bryne says, "You feel angry," while pointing to Leonard (gesture for *you*), selecting the *angry* symbol, and signing *angry* (gesture).

GATHER INFORMATION

SELf-Question: What is causing this feeling?

Mr. Bryne asks, "What is causing this feeling?" while selecting the core word *what* on his AAC device (symbol), facing his palms up (gesture to express SELf-question), and leaning in (body language to express interest and waiting). Leonard points to the bucket of cars.

Mr. Bryne provides parallel talk and says, "You feel angry because Shane is adding vehicles to the road," while pointing to Leonard (gesture for *you*), signing *angry* (gesture), and selecting the fringe word *vehicles* on his AAC device.

Leonard shakes his head *no* and signs *no*.

Mr. Bryne makes a quizzical face (facial expression to express confusion or curiosity). He says, "I need more information," while selecting the symbols on his device for *I*, *need*, and *more* (symbols) and leaning in (body language to express interest and waiting).

Leonard navigates to his vehicles page and selects *airplane*. He goes on to select the symbols for *not* and *car* on his AAC device.

Mr. Bryne says, "How do you feel? You feel angry. What is causing this feeling? You want to add airplanes, not cars. You made a runway!" while selecting symbols on his AAC device for *how*, *angry*, *what*, *airplanes*, and *cars*, pointing to Leonard (gesture for *you*), signing *angry* (gesture), and making an excited face (facial expression).

BRAINSTORM

SELf-Question: What can I do?

Following acknowledgment from Leonard that Mr. Bryne understands his message via a head nod and vocalization of "uh-huh," Mr. Bryne continues by providing parallel talk to say, "When you feel angry because our friend is adding cars instead of planes, what can you do?" while pointing to Leonard (gesture for second person singular *you*), selecting symbols on his AAC device for *feel*, *angry*, *what*, *can*, *I*, and *do* (symbols), and signing *angry* (gesture). My. Bryne leans in (body language to express interest and waiting).

Leonard looks at Shane and the cars. Mr. Bryne waits for approximately ten seconds to provide Leonard with the opportunity to respond. Mr. Bryne then presents Leonard with the sign for *stop* (gesture).

Leonard recognizes the sign, taps Shane on the shoulder, and selects the *stop* symbol on his AAC device. Shane stops adding cars.

Mr. Bryne turns toward Shane and says, "Thank you for listening to your friend when he said, 'Stop.' Leonard wants to add airplanes!" He then signs *thank you* and *friend* (gestures), selects *stop* on his AAC device (symbols), and points to the bucket of airplanes (gesture). Shane smiles and says, "Me, too!"

REFLECT

SELf-Question: Did it work?

Mr. Bryne turns toward Leonard and provides parallel talk to say, "You felt angry. What was causing this feeling? Our friend was adding cars, but you wanted to add airplanes. What did you do? You asked our friend to stop. Did it work? Yes!" Mr. Bryne says this while signing *angry* and *yes* (gestures), making an angry face (facial expression), and selecting the *what, cars, airplanes,* and *stop* symbols on his AAC device.

Throughout these steps (Identify Feelings, Gather Information, Brainstorm, and Reflect), Mr. Bryne uses multiple modes of communication. He uses verbal speech to ask and answer the structured SELf-questions, makes statements to describe Leonard's expression of an emotion, expresses an emotion, provides a cause of an emotion, requests information, provides a solution to a social problem, reflects, protests, and provides praise. He uses picture symbols on an AAC device, gestures, facial expressions, body language, and American Sign Language.

The use of multiple modes of communication promotes students' comprehension of the structured SELf-questions, causes of emotions, emotions vocabulary, requests, the problem-solving process, reflections, protests, and praise, and it also promotes the recognition of emotions and how they present in the body, which facilitates receptive language skills. It promotes the students' ability to ask and answer the structured SELf-questions, describe emotions and how they present in the body, provide a cause of an emotion, use emotions vocabulary, request information, provide a solution to a problem, reflect, protest, and provide praise which facilitates expressive language skills. Additionally, it promotes students' ability to interact with others, participate in exchanges, provide praise, and take turns, which facilitates pragmatic language skills.

Conclusion

Our students are capable of the world if we offer them the world! By taking the metacognitive strategy of structured SELf-questioning and providing students with a structure to think about their thinking, we open them up to a whole new world of independent management of their emotions. We offer them the opportunity to learn more about their feelings, what is causing them, and what they can do when they feel them. By providing students with a teacher who serves as a model and a guide in the natural environment, supported by direct teaching of the skills, we set up students for greater success in the future. As supported by the research of Jeffery Liew and colleagues (2020), "Emotional supports and instructional supports often go hand-in-hand for teachers who engage in quality and developmentally appropriate teaching practices" (p. 643). With the information in this chapter and those that follow, you will be well on your way to teaching your students how to effectively use structured SELf-questioning while providing all students with the support they need to be successful in a way that meets their developmental needs.

Parent Corner

As teachers, we know that continuity between all environments is one of the best ways to support our students inside and outside of the classroom. With that in mind, let's dive into how you can facilitate parental and caretaker use of structured SELf-questioning for emotional self-management at home. As stated at the very beginning of this chapter, when all stakeholders in a student's life are effectively able to use structured SELf-questioning to teach self-awareness and self-management, students will better understand that their environment recognizes and supports their emotional regulation and management while building positive relationships between teachers and students.

I always recommend that teachers begin by having parents start with one question that they know they can first just model at home with consistency using self-talk. This allows the parent to become familiar with the question, expanding their emotional language repertoire and showing their child that this is a strategy that they will also be using at home. This will set up your environment for success before parents even get started using the strategy with their child.

In the reproducible "SELf-Questioning 101: Teaching Self-Management to Your Child," you will find a sample conversation to serve as a taste of what using structured SELf-questioning in a naturally occurring, routine activity at home may look like.

SELf-Questioning 101: Teaching Self-Management to Your Child

In the following chart, you will find Bryce and his dad, Dave, using structured SELf-questioning to manage a snag in their morning routine—not wanting to brush his teeth before school! You can apply this model to encourage and reinforce sticking to many other similar routines that occur in the home.

SELf-Questioning Step	Parent or Caregiver Dialogue as a Model	Parent or Caregiver as a Support
Identify Feelings	**Dave models asking:** "How do I feel?" "I am feeling angry."	**Dave asks:** "How do you feel?" **Bryce responds:** "You make me mad!"
Gather Information	**Dave models asking:** "What is causing this feeling?" "I do not want to brush my teeth with this toothbrush."	**Dave asks:** "What is causing this feeling?" **Bryce responds:** "I hate this toothbrush!" and throws it.
Brainstorm	**Dave models asking:** "What can I do?" "I can pick either the blue or green toothbrush."	**Dave asks:** "What can you do?" **Bryce responds:** "I want the green toothbrush."
Evaluate	**Dave models asking:** "What strategies are supported by my circumstance?" "I have just enough time to pick a new color toothbrush, then brush my teeth."	**Dave asks:** "What strategies are supported by your circumstance?" **Bryce responds:** "I have time today to pick a new toothbrush and brush my teeth super fast!"

A Practical Guide to Social and Emotional Problem Solving

5

Be a wonderful role model, because you will be the window through which many children will see their future.

—Thomas McKinnon Wood

In the previous chapter, you continued to learn how to use the SELf-questions for emotional problem solving as a guide for student self-talk through self-management and emotional regulation. In this chapter, we look at how easy and efficient it is for students to apply these same steps and SELf-questions to resolve a social conflict in the classroom. Since it takes time and practice for students to internalize the steps and SELf-questions and even more to use the overall strategy to guide their own self-talk through academic and social problem solving independently, continued use of a gradual release approach is best practice. (See our illustration of gradual release in figure 4.1, page 72. You'll learn more about using gradual release for academic inquiry in chapter 6, page 117.)

People who work outside the preschool classroom might wonder, "What kind of social problems can arise in a preschool classroom?" Those who work in these classrooms know well the list can be quite long, with some of the most frequent social problems including sharing, making friends, being denied access to something, name calling, waiting their turn, initiating play, pushing, shoving, and biting.

In an integrated preschool classroom, there are many of these social problems that can arise as preschoolers are just beginning to develop their social skills. As stated in the *Encyclopedia of Child Behavior and Development*, "Social problem solving is the process by which individuals identify and enact solutions to social life situations in an effort to alter the problematic nature of the situation, their relation to the situation, or both" (Adrian, Lyon, Oti, & Tininenko, 2011).

As an integrated preschool teacher, Michele has seen that with each passing year, fewer students come into the classroom with the knowledge of solving social problems independently. Students tend to rely solely on adults to solve these social problems. Although this may be a developmentally appropriate strategy for students who enter the class, the goal is to promote independence on this matter throughout their time in preschool. This chapter discusses three different stages of social problem solving based on student need, with examples of what this may look like in an integrated setting. This includes modeling, guided structured SELf-questioning, and independence. These steps need to be introduced to students through modeling, as detailed in Modeling Using Self-Talk and Parallel Talk (page 53 in chapter 3). Once modeling has occurred and students are ready, teachers can practice guided questions where teachers will ask the question aloud, "What can we do?" With enough practice, the goal is for students to be able to ask themselves and answer these questions independently.

The Importance of Teaching a Metacognitive Strategy for Social Problem Solving

It is circle time in an integrated preschool classroom. A four-year-old boy named Ronan is feeling excited. His teacher just introduced a new center to him and his classmates: light table. The teacher explained that at the light table, there will be special transparent blocks that light can shine through; however, only three students can play with the light table at a time! When he heard this, Ronan's heart began to beat faster, his mouth opened wide with excitement, and his body began to wiggle with anticipation. He felt like a volcano, ready to explode. He knew he needed to be in this center! After circle time, the students transition to the table to discuss where they would like to play and what they would like to do in each center. Ronan ran right to the table to grab his seat. He was ready. Ronan was waiting patiently for his turn. With each passing name being called, Ronan grew more and more anxious with thoughts like, *Will I be able to go to the light table today? Why isn't the teacher calling my name? I'm sitting in my seat nicely.*

With all of these thoughts running through his mind, it became difficult to focus. Finally, he hears, "Ronan, what center would you like to go to?" This is it! He tells the teacher that he would like to go to the light table to build a tall tower, only to find out that the allotted three spots were already taken by the students chosen before him. His body sank into the chair, and he could feel the tears welling up in his eyes. He was feeling devastated. "I feel devastated," he stated aloud. He took one deep breath and remembered his structured SELf-questioning that he has been practicing with his teacher when a social problem arises.

His internal dialogue began: *What can I do?* He started to rack his brain on the different ways he could solve this problem. *I can take a break until my body is calm. I can pick another center and wait my turn. I can ask the teacher for a hug to help me feel better.* Many options ran through Ronan's mind. *What's the best way to solve this problem? I think waiting my turn would be the best choice. First, I will pick blocks,* he thought, *and then I will switch to the light table.*

This sequence felt like an eternity to Ronan, but in reality, only a few seconds had passed. Ronan sat up in his seat with a calm body and told the teacher that he would go to blocks first, then switch to the light table when it opened up again. Ronan transitioned to blocks, and after ten minutes, he noticed that a student who chose the light table station was now switching to another center. Again, Ronan's mouth opened wide with excitement, and his body began to wiggle with anticipation. He made his way to the light table.

As he transitioned, he asked himself, *Did it work? I waited my turn, and now I get to go to the light table. Yes, yes it did!*

Ronan went through each step of the problem-solving process. He began by identifying his feelings, the reason for those feelings, and what he could do about the situation. These are the Identify Feelings, Gather Information, and Brainstorm steps for emotional problem solving. Consequently, the final three steps Ronan works through—Evaluate, Plan and Act, and Reflect—make this social problem solving as well.

In order for him to be conscious of how others feel, he must first be able to identify these feelings. Hence, social and emotional problem solving do have some overlap, first, by identifying the feeling within oneself, and then by identifying that feeling within others. After Ronan follows the emotional problem-solving steps, he seamlessly solves social problems by completing the final steps.

How to Teach a Metacognitive Strategy for Social and Emotional Problem Solving

Although all chapters in this book reflect on each SELf-question step to some degree, notice that the previous chapters deeply explored the Identify Feelings and Gather Information actions related to SELf-questioning. In this section, we shift that deep focus and extend our knowledge to social problem solving by focusing on the steps: Brainstorm, Evaluate, Plan and Act, and Reflect. At this point, students have already worked on self-awareness and self-management, and they are starting to become more socially aware! During this time, they will ask themselves what they can do and will enter the phase where they pick the best solution and try it out. This is a good point to review the SELf-question set for emotional problem solving featured in figure 1.3 (page 18). As a quick summary, this question set progresses as follows.

1. **Identify Feelings:** How do I feel? What am I feeling? How does he, she, or they feel?
2. **Gather Information:** What do I know? What is causing this feeling? What can I control? What is my goal?
3. **Brainstorm:** What can I do? What strategies can I use?
4. **Evaluate:** Has this strategy helped me in the past?
5. **Plan and Act:** What do I do first, second, and so on?
6. **Reflect:** Did it work? How do I know?

The following sections use the gradual release framework illustrated in figure 4.1 (page 72) to show how teachers can teach preschoolers to use SELf-questioning to problem solve social problems.

Modeling Social and Emotional SELf-Questions for Students

The first thing I (Michele) focus on when introducing problem solving to my students is modeling how to use these questions for that purpose. The importance of this is for students to become even more comfortable with these steps and their associated SELf-questions. The more these students hear the question aloud, the quicker they can absorb the information and use it independently. This step is completely teacher directed and observed by students. This can be done within the natural environment or directly taught during whole-group instruction.

Let's focus on how we can teach social problem solving in the natural environment. For example, Jack and Alex are playing in the blocks center. Jack chose to play with the wooden blocks to make a ramp. Alex chose to play with the trains. The boys have been playing with their respective toys for some time when Jack hears the train "choo-choo" down the tracks. Without hesitation, Jack grabs the toy from Alex's hand and begins to drive it down the ramp.

Since this observation, the teacher has identified difficulty sharing as a social problem. This is a social problem that can be resolved in the classroom by beginning with the teacher and paraprofessional modeling it for students. The teacher calls over a paraprofessional and explains the social problem she has observed. The teacher and paraprofessional begin playing with toys. The following example is a dialogue that can happen between a teacher and paraprofessional to model social problem solving using the structured SELf questions. Thinking aloud, the teacher models what to do when a person wants a toy by speaking aloud and modeling body language.

> ***Identify Feelings: How do I feel?*** *"I'm feeling frustrated!"*
>
> ***Gather Information: What is causing this feeling?*** *"I love playing with blocks, but I really want to play with trains."*
>
> ***Brainstorm: What can I do?*** *"Hmm. What can I do? I know! I can ask them if I can play with the trains."*
>
> ***Evaluate: Has this strategy helped me in the past?*** *"Has this strategy helped me in the past? Yes! Let's try it!"*
>
> ***Plan and Act: What do I do first, second, and so on?*** *"First, I'll ask them if I can play with the trains, and then I will wait. Can I play trains with you?" The paraprofessional states, "Sure! Thank you for asking!"*
>
> ***Reflect: Did it work?*** *"Did it work? Yes, I wanted to play with the trains, I asked to play with them, and then I got them!"*

The teacher and paraprofessional proceed to model how they play with trains together.

Modeling in this setting shows students situations they will come across in their natural environment. This open dialogue can be used across all social problems and allows students to see different positive outcomes. Although you may feel silly at first, the more structured SELf-questions you speak aloud, the more your students will hear the process, practice, and internalize it.

Consequently, modeling can also happen during whole-group instruction. Just as before, this example begins with the teacher identifying a social problem within the classroom or one that may arise. When presenting these steps in a whole-group setting, it is more contrived, meaning teachers can plan it out in advance. For example, let's say the teacher has planned to do a snowman craft using glue sticks and different shapes cut out of construction paper. Each student will receive their pieces to create a snowman. During whole-group instruction, the teacher, along with a paraprofessional, review the steps to creating this craft by showing the students each step.. The teacher and paraprofessional are modeling not only how to put the pieces together but also how to share the glue stick. The teacher is contriving a situation where students are practicing sharing. The teacher will first use the glue stick and put it on the table. The paraprofessional will then take the glue stick off the table and begin to glue the pieces of the craft together. The teacher will begin modeling by stating how she feels. Let's dive deeper into what this teacher and paraprofessional dialogue could sound like using the problem-solving steps.

> **Identify Feelings: How do I feel?** *"I feel upset."*
>
> **Gather Information: What is causing this feeling?** *"I want to glue the pieces on my paper to make a snowman, but I do not have a glue stick."*
>
> **Brainstorm: What can I do?** *"Hmm. What can I do? I can take the glue stick from my friend. Or, I can ask them to share the glue stick. "*
>
> **Evaluate: Has this strategy helped me in the past?** *"Has this helped me in the past? Yes, I can ask my friend to share the glue stick."*
>
> **Plan and Act: What do I do first, second, and so on?** *"I know asking nicely has worked before. I'll try it again!" The teacher turns to the paraprofessional and says, "Can I have a turn with the glue stick?" The paraprofessional states, "Sure! Thank you for asking!"*
>
> **Reflect: Did it work?** *"Did it work? Yes, I needed a glue stick, I asked for it, and I got the glue stick!" The teacher continues to glue the pieces onto her snowman.*

Modeling is a great way to start the process of independent problem solving. In the gradual release model illustrated in figure 4.1 (page 72), this can be described as the *I do* portion of social problem solving, which has students immersed in the problem-solving steps directed by the teacher with no requirements of the students.

The next step is loosening the reins and assisting students experiencing social problems by guiding them with structured SELf-questioning. The importance of this gradual release is to promote independence within the students. This *we do* component is essential for continued internalization of the modeled skills presented to students by the teacher. Let's look at some additional examples and implementations of guided structured SELf-questioning to further engage students to use these questions to resolve social problems. Just as with modeling, this can be done in the natural environment as well as in contrived situations during whole-group instruction.

Guiding Students to Use Social and Emotional SELf-Questions

Different from modeling, guiding structured SELf-questions in the natural environment requires student input. When a social problem emerges between students, the teacher poses the questions to students, and they answer the questions in order to solve the social problem. The following is an example of a scenario involving guided questioning.

> *When walking to class and up the stairs, Alice tripped on the last step of the staircase. Consequently, she grabbed onto Noah's backpack in order to gain her balance. Accidentally, she broke off his favorite Thomas the Train keychain. Noah glared at Alice with anger. Alice looked at Noah with regret.*
>
> *"I'm sorry," cried Alice.*
>
> *Noah shouted, "I hate you!" He began to kick and scream on the floor.*
>
> *Alice froze in shock. Observing nearby is the teacher, who approached this social problem in a calm manner. She lets Noah express his feelings and, during his de-escalation, offers assistance with guided questions.*
>
> ***Identify Feelings: How do you feel?***
>
> *Teacher: "Noah, How do you feel?"*
>
> *Noah: "I am feeling angry!"*
>
> ***Gather Information: What is causing this feeling?***
>
> *Teacher: "What is causing this feeling?"*
>
> *Noah: "She broke my favorite keychain!"*
>
> ***Brainstorm: What can you do?***
>
> *Teacher: "What can you do?"*
>
> *Noah: "I can take deep belly breaths."*
>
> ***Evaluate: Is this the best way to solve this problem?***
>
> *Teacher: "That's a great idea. Let's try it."*
>
> ***Plan and Act: What do I do first, second, and so on?***
>
> *First, in unison, the teacher and Noah took three belly breaths. After a few seconds of calmness, the teacher checks in with Noah.*
>
> ***Reflect: Did it work?***
>
> *Teacher: "Did the belly breaths work?"*
>
> *Noah: "Yes, I feel calm."*
>
> *Teacher: "Now that we are feeling calm, I notice that Alice may still be feeling sad. What can we do?"*
>
> *Noah: "I can say sorry for saying I hate her. I was feeling mad."*
>
> *Teacher: "Great idea!"*

Noah approaches Alice and apologizes for saying he hates her. Alice apologizes for breaking his keychain. They begin to play together. It worked!

Using guided structured SELf-questioning during whole-group instruction can also involve student input. The following is an example of a scenario involving guided questioning during whole-group instruction in an integrated preschool classroom.

The teacher instructs the paraprofessional to sit in a spot at circle time. During the "Hello Song," the paraprofessional starts to roll around on the carpet when the expected behavior is to sit with a calm body and crisscross applesauce. The teacher approaches the paraprofessional in a calm manner.

Identify Feelings: How do I feel?

Teacher: "How do you feel?"

Paraprofessional: "I am feeling silly."

Gather Information: What is causing this feeling?

Teacher: "Your body is telling me you feel silly. I see you are rolling on the carpet."

Brainstorm: What can I do?

Teacher: "What can you do when our bodies feel silly?" (The teacher can pose this question to the class to see what solutions they can come up with.)

Student 1: "Get a fidget toy!"

Student 2: "Take a belly breath!"

Student 3: "Get a weighted ball!"

Student 4: "Take a break!"

Evaluate: Which is best?

Paraprofessional: "Those are great ideas! Which is the best?"

Plan and Act: What do I do first, second, and so on?

Paraprofessional: "First, I will try the fidget toy!"

Reflect: Did it work?

The paraprofessional chooses a fidget toy and brings it to the carpet. She models how to appropriately use the fidget toy in her lap, sitting crisscross applesauce!

To add to the guided structured SELf-questioning, the paraprofessional can also demonstrate what to do if the solution they chose does not work. If so, the paraprofessional models how *not* to use the fidget toy. For example, they may continue to roll on the carpet. During this time, the teacher may pose the question, "Did it work?" a question the students can easily answer for the paraprofessional. The teacher can encourage the paraprofessional to try another solution and demonstrate that one appropriately. Again, posing the question, "Did it work?" until the answer is *yes*, which means she found a strategy that worked.

Releasing Students to Use the Social and Emotional SELf-Questions

We have now reached the last of three phases of the gradual release approach of social problem solving: independence (release). The introduction of the problem-solving process using structured SELf-questioning through modeling and guided questioning has paid off. The overall goal of this phase of the gradual release process is for students to not require assistance when dealing with social problems. The classroom starts to feel more like a well-oiled machine where the teacher can take a step back and observe all the hard work that has been done.

For this example of independence, let's reintroduce Ronan. Throughout Ronan's time in the classroom, he encountered many social problems, but by the end of his time there, he gained independence to solve social problems. How did he do that? He made his way through the gradual release stages in which he gained independence by working through each step without guidance. This means that when a social problem arises, he can come up with a strategy, try it out, and reflect on it all on his own.

On one of Ronan's last days in the room, I overheard a conversation between him and his friend Adam. They were discussing their feelings about moving up to kindergarten and leaving their old friends, and they did so explicitly using SELf-questioning. I was so proud of their ability to maneuver through this conversation using this skill of both social and emotional problem solving, as detailed next.

Ronan was sitting on the carpet and waiting for circle time to start. Ronan, who usually had a smile on his face, was hunched over with his hand on his cheek and his elbow resting on his leg. Adam approaches Ronan and sits next to him on the carpet. Adam looks at his friend with a furrowed brow and a worried expression on his face since this is not typical for Ronan.

Identify Feelings: How do I feel?

Ronan immediately turns to Adam and says, "I'm feeling nervous."

Gather Information: What do I know? What is causing this feeling?

Ronan continued, "Mrs. Herold says kindergarten is fun, but I am going to miss my old friends."

Adam answered, "I'm nervous, too."

Brainstorm: What can I do?

Ronan explained, "When I feel nervous, I like to play with you. Do you think we could play together in kindergarten?"

Evaluate: Which is best?

Adam stated, "That's a great idea. But, today, we can play with our friends to make us feel happy!"

Plan and Act: What do I do first, second, and so on?

Ronan said, " Hooray! First, we can ask our friends to play with us today, then we can ask new friends to play with us when we go to kindergarten. That will make us feel happy."

Adam shouted, "Yes! I like that plan."

Reflect: Did it work?

During playtime, I overheard Ronan telling Adam, "I am happy now because I get to play with you."

The first part of their plan worked! They were feeling nervous but figured out independently that playing with friends could help them feel better. The boys waited all summer to see if the second part of their plan worked. Ronan and Adam started kindergarten and played with each other and their new friends every day. Their plan did, in fact, work!

Scenarios for Social and Emotional Problem Solving

The following sections offer three example scenarios for interactions between teachers and students that are focused on social and emotional problem solving. Note that the scope of these scenarios each includes its own utilization and range of steps within the metacognitive strategy for SELf-questioning, as illustrated in figure 1.3 (page 18).

Scenario 1: Social Problem Solving

Program: Integrated preschool

Objective: Solve social problems.

Standard: 0.4.6 "Demonstrate verbal or nonverbal problem-solving skills without being aggressive (e.g., talk about a problem and related feelings and negotiate solutions)" (Teaching Strategies, n.d.a, p. 4).

Teacher: Mrs. Herold

During music and movement, students are asked to keep their hands to themselves and make sure they have enough space to move their bodies. Mrs. Herold notices Oscar bumping into Eloise during a song. Notice in this scenario how she uses structured SELf-questioning for social problem solving with Oscar and Eloise.

IDENTIFY FEELINGS

SELf-Question: How do I feel?

Mrs. Herold approaches Eloise and Oscar calmly. She turns to Eloise and asks, "Eloise, how are you feeling?" Eloise folds her arms and yells, "I am feeling angry!"

GATHER INFORMATION

SELf-Question: What do I know? What is causing this feeling?

Mrs. Herold adds, " I see you are angry; your arms are folded! What is causing this feeling?" Eloise shares, "Oscar is bumping into me, and I want to dance!" Mrs. Herold has already introduced and modeled strategies (using read alouds and natural environment teachings) to help when students are feeling angry.

BRAINSTORM

SELf-Question: What can I do?

Eloise already remembers talking about what she can do when a friend is not keeping their hands to themselves, so when Mrs. Herold asks, "What can you do?" she is ready with an answer, saying, "I know! I can use my words to tell them to stop."

EVALUATE

SELf-Question: Has this strategy helped me in the past?

Mrs. Herold asks, "Has this strategy helped you in the past?"

Eloise pauses and thinks. Eloise states, "Yes! If I use my words, he will know I don't like it when he bumps into me during music."

Mrs. Herold smiles and states, "Let's try it!"

Eloise approaches Oscar, asking him to keep his hands to himself.

REFLECT

SELf-Question: Did it work?

Mrs. Herold notices Eloise and Oscar dance near each other without bumping into one another. She tells Eloise, "I see you are dancing again! Did it work?"

Eloise smiles, gives Mrs. Herold a high five, and continues to dance.

Scenario 2: Social Needs Expression

Program: Integrated preschool

Objective: Suggest solutions to and solve social problems.

Standard: 0.4.5 "Express needs verbally or nonverbally to teacher and peers without being aggressive" (Teaching Strategies, n.d.a, p. 4).

Teacher: Mr. MacLany

As center time begins, Mr. MacLany's students begin choosing their centers and dispersing through the classroom. Student Renee runs past her friends to the block area, scooping up all the farm animals. She sits with the farm animals on her lap and begins to play, but Jayden really wanted to play with farm animals, too. He stomps to the blocks, yelling at

Renee, "Hey! I want those farm animals! Gimme!" Renee turns her back to Jayden. Seeing the situation, Mr. MacLany joins the block area. Jayden immediately tugs Mr. MacLany, stating, "Those are mine!"

IDENTIFY FEELINGS

SELf-Question: How do I feel?

Mr. MacLany replies, "Jayden, how are you feeling?" Jayden states, "I am feeling frustrated. I wanted to play with the animals."

GATHER INFORMATION

SELf-Question: What is causing this feeling?

Mr. MacLany validates and expands on Jayden's information, stating, "I understand you're feeling frustrated. What is causing this feeling?" Jayden replies, "Renee has my animals."

BRAINSTORM

SELf-Question: What can I do?

Mr. MacLany and his class have spent a lot of time learning about these social situations through read alouds, role plays, and with visual supports on the wall. Mr. MacLany guides Jayden to a visual list of strategies located in the block area, which includes the question, "What can I do when a friend doesn't share?"

Jayden states, "I can . . ." and begins to look at some of the visuals. Jayden points to the icon that shows *teacher help*.

Mr. MacLany states, "I am here to help you pick a strategy. What else can we do?" prompting Jayden to try a strategy that will have him attempt to solve the problem on his own.

EVALUATE

SELf-Question: Has this strategy helped me in the past?

Mr. MacLany reminds Jayden, "We are at blocks, and we are feeling frustrated because we want to play with the animals." Mr. MacLany begins to modify the Evaluate question by asking, "What can we do at the block area when a friend doesn't want to share?" Jayden looks back at the visual and states, "I can ask for some animals?"

Mr. MacLany encourages Jayden by stating, "Let's go try it!"

Jayden approaches Renee, still clutching onto the animals bin. Jayden asked, "Can I have two animals? I really like the elephant and monkey." Renee looks at Jayden and then at the animals bin. Renee slowly hands Jayden the animals he asked for and turns back around. Jayden rejoices, holding his two favorite animals. He then takes out some wooden blocks and begins building them a habitat.

REFLECT

SELf-Question: Did it work?

Mr. MacLany approaches Jayden in the block area. "I see you asked Renee if you could have two toys. Did it work?" Jayden gives Mr. MacLany a thumbs-up, confirming that the strategy he chose was successful!

Scenario 3: Receptive, Expressive, and Pragmatic Language Skills

Program: Self-contained preschool

Objective: Comprehend and respond to books and other texts.

Standard: RL.PK.10 "Actively participate in read aloud experiences using age appropriate literature in individual, small and large groups" (Teaching Strategies, n.d.a, p. 13).

Teacher: Mr. Cortes

It is story time, and Mr. Cortes is reading *The Way I Feel* by Janan Cain (2021) to his students. To encourage active participation and facilitate language skill development for his diverse learners during a read aloud, Mr. Cortes encourages students to take turns (pragmatic language) making comments and statements (expressive language) at the end of each page. He poses questions to facilitate their understanding of the content (receptive language) as well as their ability to use single- to multi-word utterances to respond (expressive language). Mr. Cortes has access to a static board that offers picture symbols with core and fringe vocabulary words. In addition to verbal speech and picture symbols, Mr. Cortes uses facial expressions, gestures, and body language while implementing structured SELf-questioning. This use of multiple modes of communication promotes students' receptive, expressive, and pragmatic language skills.

IDENTIFY FEELINGS

SELf-Question: How do I feel?

The students are sitting and attending to the storybook. Mr. Cortes reads the page in the book about pride. He reads, "Proud! I did it! I did it! I shout to the crowd. Getting dressed by myself makes me feel proud" (Cain, 2021). The picture in the book is of a girl smiling and giving a thumbs-up as she stands proudly in her outfit.

Mr. Cortes turns to Isla (body language) and asks, "What made her feel proud?" while touching the *what* picture symbol on the core board (picture symbol), using American Sign Language by signing *proud* (gesture), and pointing to the *proud* picture symbol. He leans in (body language to express interest and waiting). Isla does not respond.

Mr. Cortes provides additional wait time while smiling (facial expression to signal support and patience). Isla's eyes begin to swell with tears, and she looks around the room at her peers. Some peers are looking at the book. Some peers are looking at her. Isla begins to cry loudly.

Mr. Cortes says, "I see you are crying. I wonder, how do you feel?" while pointing to himself (gesture for first person singular *I*), signing *cry* (gesture), pointing to Isla (gesture for second person singular *you*), and presenting her with picture symbols for possible feelings.

Isla recognizes her emotion of *sad* and points to the *sad* picture symbol. Mr. Cortes provides parallel talk by using the first person singular pronoun *I*, as it closely aligns with Isla's internal language. He says, "I feel sad," and points to himself (gesture for *I*), signs *sad*, and points to the *sad* picture symbol to let her know she functionally demonstrated self-expression of an emotion.

GATHER INFORMATION

SELf-Question: What is causing this feeling?

Mr. Cortes asks Isla, "What is causing this feeling?" and points to the *what* picture symbol on the core board. Isla responds, "I don't know the answer."

BRAINSTORM

SELf-Question: What can I do?

Mr. Cortes says, "I feel sad because I don't know the answer. When I feel sad because I don't know the answer, what can I do?" while pointing to himself (gesture for *I*), signing *sad* (gesture), frowning (facial expression to express *sadness*), touching the *what* picture symbol on the core board, and leaning in (body language to express interest and waiting).

Mr. Cortes smiles (facial expression expressing support and patience). Isla does not respond. He signs *help* (gesture) and points to the *help* picture symbol on the core board. Isla recognizes the sign and yells, "I need help!"

Mr. Cortes encourages her to ask a friend. Isla approaches Jet and says, "I need help." Jet goes on to tell Isla that the girl in the story feels proud because she got dressed by herself.

When Isla sits down again, Mr. Cortes asks, "What made her feel proud?" and touches the *what* picture symbol on the core board, signs *proud* (gesture), and leans in (body language expressing interest and patience). Isla smiles and says, "She got dressed by herself!" Mr. Cortes says, "You got it!" while smiling (facial expression) and offering Isla a high five (gesture to provide praise).

REFLECT

SELf-Question: Did it work?

Mr. Cortes provides parallel talk and says, "You felt sad because you didn't know the answer. What did you do? You asked a friend for help. Did it work? Yes or no?" Mr. Cortes points to himself (gesture for *I*), points to the *sad* picture symbol, signs *sad* and *help* (gestures), points to the *help* and *what* picture symbols on the core board, signs *yes* and *no*, points to the *yes* and *no* picture symbols on the core board, nods and shakes his head (body language), and leans in (body language to express waiting). Isla smiles, says "Yes," signs *yes*, points to the *yes* picture symbol on the core board, and nods her head.

Throughout these steps (Identify Feelings, Gather Information, Brainstorm, and Reflect), Mr. Cortes uses multiple modes of communication. He uses verbal speech to ask and answer the structured SELf-questions, reads, provides praise, uses emotions vocabulary, makes statements to describe Isla's expression of an emotion, provides a cause of the emotion, expresses the emotion, provides a self-management strategy, which was requesting assistance, and reflects. He further makes statements based on the text to provide a cause of a character's emotion. He uses facial expressions, picture symbols, gestures, and body language.

The use of multiple modes of communication promotes student comprehension of the structured SELf-questions, written text, praise, emotions vocabulary, statements, how others may express emotion, causes of emotions, self-management strategies, and reflection, which facilitates receptive language skills. It further promotes students' ability to ask and answer the structured SELf-questions, provide praise, use emotions vocabulary, make statements about one's own emotions and the emotions of others, express emotions, provide causes of emotions, provide strategies to manage those emotions, request assistance, and reflect, which facilitates expressive language skills. Additionally, it promotes students' abilities to interact with others, participate in exchanges, provide praise, take turns, and be socially aware, which facilitates pragmatic language skills.

Conclusion

We have to remember as teachers of young students that all eyes are on us. What we model, guide, and teach within the walls of our classroom leaves a lasting impression on our students. So why not use this realization to benefit the classroom by creating independent social and emotional problem solvers? As teachers, it is very easy to intervene when a problem arises in our classroom. Consequently, sheltering students from working through their problems will only create bigger problems when they are forced to handle these social problems themselves. However, if we model the expected behavior through structured SELf-questioning, slowly hand over the reins, guide students aloud with the same question set, and, with consistency, internalize this question set to gain independence when solving social problems, we can see social successes, confidence, and awareness in even our youngest students.

Parent Corner

As beneficial as structured SELf-questioning is in the classroom, it's even more beneficial when parents and caregivers support at home the work we do inside the classroom. What if a student is struggling with social problem solving when they are not in school? This is where parents' and caregivers' knowledge of the SELf-question sets is very important and can assist a child with social problem solving at home. The more a preschooler is immersed in the usage of these strategies during social situations, the more effective they can be in solving social problems independently.

In the reproducible "SELf-Questioning 101: Teaching Social and Emotional Problem Solving to Your Child," you will meet a father named Alex and his son, Robert. They are using structured SELf-questioning to help Robert play with friends on the playground. This is an example of a social problem that may arise when a child is outside of school and how a parent or caregiver can support their child using structured SELf-questioning. Provide parents with this resource to illustrate how structured SELf-questioning can be used outside the classroom.

SELf-Questioning 101: Teaching Social and Emotional Problem Solving to Your Child

At school, we use the metacognitive strategy of structured SELf-questioning throughout the day to promote your child's social and emotional problem-solving skills. You can accelerate your child's understanding and use of structured SELf-questioning at home to do the same! Please see the following example of how structured SELf-questioning helped a child initiate play with others. We encourage you to reflect on this example and use the structured SELf-questioning at home and in the community, brainstorming other ways you may be able to apply structured SELf-questioning with your child.

SELf-Questioning Step	SELf-Question Selected by Parent and Child	Parent and Child Response
Identify Feelings	"How do you feel?"	**Alex (father):** "How do you feel?" **Robert (son):** "I am feeling sad."
Gather Information	"What is causing this feeling?"	**Alex:** "What is causing this feeling?" **Robert:** "I want to play with friends on the playground."
Brainstorm	"What can you do?"	**Alex:** "What can you do?" **Robert:** "I can ask them."
Evaluate	"Has this strategy helped you in the past?"	**Alex:** "Has this strategy helped you in the past?" **Robert:** "Yes! If I ask them, then they will know I want to play."
Plan and Act	"What do you do first, second, and so on?"	**Alex:** "What do you do first?" **Robert:** "First I will ask them if they want to play with me." **Alex:** "What will you do second?" **Robert:** "Then, we can play together!"
Reflect	"Did it work?"	After Robert asks, he begins to play with friends. Later, Alex reflects with Robert: **Alex:** "Did it work?" **Robert:** "Yes! I asked them to play, and they played with me!"

6 A Practical Guide to Academic Inquiry-Based Units

Children need many opportunities to generate and discuss ideas, make plans, brainstorm solutions to problems, reflect and give reasons for their choices.

—Aikaterini Michalopoulou

In the previous three chapters, you learned about how to use structured SELf-questioning in classrooms to develop all students' self-awareness, self-management, and social-emotional problem-solving skills. In the same way the social and emotional structured SELf-question set guides students' self-talk through emotional awareness and management of their own feelings and relationships, the academic and social structured SELf-question set helps students work through complex academic inquiries in the preschool classroom easily and seamlessly. While the questions presented in the emotional problem-solving set guide students to think inward, the academic and social questions help students think outward about their learning. To illustrate, under Identify Feelings in the emotional problem-solving set, students turn inward and ask themselves, "How do I feel?" Conversely, under Select a Focus in the academic problem-solving set, the focus is external as students ask, "What is the problem?" Please be mindful that the steps in each prompt promote the same kind of thinking.

Cohen and colleagues (2021) describe how the academic problem-solving set can be misused within *emotional* contexts. To avoid this outcome, this chapter dives into the importance of teaching and how to teach a process-based metacognitive strategy for *academic* problem solving, where the key difference between it and the emotional problem-solving set is how the prompts move from thinking inward to thinking outward. From there, we offer suggestions that will help you align SELf-questions to an inquiry-based academic curriculum.

The Importance of Teaching a Metacognitive Strategy for Academic Problem Solving

Academic inquiry is key to developing all preschool students' academic intellect. Aikaterini Michalopoulou (2014) states that preschoolers "need many opportunities to generate and discuss ideas, make plans, brainstorm solutions to problems, reflect and give reasons for their choices" (p. 377). We find that Teaching Strategies' (n.d.b) *The Creative Curriculum for Preschool* is a particularly useful set of resources for achieving these outcomes. Teaching Strategies (2020b) describes the interrelatedness between the four learning domains—(1) physical, (2) cognitive, (3) social-emotional, and (4) language—and how they often overlap. The curriculum asserts how academic inquiry can be taught in tandem with social knowledge and understanding, such as being part of a group. Furthermore, Teaching Strategies (2020c) affirms findings that mental health and employment are positively impacted when social and emotional skills are embedded within academics at a young age. Since three- and four-year-old students' brains and cognitive skills are just developing, multistep processes can be complicated, especially for students with special needs. Teaching Strategies (2020b) further asserts that when students are motivated to communicate with others, language develops. The SELf-question set, which is academic, emotional, and social in nature, is a collaborative effort between students and staff. Finally, Teaching Strategies (2020b) affirms that teachers should ask open-ended questions to preschoolers and extend their responses. Teachers using the academic and social SELf-question set empower preschoolers with open-ended questions that allow for academic and social exploration and collaboration between students.

Introducing academic inquiry while preschoolers' brains are newly developing is a great opportunity, but students at this age are not ready to tackle the big questions of inquiry-driven preschool curricula independently. Thus, preschool students benefit from the metacognitive strategy of SELf-questioning because it provides a structured set of steps. Michalopoulou (2014) adds that inquiry-based learning allows students to problem solve issues that are raised by either the teacher or the student. When preschoolers are already becoming familiar with the emotional structured SELf-question set, it serves as a perfect scaffold for students to fall back on and transfer application of the strategy to new content, situations, and contexts—for our purposes in this chapter, this means academics. Preschool is a prime time to guide students' emotional and academic habits of mind development, as Michalopoulou (2014) confirms that students gain reflexivity, imagination, and persistence when they participate in meaningful inquiry-led experiences.

When students participate in inquiry-based learning, metacognition does not immediately occur. For example, students' curiosity is not only piqued through investigations (Michalopoulou, 2014). This research shows us that a teacher is needed to guide students through inquiry-based learning. In contrast, the simplicity of a problem-solving process can lead to the teaching of metacognitive strategies for academic problem solving. In the next section, you will discover how to use structured SELf-questioning for academic problem solving. Additionally, you will see that academic inquiries can engage with both academic and social problems when students interact with others around the curriculum (for example, a music study with a guest speaker or a job inquiry in which students role play professions in a presentation to parents).

How to Teach a Metacognitive Strategy for Academic Problem Solving

If the goal is to provide preschoolers with a scaffold that empowers them to thoughtfully approach and answer the multistep problems that inquiries demand, what better way to support them than with a metacognitive strategy? The academic and social SELf-question set can help preschoolers independently solve academic and social problems within preschool classrooms. From experience, preschoolers love anything interactive and exciting. Each problem-solving step that follows could be, for example, written out and pulled one at a time from a mystery box to be taped on a chart, modeled by a teacher asking and answering the questions by acting them out with puppets, associated with a color, or added to a chart or song that uses the words within the academic problem-solving set.

- **Select a Focus:** What is the problem? What is the question? What is the task? What is important? What is the user's need?
- **Gather Information:** What do I know? What do I need to know? What is important?
- **Brainstorm:** How can I solve this problem? What can I do? What are possible solutions? What is similar, and what is different?
- **Evaluate:** What is the best way to solve this problem? Does this make sense? What are possible consequences?
- **Plan and Act:** What do I do first, second, and so on? Is this working?
- **Reflect:** Did it work? How do I know?

The following section provides a number of models of how to embed these steps into inquiry-based units in any preschool class and how to sprinkle these SELf-questions into academic curriculum and instruction. The fact that the metacognitive strategy of structured SELf-questioning fits so well into any inquiry-based curricula makes it easy and practical to embed. Inquiry-based learning and structured SELf-questioning are further aligned in that they are intended to ultimately be student-led processes, where there is no wrong answer for the problem-solving steps nor within the inquiry. Because the SELf-questions are different for each step, a teacher or student's thinking process can alter along the way to fit the context.

For example, the preschool classes at Moss School use *The Creative Curriculum for Preschool* (Teaching Strategies, n.d.b), which provides student-led opportunities to "think critically and develop process skills with rich, hands-on investigations of relevant and interesting topics in the classroom." In this environment, as well as that of any other preschool, teacher choices related to inquiry topics should ideally come from student interest. To do this effectively, teachers take on the role of observer, as they notice what materials and topics students are naturally drawn to within the classroom as they gauge interest. *Long-term inquiries*, often referred to as *studies*, are defined by Teaching Strategies (2020b) as hands-on, project-based investigations that allow children to explore topics of interest while developing skills in language and literacy, mathematics, art, and technology. Thus, long-term inquiries are an ideal venue for a metacognitive approach to academic problem solving at the preschool level.

Let's take a look at how the academic set of SELf-questions can be sprinkled onto various components of just one unit through a gradual release model. Many resources advocate for the gradual release model (Cohen et al., 2021; Fisher & Frey, 2021; Pearson & Gallagher, 1983), which we first featured in this book in figure 4.1 (page 72). While there are many valid variations on the implementation of gradual release, we stand by the following.

- **I do, you watch:** Teacher models use of SELf-questioning.
- **I do, you help:** Teacher models use of SELf-questioning with students' suggestions.
- **You do, I help:** Students use SELf-questioning with teacher support and suggestions.
- **You do, I watch:** Students use SELF-questioning independently.

When using this model, as you have seen in previous chapters, teachers go through the SELf-question sets to see what the area of need is in their classroom, and it works the same way when utilizing inquiry-based learning.

One of the units of study in *The Creative Curriculum for Preschool* centers on balls (Teaching Strategies, 2020a). You will see in the following sections that a teacher must use the think aloud method to present each structured SELf-question to students. Because preschoolers are young, modeling each question and guiding students through their thinking to find out the answer provides a framework for how to think through each SELf-question. Through modeling, the ultimate goal is for students to internalize the framework as they grow, not just for emotions but also for academics. Eventually, they learn to independently apply structured SELf-questioning during academic opportunities.

Modeling Academic SELf-Questions for Students

In the first phase of the gradual release model, the teacher asks and answers many of the SELf-questions for their students. Modeling is the entirety of this phase, with students acting as observers. Cohen and colleagues (2021) add that when teachers model the SELf-questions, they demonstrate their own metacognitive thinking by thinking aloud. Using our Creative Curriculum example introduced in the previous section, this phase occurs during week 1 of the ball unit, which is focused on the inquiry question, *What do we know about balls?* (Teaching Strategies, 2020a). Conveniently, this question overlaps with the first step of the SELf-questioning process.

Select a Focus

When beginning any long-term inquiry, teachers can use the first step of structured SELf-questioning (Select a Focus) by understanding that the problem or question being asked comes from the curriculum itself. The broad inquiry question "What do we know about balls?" is answered as students participate in daily hands-on activities. While it may feel like a coincidence that this topic and question align so perfectly with the SELf-question "What do we know about ____________?" you will find that any topic or unit of instruction in a curriculum aligns similarly well.

Consider the following example of how a teacher might complete this step with students.

> *I complete the first step of the structured SELf-questioning process by selecting a focus. The question I ask students is, "What is the question?"*

> *I introduce the inquiry topic by showing photos of balls on the SMART Board. I model asking, "What is the question?" Students begin to label what they see on the board: "Tennis ball!" "Baseball!"*
>
> *I repeat, "What is the question? We need to know what we know about balls and what we want to find out about balls. Our questions are, 'What do we know about balls?' and 'What do we want to find out about balls?'"*

Gather Information

The second step in the structured SELf-questioning process is Gather Information. Here, questions include: "What do I know? What do I need to know? What is similar and what is different?" One activity that is useful for this step is creating a KWL chart during whole-group time. A teacher can model gathering information through a think aloud by asking, "What do I know?" For learners with diverse abilities, access to tactile and kinesthetic experiences proves beneficial, as in this example.

> *In my special education preschool classroom, I use a mystery bag when asking the question, "What do I know?"*
>
> *I fill the mystery bag with balls of different colors, shapes, and sizes. Some are full of air, while others are deflated. I model asking students, "What do I know?" by opening the bag and pulling out one ball. I model language for my students, "I see an orange ball with black lines. It's a basketball. Basketball starts with the letter B." I then model writing the word 'BASKETBALL' on the SMART Board. One of my students who can read shouts, "Basketball!" I affirm him: "You're right. It's a basketball. I wonder what else is in my bag."*

Brainstorm

The third step in the structured SELf- questioning process is Brainstorm. Here, teachers model asking the question, "What can I do?" Cohen and colleagues (2021) describe the significance of flexibility when problem solving through this step. They specify that when teachers allow students to come up with more than one possible solution to solving a problem, they not only become flexible thinkers but can also gain higher-order cognitive skills, as in the following.

> *"I have a mystery bag. I want to find out what else is inside. What can I do?" I model saying and pointing to the core word* open *on the giant core board behind me. Students become excited. Shouts of "My turn!" erupt from circle time. "Oh!" I say playfully. "Should Ms. Young open the bag, or should my friends?"*
>
> *Students begin to shout, "Open please!" and "I'll do it!" Paraprofessionals model the core word* open *using students' AAC devices, and students imitate their actions by touching* open *using their laminated core boards.*

Evaluate

Cohen and colleagues (2021) state that within the Evaluate step there is a reflection of the Brainstorm step. Within the first phase of the gradual release model, teachers determine the best way to solve a problem and determine if it makes sense.

> *I have a choice to make as I model asking the question, "What is the best way to solve this problem?" Should I open the bag myself? Or should I let my students do it? Does this make sense? It makes more sense for my students to open the bag, as I want them to have an active role in their learning. Giving students an active role in their learning allows for the possibility of the onus to be taken off the teacher and placed onto the students, as Cohen and colleagues (2021) describe.*

Plan and Act

During the Plan and Act step, teachers model the question, "What do I do first, second, and so on?" During this step, a teacher can verbally or visually place each step of their thinking in order.

> *"I see. It seems like my friends want to open the mystery bag! Let's think. I know. We can make a list to help us solve our problem." I ask my friends, "What do I do first? First, I will write Chris's name, and he will have a chance to open the mystery bag and share his ideas. Then I will write Brad's name, and he will get a turn." I model. "First Chris goes, then Brad." Then I ask, "Who is next?" Parker raises his hand, and I state, "First Parker, then Julie." Students watch as I, the teacher, ask and answer.*
>
> *Students are then invited to come up one at a time and pull a ball out of the mystery bag. Language is modeled for the students by myself and the paraprofessionals as they explore the balls. Students may spontaneously state the color of a ball or demonstrate how they can roll, kick, or throw the ball. As the students are talking about what they know about balls, the paraprofessionals are writing their responses next to their name on the list.*

Reflect

The final step is to Reflect. Teachers model asking the question, "Did it work?"

> *While reflecting, I point to the list we created during the Plan and Act step. I share each contribution they made. "We said that we wanted to find out what we know about balls, and we made a plan for each friend to share when Ms. Young pointed to their name on the list. Did our plan work?"*
>
> *Larry smiles. "Yes. Me and Kim both said we know a lot about balls."*
>
> *I ask, "Did it work?" and Kim answers, "Yes." I affirm the answer by stating, "Our plan worked because each student was able to share."*

Guiding Students to Use the Academic SELf-Questions

In the second phase of the gradual release model, the teacher continues to ask the SELf-questions, while the students do more of the answering, although not completely independently of the teacher or each other. In *The Creative Curriculum for Preschool*, the inquiry question at the center of week 2 of the ball unit is, "How do balls bounce?" (Teaching Strategies, n.d.a). However, as stated previously, you can adapt this approach to your own curriculum. An activity done during week 2 of the ball inquiry is a game that involves numbered ping pong balls, a bowl filled with water, and plastic tongs. Students who need a challenge are asked to pick up two numbered ping pong balls and add the sum of the numbers together. Let's add two numbered ping pong balls together using the second phase in the gradual release model and structured SELf-questioning.

Select a Focus

As aforementioned, the Select a Focus question asked to students comes from the curriculum. Teachers model asking the SELf-question and the academic question to students. This still falls under the "I do, you help" phase of the gradual release model because the teacher is asking the question, and the students are helping answer it as they repeat the answer to the question. Conversely, in the first phase, the teacher is doing all the answering and asking. Of course, in a preschool classroom, students are bound to shout out answers, but the teacher is ensuring the SELf-questioning language is used appropriately in all phases of the gradual release model.

> *First, I model pulling two ping pong balls out of the water. One ball has the number three on it. The other ball has the number six on it. The student identifies the number six and the number three. I state, "What is the problem? The problem I need to solve is, What is three plus six?" I wonder aloud, "I wonder how I can add three plus six?" I then ask myself, "What is the problem?" and my student says, "What is three plus six?"*

Gather Information

Within the Gather Information step, teachers and students learn how to become aware of and manage the application of their thinking. Cohen and colleagues (2021) point out that this step portrays an individual's ability to strategically critique the information they have at their disposal. When these questions are asked during the second phase of the gradual release model, the student might answer part of one of the questions as follows.

> *I ask my student, "What do I know?" The student points to the numbers on the balls and labels them by stating, "Three and six." I affirm the student's answer. "You're right. We know that one ball has the number three on it, and the other ball has the number six on it."*
>
> *I then model asking my student, "What do I need to know?" and answer the question aloud: "I need to know how to add three plus six. I need to know what number three and six make when they are added together."*

Brainstorm

As the Brainstorm step is where preschoolers begin to become flexible thinkers, observe in the following example how the student notices both options that the teacher lays out for him. You will notice that the teacher provides two possible solutions for the student, using the phase, "I do, you help." However, more onus is now placed on the student than in the first phase of the gradual release model.

> *I model brainstorming through a think aloud: "How can I solve this problem?" I offer two solutions using visual cue cards. A student looks at the cards and says what he sees: "This card says I can count on my fingers." He looks at the other card and says, "This card says, draw circles."*

Evaluate

Cohen and colleagues (2021) advocate for the transfer of metacognition from teacher to student. In the following Evaluate example, the teacher gives the student the opportunity to answer the SELf-question from two constructed choices.

> *I ask the student their preference for solving the problem. "What is the best way to solve this problem?" Why do I do this? Giving students choice leads to ownership over their learning! The way one student wants to solve the problem may differ from the way another student chooses to solve it. This particular student chooses to draw a picture.*

Plan and Act

During the Plan and Act step, teachers model the question, "What do I do first, second, and so on?" During the second phase of the gradual release model, the teacher asks all the questions, and the student helps as they answer guiding questions closely related to SELf-questions, such as the "How many?" question that follows. This differs from the first phase of the gradual release model, as the students watched while the teacher asked and answered each question.

> *During the Plan and Act step, I model asking the student the question, "What do I do first, second, and so on?" Again, I remind the student of the problem by guiding them through the steps. "What do I do first? Let's first draw three circles using a yellow crayon. What do I do second? How many circles will you draw with the red crayon?" The student answers, "Six!"*
>
> *I continue. "What is my last step? Finally, we can count the total number of circles." Together, the student and I count the total number of circles. The student shouts, "Nine!"*

Reflect

Cohen and colleagues (2021) acknowledge how the Reflect step helps both the teacher and the learner assess the journey thus far. In the first phase of the gradual release model, the teacher modeled both asking and answering, "Did it work?" In the second phase, the student answers the question their teacher poses. A teacher should be mindful that a student is not answering "yes" for the sake of answering "yes," rather students should be empowered to actually check their work. Say a student got a wrong answer. They might share that their strategy did *not* work. In this phase, a teacher could remind the student to go back and check their work before disputing the strategy they chose.

> *Before asking the student, "Did it work?" I reflect on the strategy they used, not just the answer they gave. It is imperative to remember that while it is fantastic the student gave the correct answer, the structured SELf-questioning process is a metacognitive strategy. We need students to think about how they get their answers! I say, "You chose to draw a picture to represent three plus six equals nine. Did it work?" The student answers, "Yes, circles." We can check that the chosen strategy worked by counting the circles with the student. Along with metacognition, this reflection activity promotes one-to-one correspondence.*

Releasing Students to Use the Academic SELf-Questions

In the third phase of the gradual release model, the teacher continues to ask the students the SELf-questions, and the students answer them as independently as possible. Cohen and colleagues (2021) utilize Pearson & Gallagher's (1983) model by associating the phrase *you do, I help* with this phase. Here, *you do, I help*, and *you do, I watch* are combined depending on a student's level of independence.

Please understand that the gradual release model does not assume that all students will be able to ask and answer each academic SELf-question independently, and it does not expect them to do so. Following a gradual release model takes each student's development and differing abilities into account. Success looks different for every student. Some students will ask and answer the SELf-questions by themselves, while others will find success with the teacher asking the questions and the student answering, similar to the second phase of the gradual release model.

Returning to our example from *The Creative Curriculum for Preschool*, the focus question for week 3 of the ball inquiry is, "How do balls roll?" and one activity for this portion of the unit is bowling (Teaching Strategies, 2020a). The purpose of this activity is for students to roll a plastic ball and count the number of pins they have knocked down. Let's take a look at bowling through the lens of the academic and social structured SELf-question set and the third phase of the gradual release model.

Select a Focus

When we Select a Focus, the concept can be as simple or complex as an individual wants. When two students in this class, Ashna and Maddie, are in the blocks center, they decide they want to bowl. It is Ashna's turn to bowl. "What is the task, Ashna?" I ask. You'll see that in this third phase, the student begins to answer in more depth than the student answered in the second phase, even asking herself an additional SELf-question that falls under the Select a Focus category.

Here, Ashna answers. "I can knock down so many pins! What is the problem? What is the number I knocked down?"

I affirm Ashna's answer. "She needs to know, how many pins is she going to knock down? Ashna's question is, 'How many pins did I knock down?'" I confirm Ashna's response and model asking the girls, "Ashna asked herself the question, 'What is the problem?' How many did she knock down?"

Gather Information

When we Gather Information, we survey the information that students have readily available to them. You will see that the teacher continues to model the question, as she did in the first and second phases. Please be aware that students may have the ability to ask themselves the questions, as Ashna did in the previous step. Ashna and Maddie Gather Information as they determine what they need to know independently in the third phase of the gradual release model.

I ask my students, "What do I know?" The girls shout out answers, labeling the colors of the bowling pins and stating, "Give me the ball."

I use parallel talk: "You are telling me that we have different color pins. You are saying that we can use the ball to knock the pins down."

"Yeah," Ashna says. "But I need to know how I can find out if it's one, two, or seven."

"What number?" Maddie asks, and Ashna continues: "How many pins will my ball hit?"

"Yes, Ashna. You need to know how you can find out the number of pins you knock down after you roll the ball," I say.

Brainstorm

When we Brainstorm, more than one possible solution should be derived. "But how?" Maddie asks. You'll notice that Maddie did not use the exact wording of the SELf-question, "What can I do?" but her language was relevant. Therefore, in the third phase, as opposed to the second or the first, more onus is placed on the student. I model asking the SELf-question, "What can I do?"

Ashna answers, independent of her teacher. "Roll it, then count the pins that are up, up, up!"

"No!" says Maddie. "We need to wait until the ball rolls and count the ones that the ball knocks over."

Maddie, who has been using SELf-questioning for a while, is able to help her friend. However, a teacher can take this one step further by not declining the wrong answer. I say, "What can we do? We can count the pins that Ashna knocks down or count the pins that are standing up now."

Evaluate

When we Evaluate, as when we go through any steps in our structured SELf-question process, we want to teach metacognition. I ask, "Does this make sense?" as I want the girls to reflect on the first step of selecting a focus. "Does it make sense to count the pins that are standing up? We said that our task is to count the pins that are knocked down."

> *"No!" cries Ashna. "We gotta roll the ball, then count the pins that it knocks over."*
>
> *I want the girls to lead and for me to help only by reminding the students of the strategies they have learned to count: "Let's think of the best way to solve this problem."*
>
> *Maddie smiles as she says, "Touch and count or line up and count."*
>
> *"Let's touch and count," answers Ashna. "That makes sense."*

Here, you can see that the girls independently evaluated their options while the teacher observed from the side.

Plan and Act

In the third phase of the gradual release model, a teacher may create a visual for their students to plan and act as independently as possible. I write the numbers one and two on a whiteboard.

> *"What should Ashna do first? Roll the ball or count the number of pins she knocked down?"*
>
> *"First roll, then count," says Ashna.*
>
> *First-then language is often used in the classroom to manage behaviors. I draw a picture of a bowling ball next to the number one on the whiteboard and the numbers one, two, three in quotes next to the number two on the whiteboard. I affirm the student's response by telling them that Ashna cannot count the number of pins knocked down until she rolls the ball. I verbalize the girls' plan out loud and present it to the students by pointing to the numbers on the whiteboard.*
>
> *Maddie says, "Ashna will roll the ball first, then touch and count the number of knocked down pins."*
>
> *Ashna follows through with the plan as Maddie points to the numbers one and two on her whiteboard.*

Reflect

In this phase of the gradual release model, the teacher may still ask the question as opposed to the students to Reflect on the learning.

As Ashna and Maddie declare "Five," I use the Reflect question as an opportunity to challenge my students as I state, "I see that you knocked down four pins! Did it work? Do you need to go back and check?"

Maddie smiles and shakes her head. "Yes! One, two, three, four. Silly Miss Young."

Reflecting on the ability to correct a person's mistakes within the process is another way that the third phase of the gradual release model can differ from the second or first phase. Of course, the use of humor and correcting the teacher can add levity and increase student confidence with their metacognitive skills.

Scenarios for Inquiry-Based Units for Academic and Social Problem Solving

The following sections offer two example scenarios for interactions between teachers and students that are focused on academic problem solving in inquiry-based units. Note that the scope of these scenarios each includes all steps within the metacognitive strategy for SELf-questioning, as illustrated in figure 1.3 (page 18).

Scenario 1: Work With Numerals and Quantities

Program: Preschool disabilities

Objective: Connect numerals with their quantities.

Standard: 4.1.2 "Recognize and name one-digit written numbers up to 10 with minimal prompting" (Teaching Strategies, n.d.a, p. 25).

Teacher: Mr. Benny

Mr. Benny pulls two students, Jeremy and Brian, for small-group instruction. The purpose of this small group is to place a quantity of marbles into the appropriate numbered container on the light table.

SELECT A FOCUS

SELf-Question: What is the question?

Mr. Benny pulls out red and blue cups labeled with the numbers three and five on them. He models asking the students the structured SELf-question, "What is the question?" Mr. Benny answers, "How many marbles should I put in this red cup?"

GATHER INFORMATION

SELf-Question: What is my goal?

Mr. Benny asks Jeremy and Brian, "What do I need to know?" He wonders aloud. "I need to know how many marbles to put in the red cup. I also need to know what the number on the red cup is."

BRAINSTORM

SELf-Question: How can I solve this problem?

Mr. Benny models asking the SELf-question, "How can I solve this problem?"

He gives the students adequate wait time until Jeremy enthusiastically states, "You have to count!" Brian wonders, "Count what?" Mr. Benny smiles and affirms, "Count the marbles!" He adds, "We need to do one more thing. We need to know what number is on my special red cup."

EVALUATE

SELf-Question: What is the best way to solve this problem?

Mr. Benny asks his students, "What is the best way to solve this problem?"

Jeremy exclaims that he will count the marbles from the pile, and Brian says that he will figure out what the number on the cup is. Then, Jeremy says he will put that many marbles in the red cup. Mr. Benny tells his students, "Great thinking!"

PLAN AND ACT

SELf-Question: What do I do first, second, and so on?

Mr. Benny tells his students that it is time to plan and act. "When we plan," he says, "we decide what we are going to do first, second, and third. When we act," he continues, "we begin to see if our plan is working. Let's make a plan."

"The red cup says number five," asserts Brian.

"OK," Mr. Benny reinforces Brian's thinking. "You're right. Brian completed our first step of identifying the number on the cup. Now, what should we do next?"

Jeremy answers his teacher excitedly. "I'll count the marbles right here!"

"One, two, three, four, five, six, seven! Seven little marbles!"

Mr. Benny gives his student a high five. "You're right! There are seven marbles. First, Brian told us the number on the cup, and then you counted the marbles. Is our plan working? Yes it is! What do we do last?"

Jeremy gives Brian a high five. "Let's drop five marbles in the red cup. Me first, then you." Together, the boys take turns dropping each marble inside the red cup.

REFLECT

SELf-Question: Did it work?

Mr. Benny congratulates his students for their fine teamwork of putting the marbles inside the cup. He models asking the SELf-question, "Did it work?" Brian and Jeremy look at each other and smile. "Yeah! The marbles are in the cup." Mr. Benny reminds his students to check their work. Together, the children acknowledge that the number on the red cup is indeed number five and that there are five marbles in the cup. Mr. Benny confirms his students' thinking: "In small group today, we worked on connecting numerals with their quantities. The cup has a five on it, and you put five marbles in the cup!"

Scenario 2: Work With Letters of the Alphabet

Grade: Integrated preschool

Objective: Identify letters.

Standard: RF.PK.1d "Recognize and name many upper and lower case letters of the alphabet" (Teaching Strategies, n.d.a, p. 15).

Teacher: Mrs. Herold

Mrs. Herold pulls two four-year-old students, Maria and Stella, who are out of centers for small-group instruction. She explains that today, the purpose of the small group is to identify letters. She continues by saying that she will lay out twenty-six cards on the floor with one letter on each card. Students are to use a fly swatter to hit the letters that they hear aloud!

SELECT A FOCUS

SELf-Question: What is the question?

Mrs. Herold models the structured SELf-question by asking the students, "What is the question?" Mrs. Herold answers, "How many letters do I know?"

GATHER INFORMATION

SELf-Question: What is my goal?

Mrs. Herold models aloud, "What is my goal?" She wonders aloud. "My goal is to identify the letters I know by hitting them with the fly swatter when Mrs. Herold says the letter name!"

BRAINSTORM

SELf-Question: How can I solve this problem?

Mrs. Herold models asking the SELf-question, "How can I solve this problem?" Maria repeats, "You can hit the letters with the fly swatter!" Stella adds, "But what if I do not know the letter?" Mrs. Herold suggests, "We can work together to find the letter!"

EVALUATE

SELf-Question: What is the best way to solve this problem?

Mrs. Herold then models, "So, what is the best way to solve this problem?" Maria states, "One of us can hit the letters with the fly swatter, and the other can help!" Mrs. Herold tells her students, "Great thinking!"

PLAN AND ACT

SELf-Question: What do I do first, second, and so on?

Mrs. Herold continues, "What do I do first?"

Stella says, "First, you can use the fly swatter."

Mrs. Herold says, "What do I do second?"

Stella continues, "Second, you can give the fly swatter to Maria, and then I can go!" Maria states, "And if you need help finding the letters, you can ask for help!" Mrs. Herold cheers, "Great, let's try it!"

Mrs. Herold goes first and models how to use the fly swatter and continues, "I will find A! There it is!" Mrs. Herold lightly taps the A on the floor with the fly swatter then passes it to Maria.

Mrs. Herold asks Maria to find H.

Maria says, "Hmmm. I don't know where H is. Can you help me?"

Stella takes a closer look and helps Maria find the letter H.

Stella yells, "Maria, I found H."

Maria walks over and hits the H on the ground with the fly swatter!

They continue to take turns and work together until they identify all of the letters in the alphabet.

REFLECT

SELf-Question: Did it work?

Mrs. Herold celebrates their amazing teamwork and perseverance when identifying letters. She models the SELf-question, "Did it work?" Stella and Maria high five and answer, "Yes!"

Mrs. Herold reiterates, "Today, our small group was about identifying letters! You made a plan to take turns and help each other identify the letter you did not know. You worked together to identify all twenty-six letters in the alphabet!"

Conclusion

This chapter discussed how preschool teachers can use the academic problem-solving set in tandem with the inquiry-based learning they already have in place. Structured SELf-questioning is *not* a curriculum, nor is it meant to add more to a teacher's plate. You may choose to begin using the academic problem-solving set during one area of your day, such as small group, then increase its usage throughout the school day. As you begin to use the SELf-questions over time, your students are more likely to generalize them across other times and areas within the classroom.

If you are in a classroom with a paraprofessional, encourage your paraprofessional to use the SELf-questions with students as they reinforce concepts you've previously taught. You and your paraprofessionals can ask the SELf-questions of each other as you deliver whole-group instruction during circle time or similar activities.

This chapter referenced the gradual release model as supported by Pearson and Gallagher (1983) and Fisher and Frey (2021). Only the educator can determine when their students are ready to move into the second or third phase. There is no timeline nor pressure for when students should be ready to adapt their thinking to the following phase.

In the next chapter, you will see how to apply additional academic problem solving within the classroom to guide students to become metacognitive readers.

Parent Corner

Just as parents and caregivers can use the resources from the Parent Corners in previous chapters to support their child's growth at home, teachers can provide the similar resources in this chapter to support their child's sense of academic inquiry.

In the reproducible "SELf-Questioning 101: Teaching Academic Inquiry to Your Child" (page 133), parents or caregivers will see how a parent, Maria, easily navigates the academic problem-solving set with her preschooler, Ellie. The reproducible chart that follows, "SELf-Questioning 101: School-to-Home Application" (page 134) takes parent or caregiver involvement a step further by offering a resource teachers can give parents to support any relevant activity. This resource is intended to guide parents on how to use the metacognitive strategy of structured SELf-questioning for academic problem solving to complete academic activities in the home environment.

SELf-Questioning 101: Teaching Academic Inquiry to Your Child

Let's take a look at how a parent or caregiver (Maria, in this example) can easily implement academic problem solving with her preschool daughter (Ellie) at home. Each week, Ellie's teacher sends home a *School-to-Home Connection Activity*. This week's activity is titled, "What was for breakfast?" (Teaching Strategies, 2017) in which students draw a representation of what they had for breakfast. Ellie's teacher provides a table of the step names and SELf-questions a parent or caregiver could use as they engage in the activity with their child.

SELf-Questioning Step	SELf-Question Selected	Parent and Child Responses
Select a Focus	What is the question?	**Maria:** "Let's get started on your homework, Ellie. Your teacher wants you to draw a picture of what you ate for breakfast. Let's select a focus by answering the question. What is the question?" **Ellie:** "I need to draw what I ate before I went to school!"
Gather Information	What do I know? What do I need to know?	**Maria:** "We can gather information by asking the question, What do I know? What do you know about your breakfast, Ellie?" **Ellie:** "I know I ate it before I saw my teacher. I know it was really yummy, but I can't remember what I ate."
Brainstorm	What can I do?	**Maria:** "Let's brainstorm. We can ask the question, 'What can I do?'" **Ellie:** "I said I can't remember!" **Maria:** "OK. When we brainstorm, we come up with more than one solution. We can ask your grandma who made your breakfast. Or, we can look in the fridge to see if seeing the food we have jogs your memory."
Evaluate	What is the best way to solve this problem?	**Ellie:** "Let's look in the fridge. I'm hungry!"
Plan and Act	What do I do first, second, and so on?	**Maria:** "It's time to plan and act. What should we do first?" **Ellie:** "Open the fridge and look inside." **Maria:** "OK. What will you do after you look in the fridge?" **Ellie:** "I will get my crayons out and draw my picture!" Maria and Ellie look in the fridge and see a carton of eggs. Ellie verbalizes that she had eggs this morning and begins to draw her picture.
Reflect	Did it work?	After Ellie's picture is finished and is proudly hanging on the fridge, Maria and Ellie reflect. **Maria:** "Did our plan of looking in the fridge work?" **Ellie (smiling):** "Yes!"

Teaching Strategies. (2017). Intentional teaching experiences: What was for breakfast? Language and Literacy, LL40. *Bethesda, MD: Author.*

SELf-Questioning 101: School-to-Home Application

We have been learning about ____.
To enhance your child's learning, please use the following resource, including examples of SELf-questions and responses to apply structured SELf-questioning while completing the provided activity.

SELf-Questioning Step	SELf-Questions	Parent and Child Responses
Select a Focus	What is the problem? What is the question? What is the task? What is important? What is the user's need?	**Parent:** **Child:**
Gather Information	What do I know? What do I need to know? What is important?	**Parent:** **Child:**

SELf-Questioning Step	SELf-Questions	Parent and Child Responses
Brainstorm	How can I solve this problem? What can I do? What are possible solutions? What is similar, and what is different?	**Parent:** **Child:**
Evaluate	What is the best way to solve this problem? Does this make sense? What are possible consequences?	**Parent:** **Child:**

SELf-Questioning Step	SELf-Questions	Parent and Child Responses
Plan and Act	What do I do first, second, and so on? Is this working?	**Parent:** **Child:**
Reflect	Did it work? How do I know?	**Parent:** **Child:**

page 3 of 3

A Practical Guide to Developing Metacognitive and Self-Monitoring Readers

7

Schools must take steps to shift away from a siloed approach. . . . Instead, the focus should be on an integrated, systemic framework, in which parallel processes of interrelated competencies for both educators and students are identified, built, and sustained.

—Nadja N. Reilly

We are big fans of the epigraph for this chapter for a number of reasons. First, it emphasizes the need to design and provide interdisciplinary curriculum and instruction that is utilized not only by preschool students but also by adults, whether they be teachers, administrators, or parents. Second, the strategy can be promoted and modeled easily by parents in the home to support students' development and transfer of the strategy from school to home, as we will explain in the Parent Corner section at the end of this chapter (page 156). Third, it shines a light on the importance, power, and potential of our two SELf-question sets as parallel processes of interrelated competencies within an integrated systemic framework.

The key to success with using the SELf-question sets as parallel processes in preschool is to thoughtfully begin teaching students how to strategically transfer their developing metacognitive and self-monitoring skills across social-emotional contexts (as explained in chapters 3–5) to academic content (as explained in chapter 6 and in this chapter). To that end, this chapter dips its toes into transfer theory and shows how and why the metacognitive strategy of structured SELf-questioning can transition seamlessly from self-monitoring and social-emotional contexts to developing metacognitive and self-monitoring readers.

The Importance of Teaching a Metacognitive Strategy in Reading

You have likely noticed, by this point, how the content progression in this book for using SELf-questions has progressed from implementing from the emotional spectrum to social to academic (in the form of inquiry). This chapter continues that progression by demonstrating how, in just the first few weeks, you can support the transfer of the knowledge and skills learned already to the learning and application of the academic and social SELf-question set through the lens of reading instruction. In addition to learning how this one strategy and SELf-question set further develop the SEL competency of responsible decision making, this chapter also demonstrates how embedding this strategy into reading instruction also further enhances the SEL competency of social awareness as well as the character trait of empathy. To be able to accomplish all this with just one strategy and question set in just one academic content area, we'll examine how the strategy and question set can be used in three aspects of any and every preschool reading program and curriculum.

As a reminder, structured SELf-questioning is not designed to replace or supplant any preschool reading program or curriculum. We recommend that the structure and SELf-questions from both SELf-question sets should instead be sprinkled on top of already existing programs and routines. In the following sections, we'll look at the components of an effective preschool reading program and show how those connect with structured SELf-questioning.

Components of Preschool Reading Programs

There are three distinct components of any and every effective preschool reading program and curriculum.

1. **Picture clues:** The strategy supports students' ability to read and make inferences about the feelings of characters in the story by asking themselves, "How do they feel?"
2. **Decoding:** The strategy supports students' ability to problem solve unknown words, prompting their already learned reading decoding strategies and skills by asking themselves, "What do I know?"
3. **Reading comprehension:** The strategy supports students' ability to identify the plot and make meaning of events in stories and children's literature by asking themselves a combination of SELf-questions to prompt deeper understanding and comprehension.

Just like with the social and emotional SELf-question set, the best and most effective way to use the academic and social SELf-question set is to incorporate eye-dropper doses of the strategy and SELf-questions into these three components of sound reading instruction. By teaching these components, teachers help students not only develop the habits of mind of more persistent, independent readers but also practice the strategy of structured SELf-questioning across different tasks and challenges they come across as readers. When practice is applied during small group or one-to-one guided reading sessions, the teacher can provide timely feedback on student application and prompt transfer of the SELf-questions across academic, social, and emotional contexts in numerous ways. For example, teachers can use the SELf-questions to prompt students to make text to self connections about the feelings of the characters in the story, problems and events of the story, and social problems that occur in small group or at the independent reading or library center.

On that note, let's start first with how to utilize the metacognitive strategy of structured SELf-questioning to develop the kind of social awareness and empathy conducive to caring classrooms in the first few weeks of school.

Reading and the SELf-Questions

We start this exploration by talking about utilizing structured SELf-questioning for picture clues, because that is where we strongly recommend all preschool teachers start using the strategy in their reading instruction (before utilizing the strategy for decoding or reading comprehension). By teaching students right at the start of the school year how to use SELf-questions to be both better readers of books and better readers of the feelings of others, becoming more socially aware of and empathic to the feelings of others in their own classrooms, the classroom environment will improve even in that first month. Just as preschoolers are learning morning routines such as using the social and emotional SELf-question set in morning meeting time to read their own feelings and the feelings of their classmates, showing them simultaneously how to use SELf-questions to read the feelings of characters is extremely efficient. Embedding multiple applications of SELf-questions for reading the feelings of others at a time when preschool classrooms are building and establishing relationships is a huge key to successfully establishing caring classroom cultures built on the value of empathy.

Recall the academic and social SELf-questions introduced in the first chapter about the evidence-based underpinnings of this approach (see figure 1.3, page 18). As a quick reminder, the questions break down as follows.

- **Select a Focus:** What is the problem? What is the question? What is the task? What is important? What is the user's need?
- **Gather Information:** What do I know? What do I need to know? What is important? How does he, she, or they feel?
- **Brainstorm:** What can I do? How can I solve this problem? What are possible solutions? What is similar, and what is different? What connections can I make?
- **Evaluate:** What is the best way to solve this problem? Does this make sense? What are the possible consequences?
- **Plan and Act:** What do I do first, second, and so on? Is this working?
- **Reflect:** Did it work? How do I know?

Since most of the initial exposure to structured SELf-questioning that occurs in the first few weeks of preschool is focused on the social and emotional SELf-question set, focusing students on one SELf-question from that set—"How does he, she, or they feel?"—also has numerous advantages as the place to start exposing students to the academic and social SELf-question set. First, the SELf-question "How does he, she, they feel?" is found in both SELf-question sets. Since this may be the first experience preschool students will have using SELf-questions for academic instruction and academic skill development, using a familiar question that they have already applied during morning meeting or circle time is less overwhelming and less confusing to preschoolers.

Second, one very important construct of teaching the strategy of structured SELf-questioning is the concept of transfer. There are different forms of transfer, and there are many different definitions of transfer. The definition of *transfer* we like best for all levels of education but especially for preschool is applying skills, knowledge, or attitudes learned in one content area, context, or situation to another content area, context, or situation (Perkins & Solomon, 1992). Susan Olsen Stevens writes about the different forms of transfer in the "Transfer Theory and SELf-Questioning" chapter of *The Metacognitive Student*:

> Transfer can take place between situations that are quite similar (near- or low-road transfer) and also between situations that share some qualities but are dissimilar (far- or high-road transfer). Transfer can also take place from problem to problem, class to class, home to school, or school to work. When teachers refer to students utilizing prior knowledge to complete or further a task, they're referring to transfer. It is a key ability for learning and developing competencies for life. (Cohen et al., 2021, p. 139)

We utilized this guidance to develop a cohesive and comprehensive scope and sequence for the embedding of structured SELf-questioning into any reading programming. Toward this far-reaching end of teaching students how to independently apply their metacognitive problem-solving and self-monitoring skills learned from social-emotional contexts to reading, the process of teaching preschool students transfer is recommended to begin with near transfer. Therefore, challenging preschoolers to apply one common SELf-question of "How does he, she, or they feel?" to "read" the feelings of characters in a story (as a reading comprehension strategy) is very similar to the way students can be challenged to apply that same SELf-question in think-pair-share exercises in morning meeting or circle time (as an SEL competency of social awareness).

To understand the importance of, and the unique opportunities presented by, the use of structured SELf-questioning for decoding, let's take a look at some of the teachings of both Deanne Kildare Opatosky and Susan Olsen Stevens from "Structured SELf-Questioning in Reading Decoding":

> Although much of decoding is more cognitive than metacognitive, metacognition enters the picture when students determine if a word makes sense or sounds right in a given context. Although parents often encourage their children to sound out or stretch words out to decode, teachers need to empower readers with a broader repertoire of decoding strategies to identify unknown words in a text. Because parents seldom prompt their children to use any other strategies besides producing the sounds for each individual letter in a word, it is essential that educators teach students other strategies, model those strategies, and query students . . . to think about how the strategies interact with each other and reflect on why a particular strategy was or was not successful in identifying an unknown word. (Cohen et al., 2021, p. 77)

Do preschoolers being strategic in their reading sound too optimistic? It is not the expectation that all preschoolers master numerous decoding strategies and also master the ability to take a step back and have a think about, analyze, and evaluate the strategies available to them, or reflect on why one strategy is better suited than another in a particular text. However, we have seen that many kindergartners can master such a far-reaching metacognitive skill set. Exposing preschoolers through a guided release approach—the teacher using the SELf-questions in *you* format—not only strengthens preschoolers as emerging readers but also reinforces and provides practice opportunities for the overall strategy of structured SELf-questioning.

In the next section, we will show how teachers can model the application of the metacognitive strategy in decoding unknown words and how to use the academic and social SELf-questions in the second person *you* format to select one decoding strategy over another. In other words, we show how preschool teachers teach students how to be strategic about their strategies to figure out unknown words. But first, let's focus on how, in *The Metacognitive Student*, Opatosky and Stevens also teach how metacognition plays a vital role in developing young readers' comprehension skills:

> Metacognition is what readers use to monitor their understanding and make adjustments as they read. It comes into play in additional components of reading, such as making connections, questioning, visualizing, inferring, synthesizing information, and evaluating. Metacognitive thinking also helps readers choose when to apply a certain strategy. Annemarie Sullivan Palincsar and Ann L. Brown of the Center for the Study of Reading at the University of Illinois find, "Metacognitively skilled readers seek to establish 'meaningfulness' in their reading and value careful selection of appropriate strategies and careful monitoring of their comprehension" (as cited in Kolencik & Hillwig, 2011, p. 88).
>
> When reading, metacognition is what takes readers beyond mere identification of words into a sphere where they truly understand what the author has written, discuss (internally or out loud) the author's ideas or messages as they read. (Cohen et al., 2021, pp. 59–60)

Does this also sound too optimistic for preschoolers? As with decoding, kindergartners have shown the ability to be strategic about their reading comprehension strategies to develop habits as meaning makers as they read. Therefore, teacher modeling of the metacognitive strategy of structured SELf-questioning to comprehend stories and children's literature as they read, as well as engaging preschoolers in SELf-questioning while reading, helps in the multi-year process of developing metacognitive readers. The next section not only shows you how the academic and social SELf-question set can teach preschoolers how to be strategic about their decoding strategies but also about comprehension strategies.

How to Teach a Metacognitive Strategy in Reading

This section aims to show clearly and simply the road map to achieve what Nadja N. Reilly (2017) refers to in the epigraph of this chapter as the perfect example of an "interrelated academic, personal and social competency." Reading instruction is the perfect platform to marry the CASEL (n.d.) SEL competencies of social awareness and responsible decision making for academic, personal, and social applications through the use of the academic and social SELf-question set. The SEL competency we recommend preschool teachers marry across academic, personal, and social contexts first is social awareness. To build the skill of reading emotions in academic contexts, we strongly recommend you begin doing so with preschool students by teaching the decoding strategy of using picture clues using the SELf-question "How does he, she, or they feel?"

Modeling for Self-Awareness, Self-Monitoring, and Far Transfer

Modeling for preschoolers how to use this SELf-question actually begins in the very first days of school when preschool teachers model for students how to use the social and emotional SELf-question, "How do I feel?" and requires a little bit of both near and far transfer as described in Reading and the SELf-Questions (page 139). In the first few weeks of preschool, we recommend in previous chapters that teachers model via think alouds during the morning meeting, asking themselves the SELf-question, "How do I feel?" Through the use of a gradual release approach (see figure 4.1, page 72), students then begin to start asking and answering for themselves these same SELf-questions while reading to develop their ability to take a step back, look inward, read their bodies or thoughts, and identify their own emotions. This helps develop the habits of mind of self-monitoring as readers. In this case of near transfer, students extend their ability to read their own emotions each morning to identify how they feel as they start their school day to their ability to read their feelings while reading. In so doing, students are self-monitoring, noticing if they are feeling confused, frustrated, or connected to the text in any way.

Next, preschool teachers model some far transfer in order to teach students how to read emotions, not by looking inward, but rather by looking outward. In this case of far transfer, students are challenged to apply their skills of identifying feelings by gathering information via a completely different path. Using self-awareness of one's own emotions while reading requires "reading emotions" to occur through a very different method than "reading emotions" of characters in a text, as discussed in chapter 1 (page 13). There are many ways to teach preschoolers how to read the emotions of others, but like any new skill, the key is modeling. Some ways preschool teachers model social awareness through the reading of the feelings of others is by doing some role play during the morning meeting with either another adult or a student volunteer.

For example, the teacher may ask the volunteer to make a sad face. Then the teacher thinks aloud, saying out loud, as if to themselves, "Hmm, something doesn't look good for our friend today. How does she feel? Well, it looks like she has a frown, and she is looking down at her shoes. I think her body and mouth are telling me she is sad." This practice of asking oneself the SELf-question and reading the facial expressions and body language of others models what far transfer of SELf-questioning for self-awareness looks and sounds like for social awareness. This practice also sets the stage for another near transfer of this same skill toward reading.

Modeling for Near Transfer

Before diving into reading, the next best step toward teaching preschoolers social awareness through SELf-questioning involves modeling how to read the facial expressions and body language of other people (not characters in a story) using visuals or photos of real faces. Preschool teachers model the near transfer of using the SELf-question, "How does he, she, or they feel?" in morning meeting time by holding up photos of children's faces and thinking aloud.

One by one, the teacher holds up a photo of a child with a clear facial expression and thinks aloud in a very similar pattern to the model in the preceding role play. The teacher may hold up a photo of a boy with a very big smile on his face. The teacher says out loud, "Wow, this student looks like he is having a very strong emotion in this picture. How does he feel? Well, I see he has a very big smile on his face, so I think he is very happy." By applying this same dialogue using many different photos of different facial expressions displaying a variety of different emotions, preschool teachers not only model thoroughly what the metacognitive strategy of SELf-questioning looks and sounds like but also develop their students' emotional vocabulary. Building preschoolers' emotional vocabulary is core to building their social awareness and, of course, is a best practice for building vocabulary. By doing this, preschool teachers have made the near transfer of the SELf-question of "How does he, she, or they feel?" go from a social skill to an academic skill.

Modeling a Picture Walk

Preschoolers are now ready to be shown how good readers use self-questioning and picture clues together to make inferences about the feelings of characters in a story. The need for this skill became more apparent than ever during school lockdowns in the spring of 2020 due to COVID-19. After a few weeks of remote instruction, all educators missed seeing their students in person and connecting with them. To lift his own spirits and to reinforce his students' development of social awareness as well as the habits of mind of good readers in challenging times, Rick asked coauthors Katie and Emily if he could do a virtual lesson for their students. They enthusiastically said, "Yes!"

Rick chose the book *When Sophie Gets Angry—Really, Really Angry* by Molly Bang (1999), which served as a great tool to model via a shared read aloud and think aloud of near transfer of the SELf-question "How does he, she, or they feel?" and picture clues to read the emotions of characters in a story.

Rick holds up the cover of the book and tells students the first thing good readers do before reading a book is to do a picture walk or book look, and ask themselves some SELf-questions. Rick points out that there is a picture on the cover of a girl and asks himself out loud, "How does she feel?" Rick then models some thinking dispositions by putting a finger on his chin, looking up, and asking himself the same SELf-question again out loud, "How does she feel?" He then looks back at the cover photo of Sophie's face and points to her eyebrows. Rick says out loud, "Well, I see her eyebrows are pointing downward." Rick then points at her mouth and says, "And I see her mouth is small, all crunched up. I think she looks mad. I am not sure, though, so I am going to do a picture walk of a few pages in the book and see." Rick then conducts a picture walk, stopping at the pages with pictures of Sophie's face and repeating the same process of asking the one SELf-question out loud, looking closely for picture clues, and making inferences about how Sophie may be feeling.

At this time, students can be challenged to apply SELf-questioning as both a reading skill and a social skill to practice near transfer of the one strategy. By asking students to do a picture walk of the last few pages and directing them to ask themselves the SELf-question "How does she feel?" and share their own inferences based on the picture clues they found, preschoolers are using a reading strategy of SELf-questioning and picture clues to make inferences. These are all incredibly powerful skills to develop for emerging readers. Students can then practice near transfer by choosing an emotion and making a face that displays that emotion. Students are then told to ask themselves, "How do they feel?" and share their inferences of what emotion a friend's face is displaying by looking at facial clues the exact same way they looked at the picture clues in books.

Gradually Releasing Responsibility With Student-to-Student Interviews

Once students have demonstrated success utilizing the SELf-question to read the emotions of others across academic and social contexts, they are ready for some more gradual release. When teachers feel that routines for think-pair-shares or turn and talks are in place, preschool teachers are able to model via role play during morning meetings how to use the SELf-question, "How does he, she, or they feel?" to gather information and read, or infer, the feelings of others.

Since they may take many weeks or even months, the far transfer of this SELf-question from an internal process to an interpersonal process may be practiced during morning meeting via student-to-student interviews, and sharing out may need to occur after the teaching of picture clues is taught explicitly in reading. As always, we strongly recommend modeling first through role play, as explained in the previous section.

After modeling has occurred, students can be released to turn to a partner and ask them a modified version of the SELf-question, "How do you feel?" Students are then forced to practice their self-awareness skills, asking themselves how they feel and reading their own emotions. Once both students have had a turn interviewing each other, the teacher then asks students to share with the class. Here is where there is a ripe opportunity to take SELf-questioning one step further, adding another SELf-question found in both question sets, "How do I know?"

It's exciting as preschoolers go from SELf-questioning across academic and social contexts to structured SELf-questioning in academic and social contexts (via the SELf-questions, "How does he, she, or they [their partner] feel?" and "How do I know?"). As this happens, the preschool teacher should model using SELf-questions in sequence out loud:

> *"How does he (my partner) feel? My partner feels excited. How do I know he feels proud? I know he feels excited about letting our butterflies out in our*

butterfly garden today because he said he told me that just now. But I also know he feels excited because I could see his eyes get very big when he talked about letting the butterflies go today."

Once students have conducted their interviews of how each other is feeling, they can be asked to share out with the whole class via think alouds following this same format modeled by the teacher. Students are then able to apply near transfer of the SELf-question "How does he, she, or they feel?" to identify the feelings of others learned from reading, and be introduced to far transfer of the SELf-question "How do I know?" as an "interrelated academic, personal and social competency" of structured SELf-questioning that Reilly (2017) challenges all educators to teach all students. This leads us to our next application of structured SELf-questioning in reading instruction: decoding.

Expanding to Multiple Strategies for Decoding

We just learned in detail how to teach a powerful reading decoding strategy by using picture clues. In *The Metacognitive Student*, we learned an important perspective to keep in mind from Opatosky and Stevens about why students need to learn multiple decoding strategies, stating, "Many decoding skills develop concurrently and are interdependent with one another, meaning readers need to learn how to use multiple decoding strategies simultaneously to identify an unknown word" (Cohen et al., 2021, p. 76). Does teaching preschoolers how to use multiple decoding strategies simultaneously sound daunting? Let's look at how moving from using one SELf-question to two SELf-questions in a structured sequence helps preschoolers do just that. Like many things in life, just a little bit of structure can go a long way.

Let's zoom back, literally and figuratively, to that spring in 2020 when Rick missed his students and reconnected with them via some remote instruction on structured SELf-questioning in reading for his preschoolers. After modeling for students how to use the SELf-question "How does he, she, or they feel?" for picture clues, Rick designed his next lesson to include the SELf-question "How do I know?" to help structure preschoolers' ability to problem solve unknown words when the picture clues alone don't work.

Rick brought back out the same book as his first lesson, *When Sophie Gets Angry—Really, Really Angry* (Bang, 1999). This time, Rick reminded his students of how to do a picture walk while asking aloud the SELf-question, "How does he, she, or they feel?" Next, Rick went back to the cover, showed students the title, read off the first few words, and then got "stuck" on the word *angry*. This was the optimal opportunity to model via a read aloud and think aloud how two SELf-questions used in sequence can help preschoolers be decoding detectives.

When Rick got stuck on the word *angry*, his think aloud went like this:

Select a Focus

SELf-Question: *What is the problem?*

Rick: "When Sophie Gets A . . . a . . . a. Uh oh, I don't know what this word is. I want to read this book, but I am already stuck on a word in the title. I have a problem, but I know when I get stuck because I don't know a word, I have to stop and use my problem-solving steps and SELf-questions to solve the problem of the unknown word."

Gather Information

SELf-Questions: *What do I know? How does he, she, they feel? How do I know?*

Rick: "Now that I know what the problem is, I am going to gather information by asking myself some SELf-questions. I asked myself 'How does she feel?' during my picture walk. I looked at some picture clues, and I inferred that she feels mad. But I know that the word I am stuck on is not mad.

"Now I have to ask myself, 'How do I know?' I know Sophie is not mad because mad starts with the letter m, and the word I am stuck on starts with the letter a. Now, I need to ask myself, 'What else do I know?' and use some other strategies to gather more information. I know I used picture clues and the popper [the initial letter and sound for a]. What else do I know? Well, I know the ending letter is y. Do I know any other words for mad that start with a and end with y? Hmm, I know—angry!"

Reflect

SELf-Questions: *Did it work? How do I know?*

Rick: "I know angry starts with a, ends with y, and when I look at the picture clues, Sophie's face does look angry! So angry does work! Yeah, I got unstuck. Now I can read all the words in the title, When Sophie Gets Angry—Really, Really Angry.*"*

Here is a perfect example of how sprinkling on just an eye-dropper dosage of the metacognitive strategy of structured SELf-questioning makes a far-reaching objective, such as teaching preschoolers how to use multiple decoding strategies simultaneously to identify an unknown word.

It is important to take a step back ourselves and recognize two things.

1. Preschoolers are not expected to master structured SELf-questioning by the end of prekindergarten. By modeling structured SELf-questioning for reading decoding via think alouds and read alouds, we are modeling for students what the habits of good readers are and what self-questioning looks and sounds like as a reading self-monitoring strategy. At the same time, we are modeling for students how self-questioning is an effective strategy to guide our self-talk through problem solving unknown words.
2. This example of structured SELf-questioning used only three steps, skipping over Brainstorming, Evaluate, and Plan and Act entirely. As you have seen in

> the chapter scenarios throughout this book, it is important to know that all steps do not have to be used every time for every situation. Over multiple years of modeling, practice, feedback, success, and failure, students will become proficient in using the SELf-questions as selected internal mediators that are most helpful for the problem at hand, until the internal mediator itself is no longer needed and students are able to guide their self-talk through reading decoding without the need for any mediators.

With this in mind, we are able to take the next step forward using structured SELf-questioning in reading to help students become fluent readers capable of making meaning and comprehending the text. Toward those ends, there are more invaluable lessons from Opatosky and Stevens from *The Metacognitive Student*:

> Taking a step back is an asset for students engaged in decoding and comprehending text. *Decoding* has to do with understanding the individual words on the page and includes phonics, sight words, and sounding out words. *Comprehending* moves beyond decoding to include the understanding and interpretation of the text. In other words, comprehending involves what the individual words mean when readers put them together into sentences, paragraphs, and chapters. According to Reading Rockets (n.d.), an initiative dedicated to supporting child literacy: "To be able to accurately understand written material, children need to be able to (1) decode what they read; (2) make connections between what they read and what they already know; and (3) think deeply about what they have read." (Cohen et al., 2021, p. 59)

The academic and social SELf-question set helps in all three of these areas.

SELf-Questioning for Reading Comprehension

Time to zoom back one more time to that same book, *When Sophie Gets Angry—Really, Really Angry* (Bang, 1999). Rick learned from Opatosky when she was first hired as a literacy consultant for Metuchen School District back in 2012 that reading the same book multiple times was an effective strategy for reading instruction. He also learned that the first time students read a book, they are practicing decoding or fluency; on rereads, students can be challenged to practice reading comprehension.

To that end, Kelsee chose to show the video of Rick conducting the read aloud of *When Sophie Gets Angry—Really, Really Angry* (Bang, 1999) to model SELf-questioning for decoding. She then conducted a follow-up read aloud of that same book with her students to model how structured SELf-questioning can also be used to identify feelings and solve problems. In the example that follows, Kelsee models how structured SELf-questioning can be combined to teach social awareness and responsible decision making while teaching reading comprehension.

Ms. Young (Kelsee) reads *When Sophie Gets Angry—Really, Really, Angry* each September to her special education preschool classroom. Her goal is for students to comprehend and respond not just to this book but also for any book or other text. The story Ms. Young chose, as you'll recall, centers on Sophie, a young girl who becomes angry and runs away when her sister takes her stuffed gorilla from her. She emphasizes the pictures on the pages with symbols of core words and picture cues and proceeds to use SELf-questioning with her students.

Select a Focus

SELf-Question: *How does he, she, or they feel?*

Ms. Young shows the students an illustration of a blonde girl with braids. The girl's blue eyes are wide-set, and her mouth depicts a frown. After telling the students that the child's name is Sophie, she models asking the structured SELf-question, "How does she feel?" Ms. Young's friends begin to shout out answers, including grumpy, angry, and mad.

Gather Information

SELf-Question: *What is causing this feeling?*

Ms. Young affirms her students' thinking. "I see that Sophie feels angry. Angry is another word for mad. I can tell that Sophie feels angry because her mouth is frowning, and her cheeks are turning pink." Now, she models asking the SELf-question, "What is causing this feeling?"

Ms. Young flips the storybook back a few pages to show her students the picture clue. There is an illustration of Sophie's sister pulling the stuffed gorilla from Sophie's hands. The students answer, "Not sharing!" and "Oh no!" They show the sign for the classroom rule, "Be kind to friends and share toys."

Brainstorm

SELf-Question: *What can he, she, or they do?*

Ms. Young agrees. "Sophie is mad because her sister took her toy from her. I can see that her body feels like a volcano. I see smoke coming out of her ears." Next, she models asking the structured SELf-question, "What can Sophie do?" She uses a think aloud: "When my friends take my toys, I can tell them, 'Please don't do that.' Or, I can tell them to ask me for a turn." Ms. Young diverts her attention to two students on the carpet. Xander turns to Lola, who is holding a pop-it. "Can I have a turn?" he asks, reflecting on the strategy that his teacher modeled.

Reflect

SELf-Question: *Did it work?*

At the end of the story, Ms. Young explains how Sophie decided to draw a picture of her family and do a puzzle to calm her body. She acknowledges that although the strategy the character in the book chose was different, the strategies of saying, "Please don't do that," and asking for a turn are valid.

The examples in this section show how rich the strategy of structured SELf-questioning can truly be. While the variety of problems students can come across while reading can vary in diversity and complexity, structured SELf-questionings is one simple strategy they can internalize and use to address all kinds of reading challenges they come across as emergent readers and throughout their future schooling years.

Scenarios for Developing Metacognitive and Self-Monitoring Readers

Let's take a look at how different teachers have used the academic and social structured SELf-question set to develop emergent readers across a variety of preschool classrooms, settings, and literacy-related learning objectives. The following sections offer four example scenarios for interactions between teachers and students that are focused on enhancing preschoolers' abilities to be metacognitive and self-monitoring readers. Note that the scope of these scenarios each includes all steps within the metacognitive strategy for SELf-questioning, as illustrated in figure 1.3 (page 18).

Scenario 1: Comprehend an Emotion During a Read Aloud

Program: Integrated preschool

Objective: Comprehend and respond to books, other texts, and emotional cues.

Standards: RL.PK.10 "Actively participate in read aloud experiences using age appropriate literature in small and large groups" (Teaching Strategies, n.d.a, p. 13); 0.3.1 "Recognize and describe a wide range of feelings, including sadness, anger, fear, and happiness" (Teaching Strategies, n.d.a, p. 3).

Teacher: Mrs. Herold

The students in this prekindergarten integrated classroom are introduced to a variety of emotions during read alouds. One of the feelings Mrs. Herold discusses is the idea of *worry*. She finds that a great book to discuss this feeling is *Wemberly Worried* by Kevin Henkes (2000). On its cover, there is a girl mouse with wide-set eyes clenching onto her stuffed animal.

SELECT A FOCUS

SELf-Question: How does he, she, or they feel?

During story time, Mrs. Herold sits in front of the class. She states, "Today we are reading the story titled *Wemberly Worried*. We will meet a girl mouse named Wemberly. Let's take a look at the cover of the story! How does Wemberly feel?"

The students guess a variety of feelings, including scared, nervous, and sad.

The teacher adds, "Those are all great guesses, but Wemberly is feeling worried. Worried is a new feeling we will learn about throughout the story. We can feel worried when we are unsure of what is going to happen. It is a similar feeling to nervousness."

GATHER INFORMATION

SELf-Question: What is causing this feeling?

Mrs. Herold continues to read and finds that Wemberly is worried about a lot! She asks the class, "What is causing Wemberly to feel worried?"

The students give examples they remember from the book.

Clara says, " She's worried she will shrink!"

Eddie says, "She's worried the tree will fall!"

Gilly says, "She's worried about starting school!"

BRAINSTORM

SELf-Question: What can he, she, or they do?

Mrs. Herold agrees, "You are right. Wemberly is worried about a lot of things in this story. What can she do if she is feeling worried?"

Mrs. Herold waits for students to come up with suggestions and adds some of her own. As students show they are reluctant to answer, she continues, "When I am worried, I like to talk to a friend. She can talk to a friend!"

This gets students' creativity flowing, and Clara suggests, "She can squeeze her stuffed animal," and Eddie suggests, "She can hug her mom!"

REFLECT

SELf-Question: Did it work?

At the end of the story, Mrs. Herold explains how Wemberly made a friend and how that helped her when she felt worried. She acknowledges that although the strategy the character in the book chose was different, the other strategies would also be great solutions!

Scenario 2: Engage With Emotional Self-Management Through Story

Program: Integrated preschool

Objective: Comprehend and respond to books, other texts, and emotional cues.

Standards: RL.PK.10 "Actively participate in read aloud experiences using age appropriate literature in small and large groups" (Teaching Strategies, n.d.a, p. 13); 0.3.1 "Recognize and describe a wide range of feelings, including sadness, anger, fear, and happiness" (Teaching Strategies, n.d.a, p. 3).

Teacher: Mrs. Herold

The students in the Moss prekindergarten integrated classroom discuss many things during their read aloud, including character, setting, plot, and emotions. One of the student's favorite stories is *The Pout-Pout Fish* by Deborah Deisen (2008), in which they meet a fish with an "ever-present pout." This fish believes he is destined to be sad until, one day, he realizes he can turn his frown upside down. The following sections show how Mrs. Herold models the academic and social SELf-question set to her students to engage them with the emotions expressed through the story.

SELECT A FOCUS

SELf-Question: How does he, she, or they feel?

When reading the story, Mrs. Herold identifies how the Pout-Pout Fish is feeling by pointing to his face. Mrs. Herold thinks aloud, "The title of our story today is *The Pout-Pout Fish.* Before we open the story, let's take a closer look at the book's cover to see if it can tell us what the story is about." She pauses to let the students begin to look over the cover, and continues, "On the cover, I see a fish who is frowning. How does he feel?" She pauses again and taps her finger on her chin before continuing, "He feels sad. I know that when we are sad, we frown."

GATHER INFORMATION

SELf-Question: What is causing this feeling?

Mrs. Herold says, "Let's gather information. I wonder what is causing this feeling." She starts to read the book and finds out that the Pout-Pout Fish doesn't like that he has a pout on his face but does not know how to turn his frown upside down. He thinks he has to feel sad forever. The teacher explains, "I see what is causing this feeling. He has a pout, and he needs help turning his frown upside down."

BRAINSTORM

SELf-Question: What can he, she, or they do?

Mrs. Herold says, "What can he do? He can ask for help from a friend, ask for a hug, or maybe take deep breaths. These are all great ideas. I wonder what the Pout-Pout Fish will do." She continues reading to find out that a friend of the Pout-Pout Fish gave him a kiss, which makes him realize he doesn't have to have his ever-present pout and feel sad. She says, "He can use his pout to kiss! He is a Kiss-Kiss Fish!"

REFLECT

SELf-Question: Did it work?

At the end of the story, Mrs. Herold explains, "Did it work? Yes! Pout-Pout Fish was sad that he had an 'ever-present pout,' but he felt happy when his friend gave him a kiss, and he realized he could be a Kiss-Kiss Fish! It worked!"

Scenario 3: Discover the Plot of a Story

Program: Integrated preschool

Objective: Interact during reading experiences, book conversations, and text reflections.

Standard: RL.PK.3 "With prompting and support, identify characters, settings, and major events in a familiar story" (Teaching Strategies, n.d.a, p. 12).

Teacher: Mrs. Herold

In this example, Mrs. Herold uses the same book as in scenario 2 (page 150), *The Pout-Pout Fish* (Diesen, 2008), but instead of focusing on the emotions of the character in the story, she uses the SELf-question set to engage students more directly with comprehending the story's plot.

SELECT A FOCUS

SELf-Question: What is the question?

Mrs. Herold shows the story *The Pout-Pout Fish* to her students during whole-group instruction. She adds, "Today, we will be reading the story titled *The Pout-Pout Fish.* I need to answer a question. What is the question? The question is, 'What is the plot of the story?'"

GATHER INFORMATION

SELf-Question: What do I know?

Mrs. Herold continues, "Before I can identify the plot, I need to figure out what I know. What do I know?" She points to the cover of the story and sees a frowning fish, blue water, yellow sand, and other sea creatures. She states aloud, "I know this story has a fish in it. It takes place underwater, and the fish looks sad with his frown or pout. But I need more information."

BRAINSTORM

SELf-Question: What can I do?

Mrs. Herold continues to think aloud, "What can I do if I need more information? I can read more pages to see what the story is about. I can ask a friend if they have read this book before. I can look at the back of the book."

EVALUATE

SELf-Question: What is the best way to solve this problem?

Mrs. Herold asks, "What is the best way to solve this problem? I think reading the story is the best way to solve this problem."

PLAN AND ACT

SELf-Question: What do I do first, second, and so on?

Mrs. Herold continues to speak aloud, "What do I do first? I will read the story. What will I do next? I will check if I have more information to tell me about the plot of the story." She begins to read the story and stops halfway to ask the question, "Is this working? Yes, it is working because now I know that the Pout-Pout Fish is sad that he has an 'ever-present pout.' Also, friends ask him what is wrong, and he does not know how to solve the problem."

REFLECT

SELf-Question: Did it work? How do I know?

The teacher reads until the end and states, "Did it work? Yes it worked! How do I know? I know it worked because I know the plot of the story is that the Pout-Pout Fish was sad and that he had an 'ever-present pout,' but his frown turned upside down when his friend gave him a kiss, and he realized he could be a Kiss-Kiss Fish!"

Scenario 4: Receptive, Expressive, and Pragmatic Language Skills in Preschool

Program: Integrated preschool

Objective: Demonstrate phonological awareness.

Standard: RF.PK.2c "Identify many initial sounds of familiar words" (Teaching Strategies, n.d.a, p. 15).

Teacher: Mr. Darmah

Mr. Darmah's preschool class is working on phonological awareness by identifying initial sounds. Students will be encouraged to produce, imitate, or listen to a word and produce, imitate, or listen to the initial sound. To increase engagement and make this objective meaningful, Mr. Darmah decides to use student names as the target words. He organizes a small group of two students, Jenna and Faye. In addition to written names, his materials include static boards that offer picture symbols with written words of high-frequency core vocabulary words and topic-specific fringe vocabulary words. He uses verbal speech, picture symbols, facial expressions, gestures, and body language while implementing structured SELf-questioning. The use of multiple modes of communication is implemented to facilitate the students' receptive, expressive, and pragmatic language skills.

SELECT A FOCUS

SELf-Question: What is the question?

In the small group, Mr. Darmah exclaims to Jenna and Faye, "We are going to learn about phonological awareness!" He goes on, "What is phonological awareness?

Phonological awareness is our awareness of sounds. Sounds make up words! So, we are going to learn about initial sounds. An initial sound is the first sound in a word. It's the sound that starts the word! We are going to listen for the first sound in our names. So, what is the question? We can ask ourselves, 'What is the first sound in my name?'" Mr. Darmah says all this while touching the *what* picture symbol on the core board, using American Sign Language to sign *learn* (gesture), holding up one finger for *one* (gesture), signing *name* (gesture), and smiling (facial expression).

GATHER INFORMATION

SELf-Question: What do I know?

Mr. Darmah provides self-talk and says, "What do I know? I know my name is Mr. Darmah. My name is Darmah." He turns his body toward Jenna (body language to express turn) and says, "What do you know? You can say, 'I know my name is . . . ?" Jenna smiles and says, "Jenna."

He turns his body toward Faye (body language to express turn) and says, "Faye, what do you know?" Faye answers, "I know my name is Faye." He gives them both a high five (gesture).

Again, as Mr. Darmah poses these SELf-questions and presents the carrier phrase ("You can say my name is . . . ?"), he touches the *what* picture symbol on the core board (picture symbol), points to himself and Jenna (gesture for first person singular *I* and second person singular *you*), signs *name* (gesture), and smiles (facial expression).

BRAINSTORM

SELf-Question: What can I do?

Mr. Darmah provides self-talk and says, "I know my name is Darmah. What can I do? I can say the first sound in my name. If I need help, what can I do? I can look at my written name." As he says this, he points to himself (gesture for *I*), touches the *what* symbol on the core board, holds up one finger for *first* (gesture), and signs *name* (gesture). He turns his body toward Jenna (body language to express turn) and says, "You know your name is Jenna. What can you do?"

Jenna says, "I can say the first sound in my name!"

He answers, "You sure can!" as he smiles (facial expression). He turns his body toward Faye (body language to express turn) and poses the same question using verbal speech, gestures, and picture symbols. Faye says, "I can say the first letter in Faye!"

Mr. Darmah says, "We can do it!" while smiling (facial expression) and leaning in (body language to express excitement and engagement).

PLAN AND ACT

SELf-Question: What do I do first, second, and so on?

"What do I do first, second, and third?" Mr. Darmah asks, using self-talk. He touches the *what* picture symbol on the core board, points to himself (gesture for *I*), and holds up one, two, and three fingers for *first, second*, and *third* (gesture).

Mr. Darmah says, "First, I will say my name. Second, I will say the first sound in my name three times. Third, I will say the first sound in my name. I can do it! Darmah. D-d-d-Darmah. /d/. What is the first sound in my name? /d/. The letter *D* makes the /d/ sound! The first letter in my name is D." He holds up fingers for *first, second,* and *third* (gesture), signs *name* (gesture), points to himself (gesture for *I*), and touches the *can, do,* and *it* picture symbols on the core board.

Mr. Darmah turns his body toward Jenna (body language to express turn) and says, "Jenna, what will you do first?" while touching the *what* picture symbol on the core board and holding up one finger for *first* (gesture). She says, "I will say my name. Jenna."

He says, "What will you do second?" while touching the *what* picture symbol on the core board and holding up two fingers for *second* (gesture). Jenna looks at Mr. Darmah. He uses first person singular *I* to more closely align with her internal language and says, "I will say the first sound in my name one or three times?" while signing *name* (gesture) and holding up one and three fingers for *one* and *three* (gestures). "Three times!" Jenna shouts and smiles.

"Yes! What will you do third?" asks Mr. Darmah while touching the *what* picture symbol on the core board and holding up three fingers for *third* (gesture). Jenna says, "I will say the first sound in my name."

"Fantastic!" says Mr. Darmah as he provides Jenna with a carrier phrase to prompt her through the sequence (first, second, and third). He then asks, "What do I do first? First, I . . . ?" Jenna says, "I say my name. Jenna."

He asks, "What do I do second? Second, I will say the first sound in my name . . . ?" "I will say it three times! J-j-j-Jenna," says Jenna.

Mr. Darmah asks, "What will I do third? Third, I will . . . ?" Jenna says, "I will say the first sound in my name. J-j-j-Jenna! /j/."

Mr. Darmah exclaims, "You did it! The first sound in your name is /j/. The letter J makes the /j/ sound! The first letter in your name is J." While providing this self-talk, Mr. Darmah touches the *what* picture symbol on the core board, holds up one, two, and three fingers for *first, second,* and *third* (gesture), and leans in (body language to express support and waiting). He then encourages Jenna to answer the structured SELf-question ("What do I do first, second, and third?") to say the first sound in her name.

Using this same process, Faye was also successful when given the carrier phrases, picture symbols, gestures, and body language.

REFLECT

SELf-Question: Did it work?

Mr. Darmah says, "We learned about the first sound in our names! What was the question? What is the first sound in my name? What did I know? I know my name. What can I do? I can say the first sound in my name! What did I do first, second, and third? First, I said my name. Second, I said the first sound in my name three times. Third, I said the first sound in my name!" He says this while touching the *what* picture symbol on the core board, holding up one, two, and three fingers for *first*, *second*, and *third* (gesture), signing *name* (gesture), and smiling (facial expression).

He asks, "Did it work? Yes or no?" while touching the *yes* and *no* picture symbols on the core board. "Yes!" shout both students. "It did! High five!" says Mr. Darmah as he gives them each a high five (gesture).

Throughout these steps (Select a Focus, Gather Information, Brainstorm, Plan and Act, and Reflect), Mr. Darmah uses multiple modes of communication. He uses verbal speech to ask and answer the structured SELf-questions, explain tasks, describe material, provide praise, make a plan, act on the plan, and reflect on a plan. He uses picture symbols, gestures, facial expressions, body language, and American Sign Language. The use of multiple modes of communication promotes the students' comprehension of the structured SELf-questions, tasks, descriptions, praise, and planning process, and reflection facilitates receptive language skills. It promotes the students' abilities to ask and answer the structured SELf-questions, explain, describe material, praise, make a plan, act on a plan, and reflect, which facilitates expressive language skills. Additionally, it promotes the students' abilities to interact with others, participate in exchanges, provide praise, and take turns, which facilitates pragmatic language skills.

Conclusion

In chapter 2 (page 29), you learned from Goleman (2022) that the more activity in the prefrontal lobe, the greater the emotional resilience. To that end, years of teaching our youngest students how to transfer the metacognitive strategy of structured SELf-questioning from social and emotional contexts to reading is resulting in more resilient readers. As young readers develop the habit of mind of taking a step back when stuck as a reader and asking themselves SELf-questions in a logical sequence, the result is most commonly students who refuse to give up as readers. Instead of getting frustrated and stopping, emerging readers develop as persistent, gritty problem solvers in reading. Early learners learn from the very start that when they are stuck on a word, stuck on a sentence, or struggling with comprehension, they can use their problem-solving strategy to get themselves unstuck.

Parent Corner

The importance of parents and caregivers reading at home to their children cannot be overstated. According to an article posted by the South Carolina Reading Project (2021), parents and caregivers reading at home to their child at an early age "has been shown to contribute to children's academic successes, their critical thinking abilities and their creativity and inquisitiveness. Also, early exposure to books is proven to help increase a child's brain development and better prepares them to learn."

While getting every parent and caregiver to read to their preschooler at home is beyond the control of preschool teachers and administrators, what is within our control are the resources we provide to make the most of this rich at-home support. One of the best resources for parents and caregivers we can recommend when it comes to supporting structured

SELf-questioning while reading at home is to provide them with an academic and social SELf-question set bookmark with visual icons. For parents and caregivers, having the steps and SELf-questions at their fingertips makes for a great visual reminder and prompt and is practical (by marking the page for reading the next night). You can, of course, use the chapter 2 reproducible "SELf-Questioning 101: A Parent and Caregiver's Guide to the Process" (page 42), but for reading purposes, we recommend using the reproducible "SELf-Questioning 101: Bookmark for Reading With Your Child" (page 158), or any version like it that you might design. This bookmark serves as a great resource for parents and caregivers who are not confident they know how to support their child when their child gets stuck as an emerging reader.

As we learned in chapter 1 (page 13), the facilitative approach of asking open-ended questions first transfers over from teachers to parents. Parents are their child's first teacher, right? The bookmark will turn your parents into instructional assistants for emerging readers when they apply a best practice without the need for special training.

SELf-Questioning 101: Bookmark for Reading With Your Child

While reading with your child, use this bookmark to pose relevant SELf-questions from the academic and social structured SELf-question set to encourage their understanding of the story. You can pose these SELf-questions to elicit information about the story or even pose them from the perspective of a character. For example, if a character encounters a problem, you can model for your child by saying, "What if this character asked themself, 'What can I do?'"

In addition, you can use the SELf-questions in this handy bookmark to promote your child's ability to decode words! While reading with your child, select a few words to "read" using structured SELf-questioning.

There are many opportunities to facilitate your child's reading comprehension using the SELf-questions to enhance your child's participation in book reading and support the work we do in the classroom to increase their literacy skills!

SELf-Questioning Step	Academic and Social SELf-Questions
Select a Focus	What is the problem?
Gather Information	What do I know? How does he, she, or they feel?
Brainstorm	What can I do?
Evaluate	What is the best way to solve this problem?
Plan and Act	What do I do first, second, and so on?
Reflect	Did it work?

EPILOGUE

The Importance of the Metacognitive Adult

Social and emotional learning (SEL) is the process through which ***all young people and adults*** *acquire and apply the knowledge, skills, and attitudes to develop healthy identities, manage emotions and* ***achieve personal and collective goals****.*

—CASEL [emphases added]

The more we learn about how to teach students SEL competencies, the more we learn about the importance of adults' SEL competencies. This is especially true when considering the importance of modeling, thinking aloud, and using gradual release of responsibility from adult to student as the most effective methods of instruction. In addition, we all know that any teacher who tries to teach students emotional regulation cannot do so effectively if they yell in frustration at the students who act out due to a lack of emotional or impulse regulation. The same holds true when it comes to teaching students how to become metacognitive. In order for our youngest students to learn to be metacognitive across academic, social, and emotional contexts, the adults in the room need to *show* (model) what being metacognitive looks like and sounds like across academic, social, and emotional contexts.

Being an educator or administrator in any school can be extremely stressful. Our students' many needs can be overwhelming, making it challenging for preschool teachers, paraprofessionals, educational specialists, and school administrators to keep their calm and be at their best day in and day out. Even though it is as hard as ever for adults in education to feel mentally healthy on a regular basis, the need for them to model mental health has never been greater. To that end, we strongly recommend making structured SELf-questioning a personal strategy for every adult—not just for every adult that reads this book or that works in education, not just for every parent or caregiver dealing with the stressors of raising young children, but for *every* adult, everywhere.

Let's go back one last time to September 2020, but this time, for a wonderful example of success. Student Lee is about to start his first day in kindergarten. Lee had attended Moss School's preschool intervention program. As a result, Lee had been taught the metacognitive strategy of structured SELf-questioning by coauthors Katie, Emily, and Michele over a period of two years before entering his new inclusion kindergarten classroom.

Lee stands outside his kindergarten classroom door after all the other students enter the classroom. Lee is understandably nervous about having a new teacher, new classroom, and new classmates. To make emotions even more intense, stress and anxieties are even higher as COVID-19 is still prevalent and on everyone's minds. Lee is standing motionless with his head down, staring at his feet.

Rick is equally anxious about opening up the school for in-person learning. So when Rick sees Lee frozen outside his new classroom door, Rick begins practicing his own structured SELf-questioning to make sure he is in the best place emotionally and mentally to perform at his best for Lee. Rick's guided self-talk goes like this:

> ***What am I feeling?*** *Extremely nervous.*
>
> ***What is causing this feeling?*** *Well, besides the fact that I am nervous about everyone getting COVID-19, again, I am also fearful that Lee will refuse to go into the classroom and have an emotional breakdown that will have a radioactive effect on all the other nervous students in their first moments of this school year.*
>
> ***What can I do?*** *To calm myself down, while I walk this short hallway to Lee, I can count to ten, quickly, or five—one, two, three.... Oh! And I can use structured SELf-questioning not only for myself but also with Lee.*

Throughout his preschool career, Lee had daily opportunities to internalize and practice structured SELf-questioning to guide his own thinking through all kinds of problem solving. In so doing, he is well prepared for success outside his preschool classroom and is more school-ready for success in kindergarten than his peers who had attended other preschool programs outside of Moss School (or no preschool at all). In addition, Lee's parents had been able to support the use of the metacognitive strategy at home during remote learning.

Even though Lee had not been in the building for the past six months, Rick is able to fall on just two steps and SELf-questions to scaffold and prompt Lee's self-awareness and self-management competencies with great ease.

> *Rick: "How are you feeling?"*
>
> *Lee: "Nervous?"*
>
> *Rick: "What can you do?"*
>
> *Lee: "Take deep breaths."*

Lee and Rick take a few deep breaths together. After just a few seconds, feeling much less nervous, Lee looks into the window of his new kindergarten inclusion classroom, turns the doorknob, pulls the big, heavy door open, and walks in on his own will and power.

Practice makes perfect, and each time we try out the strategy for ourselves, we find that the practice provides us with more examples to share and use as models with our students or colleagues. Whether the outcome is a major success or not, it is the application of the strategy that builds our mastery of guiding our own self-talk, thereby making us, by default, models of the strategy. Modeling is the key and the first step in any gradual release model. So SELf-question away, and may this strategy help bring you and your students personal growth, health, and success atop our collective goal of greater peace.

References & Resources

Adrian, M., Lyon, A., Oti, R., & Tininenko, J. (2011). Social problem solving. In S. Goldstein & J. A. Naglieri (Eds.), *Encyclopedia of child behavior and development* (pp. 1399–1403). Springer, Boston, MA. Accessed at https://link.springer.com/referenceworkentry/10.1007/978-0-387-79061-9_2703 on January 25, 2024.

Aggleton, J. P. (Ed.). (1992). *The amygdala: Neurobiological aspects of emotion, memory, and mental dysfunction*. New York: Wiley-Liss.

American Speech-Language-Hearing Association. (n.d.). *Augmentative and alternative communication (AAC)*. Accessed at www.asha.org/practice-portal/professional-issues/augmentative-and-alternative-communication/#collapse_1 on January 25, 2024.

Bang, M. (1999). *When Sophie gets angry—Really, really, angry. . . .* New York: Blue Sky Press.

Barrett, L. F. (2018). *Try these two smart techniques to help you master your emotions*. Accessed at https://ideas.ted.com/try-these-two-smart-techniques-to-help-you-master-your-emotions on October 2, 2023.

Blackburn, B. (2018). Productive struggle is a learner's sweet spot. *Productive Struggle for All, 14*(11). Accessed at https://ascd.org/el/articles/productive-struggle-is-a-learners-sweet-spot on January 23, 2024.

Brackett, M. (2019). *Permission to feel: Unlocking the power of emotions to help our kids, ourselves, and our society thrive*. New York: Celadon Books.

Butler, L. B., Romasz-McDonald, T., & Elias, M. J. (2011). *Social decision making/social problem solving: A curriculum for academic, social, and emotional learning—Grades K–1*. Champaign, IL: Research Press.

Cain, J. (2021). *The way I feel* (J. Cain, Illus.). Seattle, WA: Parenting Press.

Centers for Disease Control and Prevention. (2023). *U.S. teen girls experiencing increased sadness and violence*. Accessed at https://cdc.gov/media/releases/2023/p0213-yrbs.html on March 5, 2024.

Cohen, R. K., Opatosky, D. K., Savage, J., Stevens, S. O., & Darrah, E. P. (2021). *The metacognitive student: How to teach academic, social, and emotional intelligence in every content area*. Bloomington, IN: Solution Tree Press.

Collaborative for Academic, Social, and Emotional Learning. (n.d.). *What is the CASEL framework?* Accessed at https://casel.org/fundamentals-of-sel/what-is-the-casel-framework on September 27, 2023.

Deisen, D.(2008). *The pout-pout fish* (D. Hanna, Illus.). New York: Farrar, Straus & Giroux..

Ding, X., Liu, H., Wang, H., Song, Q., Wanying, S., Li, N., et al. (2022). COVID-19 pandemic impact on family life and exacerbated emotional and behavioral health among preschool children: A longitudinal study. *International Journal of Clinical and Health Psychology, 22*(3), 100327.

Drevets, W. C., & Raichle, M. E. (1998). Reciprocal suppression of regional cerebral blood flow during emotional versus higher cognitive processes: Implications for interactions between emotion and cognition. *Cognition and Emotion, 12*(3), 353–385.

Durlak, J. A., Weissberg, R. P., Dymnicki, A. B., Taylor, R. D., & Schellinger, K. B. (2011). The impact of enhancing students' social and emotional learning: A meta-analysis of school-based universal interventions. *Child Development, 82*(1), 405–432.

D'Zurilla, T. J., & Nezu, A. M. (1999). *Problem-solving therapy: A social competence approach to clinical intervention* (2nd ed.). New York: Springer.

Elias, M. J., & Arnold, H. (Eds). (2006). *The educator's guide to emotional intelligence and academic achievement: Social-emotional learning in the classroom.* Thousand Oaks, CA: Corwin Press.

Fey, M. (1986). *Language intervention with young children.* Worthing, England: College-Hill Press.

Fisher, D., & Frey, N. (2021). *Better learning through structured teaching: A framework for the gradual release of responsibility* (3rd ed.). Alexandria, VA: ASCD.

Fisher, D., Frey, N., & Hattie, J. (2016). *Visible learning for literacy, grades K–12: Implementing the practices that work best to accelerate student learning.* Thousand Oaks, CA: Corwin.

Fox, N. A., & Davidson, R. J. (1984). Hemispheric substrates of affect: A developmental model, In N. A. Fox & R. J. Davidson (Eds.), *The psychobiology of affective development* (pp. 353–381). Hillsdale, NJ: Erlbaum.

Goleman, D. (2020). *Emotional intelligence: Why it can matter more than IQ* (25th Anniv. ed.). London: Bloomsbury.

Goleman, D. (2022, March 15) *Emotional intelligence: Myths, applications and upcoming events.* Accessed at www.linkedin.com/pulse/emotional-intelligence-myths-applications-upcoming-events-goleman on October 2, 2023.

Henkes, K. (2000). *Wemberly worried.* New York: Greenwillow Books.

Jarvers, I. Ecker, A., Schleicher, D., Brunner, R., & Kandsperger, S. (2023). *Impact of preschool attendance, parental stress, and parental mental health on internalizing and externalizing problems during COVID-19 lockdown measures in preschool children.* Accessed at https://journals.plos.org/plosone/article?id=10.1371/journal.pone.0281627 on September 27, 2023.

Jo, Y., Tomar, G., Ferschke, O., Rosé, C. P., & Gaševic, D. (2016). *Expediting support for social learning with behavior modeling.* Accessed at https://educationaldatamining.org/EDM2016/proceedings/paper_70.pdf on March 5, 2024.

Kapa, L. L., & Mettler, H. M. (2021). Language and executive function in preschoolers with developmental language disorder: The role of self-directed speech. *Perspectives of the ASHA Special Interests Group, 6,* 1315-1326.

Kato, T. (2015). Testing of the coping flexibility hypothesis based on the dual-process theory: Relationships between coping flexibility and depressive symptoms. *Psychiatry Research, 230*(2), 137–142.

Kolencik, P. L., & Hillwig, S. A. (2011). *Encouraging metacognition: Supporting learners through metacognitive teaching strategies.* New York: Lang.

Kuhn, D., & Dean, D., Jr. (2004). Metacognition: A bridge between cognitive psychology and educational practice. *Theory Into Practice, 43*(4), 268–273.

Kusche, C. A., & Greenberg, M. T. (2006). Brain development and social-emotional learning: An introduction for educators. In Maurice J. Elias and H. Arnold(Eds.). *The educator's guide to emotional intelligence and academic achievement* (pp. 15–34). Thousand Oaks, CA: Corwin Press.

Lidstone, J. S. M., Meins, E., & Fernyhough, C. (2012). Verbal mediation of cognition in children with specific language impairment. *Development and Psychopathology, 24*(2), 651–660. https://doi.org/10.1017/s0954579412000223

Lieberman, M. D. (2009). The brain's braking system (and how to 'use your words' to tap into it). *NeuroLeadership Journal, 2*, 9–14.

Liew, J., Erbeli, F., Nyanamba, J. M., & Li, D. (2020). Pathways to reading competence: Emotional self-regulation, literacy contexts, and embodied learning processes. *Reading Psychology, 41*(7), 633–659.

Lopes, S., Masters, S., McKenna, K., Presuto, E., & Young, K. (2022, October 10). *Teaching all students independent coping skills, a district wide tiered approach* [PowerPoint slides]. Metuchen, NJ: Metuchen School District.

Luria, A. R. (1976). *Cognitive development: Its cultural and social foundations.* Cambridge, MA: Harvard University Press.

Macrine, S. L., & Fugate, J. M. B. (Eds.). (2022). *Movement matters: How cognition informs teaching and learning.* Cambridge, MA: MIT Press.

Mahler, K. (n.d.). *What is interoception?* [Handout]. Accessed at www.kelly-mahler.com/printable-resources on January 24, 2024.

Mahler, K., Hample, K., Jones, C., Sensenig, J., Thomasco, P., & Hilton, C. (2022). Impact of an interception-based program on emotion regulation in autistic children. *Occupational Therapy International*, 9328967. https://doi.org/10.1155/2022/9328967

McBrien, J. L., & Brandt, R. S. (1997). The nature of curriculum. In J. L. McBrien, R. S. Brandt, & R. W. Cole (Eds.). *The language of learning: A guide to education terms.* Accessed at www.sagepub.com/sites/default/files/upm-binaries/44334_1.pdf on October 3, 2023.

Michalopoulou, A. (2014) Inquiry-based learning through the creative thinking and expression in early years education. *Creative Education, 5*(6), 377–385.

Mondi, C. F., Giovanelli, A. & Reynolds, A. J. (2021). Fostering socio-emotional learning through early childhood intervention. *International Journal of Child Care and Education Policy, 15*(6). https://doi.org/10.1186/s40723-021-00084-8

Mulvihill, A., Carroll, A., Dux, P. E., & Matthews, N. (2020). Self-directed speech and self-regulation in childhood neurodevelopmental disorders: Current findings and future directions. *Development and Psychopathology, 32*(1), 205–217.

National Governors Association Center for Best Practices & Council of Chief State School Officers. (2010). *Common Core State Standards for English language arts and literacy in history/social studies, science, and technical subjects.* Washington, DC: Authors. Accessed at www.thecorestandards.org/wp-content/uploads/ELA_Standards1.pdf on September 29, 2023.

National Scientific Council on the Developing Child (2020). *Connecting the brain to the rest of the body: Early childhood development and lifelong health are deeply intertwined.* Accessed at https://developingchild.harvard.edu/resources/connecting-the-brain-to-the-rest-of-the-body-early-childhood-development-and-lifelong-health-are-deeply-intertwined on March 5, 2024.

Niemi, K. (2020). *Niemi: CASEL is updating the most widely recognized definition of social-emotional learning. Here's why.* Accessed at www.the74million.org/article/niemi-casel-is-updating-the-most-widely-recognized-definition-of-social-emotional-learning-heres-why on September 27, 2023.

Özkan, B., & Tuğluk, M. N. (2022). *The effect of the brain-based environmental education program applied to 5-6 years of pre-school children on their sustainable environmental behaviors.* Accessed at https://files.eric.ed.gov/fulltext/EJ1331605.pdf on March 5, 2024.

Paul, R., Norbury, C., & Gosse, C. (2018). *Language disorders from infancy through adolescence: Listening, speaking, reading, writing, and communicating* (5th ed.). Amsterdam, Netherlands: Elsevier.

Pearson, P. D., & Gallagher, M. C. (1983). The instruction of reading comprehension. *Contemporary Educational Psychology, 8*(3), 317–344.

Perkins, D. N., & Salomon, G. (1992). *Transfer of learning*. Accessed at https://jaymctighe.com/wp-content/uploads/2011/04/Transfer-of-Learning-Perkins-and-Salomon.pdf on March 5, 2024.

Price-Mitchell, M. (2015, April 7). *Metacognition: Nurturing self-awarness in the classroom* [Blog post]. Accessed at www.edutopia.org/blog/8-pathways-metacognition-in-classroom-marilyn-price-mitchell on January 7, 2023.

Reilly, N. N. (2017). The bonds of social-emotional learning. *Educational Leadership, 75*(4), 56–60. Accessed at www.ascd.org/publications/educational_leadership/dec17/vol75/num04/The_Bonds_of_Social-Emotional_Learning.aspx on August 7, 2020.

Shure, M. B. (2001). *I can problem solve: An interpersonal cognitive problem-solving program, preschool* (2nd ed.). Champaign, IL: Research Press.

Siegel, D. [Dalai Lama Center]. (2014, December 8). *Dan Siegel: Name it to tame it* [Video file]. Accessed at https://youtu.be/ZcDLzppD4Jc on November 16, 2023.

Sippl, A. (2023, January 21). *Teaching the IDEAL problem-solving method to diverse learners* [Blog post]. Accessed at https://lifeskillsadvocate.com/blog/teaching-the-ideal-problem-solving-method-to-diverse-learners on September 29, 2023.

South Carolina Reading Project. (2021). *Importance of reading at home*. Accessed at www.screadingproject.org/importance-of-reading-at-home on October 6, 2023.

Sylwester, R. (1995). *A celebration of neurons: An educator's guide to the human brain*. Alexandria, VA: ASCD.

Taylor, R. D., Oberle, E., Durlak, J. A., & Weissberg, R. P. (2017). Promoting positive youth development through school-based social and emotional learning interventions: A meta-analysis of follow-up effects. *Child Development, 88*(4), 1156–1171.

Teaching Strategies. (n.d.a). *Alignment of teaching strategies GOLD objectives for development and learning: Birth through kindergarten*. Accessed at https://teachingstrategies.com/wp-content/uploads/2017/03/NJ-GOLD-Alignment-PS-2014-2.pdf on October 2, 2023.

Teaching Strategies. (n.d.b). *The creative curriculum for preschool*. Accessed at https://teachingstrategies.com/product/the-creative-curriculum-for-preschool on October 5, 2023.

Teaching Strategies. (2017). Intentional teaching experiences: What was for breakfast? *Language and Literacy, LL40*. Bethesda, MD: Author.

Teaching Strategies. (2020a). *The creative curriculum for preschool: Balls teaching guide*. Bethesda, MD: Author.

Teaching Strategies. (2020b). *The creative curriculum for preschool: Volume 1—The foundation* (7th ed.). Bethesda, MD: Author.

Teaching Strategies. (2020c). *The creative curriculum for preschool: Volume 3— Social-emotional, physical and cognitive development* (7th ed.). Bethesda, MD: Author.

Teaching Strategies. (2021, March 12). *Introducing the digital children's library in the Creative Curriculum* [Blog post]. Accessed at https://teachingstrategies.com/blog/introducing-the-digital-childrens-library-in-the-creative-curriculum on October 5, 2023.

Tough, P. (2009, September 25). Can the right kinds of play teach self-control? *The New York Times Magazine*. Accessed at www.nytimes.com/2009/09/27/magazine/27tools-t.html on September 27, 2023.

Tough, P. (2012). *How children succeed: Grit, curiosity and the hidden power of* character. Boston: Houghton Mifflin Harcourt.

Tutt, P., Boryga, A., & Gonser, S. (2023). *2023 in review, from your point of view*. Accessed at www.edutopia.org/article/2023-in-review-from-your-point-of-view on January 7, 2023.

Uhrich, B. B., Rogelberg, S. L., Rogelberg, S. G., Kello, J. E., Williams, E. B., Gur, S S., et al. (2023). The power of inner voice: Examining self-talk's relationship with academic outcomes. *American Journal of Education, 130*(1).

U.S. Department of Health and Human Services. (n.d.). *Co-regulation in human services.* Accessed at www.acf.hhs.gov/opre/project/co-regulation-human-services on January 25, 2024.

Vygotsky, L. S. (1978). *Mind in society. The development of higher psychological processes.* Cambridge: Harvard University Press.

Weir, K. (2020). Nurtured by nature. *Monitor on Psychology, 51*(3), 50. Accessed at www.apa.org /monitor/2020/04/nurtured-nature on October 3, 2023.

White, S. H. (1970). Some general outlines of the matrix of developmental changes between five and seven years. *Bulletin of the Orton Society, 20*(1), 41–57.

Wilson, D., & Conyers, M. (2016). *Teaching students to drive their brains: Metacognitive strategies, activities, and lesson ideas.* Alexandria, VA: ASCD.

Zadina, J. N. (2023). The Synergy Zone: Connecting the mind, brain, and heart for the ideal classroom learning environment. *Brain Sciences, 13*(9), 1314. https://doi.org/10.3390/brainsci13091314

Zins, J. E., Bloodworth, M. R., Weissberg, R. P., & Walberg, H. J. (2007). The scientific basis linking social and emotional learning to school success. *Journal of Educational and Psychological Consultation, 17*(2–3), 191–210.

Index

The Metacognitive Student
Richard K. Cohen, Deanne Kildare Opatosky, James Savage, Susan Olsen Stevens, and Edward P. Darrah
What if there was one strategy you could use to support students academically, socially, and emotionally? It exists—and it's simple, straightforward, and practical. Dive deep into structured SELf-questioning and learn how to empower students to develop into strong, healthy, and confident thinkers.
BKF954

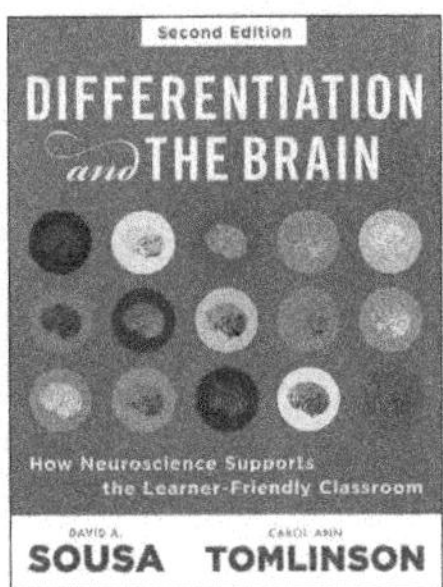

Differentiation and the Brain
David A. Sousa and Carol Ann Tomlinson
The second edition of this best-selling resource will help you create truly effective, brain-friendly classrooms for all learners. The authors share an array of updated examples, scenarios, and exercises, as well as the latest research from cognitive psychology, neuroscience, and pedagogy.
BKF804

Raising Equity Through SEL
Jorge Valenzuela
Activate social-emotional learning effectively in your classroom with this trusted source for sound pedagogy that addresses the academic and SEL needs of diverse learners. Each strategy, tool, and template shared is meant to facilitate your practice by making SEL easier to implement.
BKG041

Behavior Academies
Jessica Djabrayan Hannigan and John Hannigan
With its practical behavior intervention method, this book replaces problematic behaviors with essential life skills for school and beyond. Educators can implement effective targeted interventions in twenty-five minutes or less using eight predefined behavior academies and a process to create their own.
BKG114

Success for Our Youngest Learners
Barbara W. Cirigliano
Put preK learners on the path to a great education by embracing the professional learning community (PLC) process. Designed specifically for early childhood educators, this practical resource details the foundational ideas and concepts of a successful PLC.
BKF892